TO THE PRAISE OF HIS GLORY

B. MYRON CEDARHOLM

THELMA M. CEDARHOLM

Larry R. Oats

© 2018 Maranatha Baptist Press
A Ministry of Maranatha Baptist University
745 West Main Street, Watertown, Wisconsin 53094

Printed in the United States of America

Larry R. Oats, Author

To the Praise of His Glory
B. Myron Cedarholm and Thelma M. Cedarholm

ISBN: 978–0–9821426–5–3 (paper)

Cover design by Jonathan Williquette

CONTENTS

PREFACE

God raises up special people for special missions. B. Myron and Thelma M. Cedarholm were special people whom God chose for special ministries. This author had the privilege of spending almost all his adult life in association with Dr. and Mrs. Cedarholm. He attended Pillsbury Baptist Bible College from 1966 to 1968, and his wife attended Pillsbury from 1965 to 1968, the years the Cedarholms were there. Both transferred to Maranatha Baptist Bible College in 1968. They left Maranatha for the 1971–1972 school year, awaiting the start of the Master of Divinity program, but otherwise they were a part of Maranatha in some way for 49 of its first 50 years.

The Fiftieth Anniversary celebration of Maranatha Baptist University was the occasion for the writing of this book. The Cedarholms did not write very much about themselves, and with the Cedarholm generation nearly gone, it is time their story is told.

The reader may assume that the writer's close association with the Cedarholms would bring about inevitable bias. That assumption is true. The writer understands the Cedarholms were merely human, with all the frailties of humanity, but they wanted only to please their Lord. They were leaders, but humble; innovators, but tied to the Word; at times impatient, but willing to wait on the Lord.

This author expresses his gratitude toward Dr. Marty Marriott, Maranatha's President, for allowing him the time necessary to research and write this volume. He is thankful for the help he received from the Maranatha Library Archives (scanned and organized by Lois Oetken). Charlotte Cedarholm, daughter of Dr. and Mrs. Cedarholm, provided a wealth of material and photos. Kim Ledgerwood, author of *Rich in Mercy*, provided a history of Maranatha's first forty years. Sections of this book depend heavily upon the organization of those materials by Ledgerwood. As often as possible, the sources of information appear in the footnotes.

Uncited sources of information originate from the Maranatha Library Archives.

The Cedarholms were integrally involved in the Conservative Baptist Association of America, Pillsbury Baptist Bible College, and Maranatha Baptist Bible College (now Maranatha Baptist University). This book, however, is not a history of any of those movements; it is a history of the Cedarholms, two of God's most industrious and humble servants.

INTRODUCTION

While several short articles and two college presentations have focused attention on Blaine Myron and Thelma Melford Cedarholm, no significant work has been written on their fruitful lives. This is an attempt to correct that. They were an uncommon couple—humble in the midst of honor, steadfast in the face of testing, and mindful of one purpose—the praise of His glory.

Myron and Thelma Cedarholm lived in tumultuous and wonderful times. Both from devout families, they experienced firsthand the pseudo-intellectual discrediting of the Bible as the Word of God, yet saw great revivals in the 20th century. They both came from ministry families and committed themselves to ministry early in their lives, and God used them in a variety of ways.

Myron grew up in the home of a Baptist evangelist. Thelma grew up in the home of a Lutheran pastor. During Myron's early childhood his father, Anton, was gone much of the time. Thelma grew up developing a close relationship to her father. Myron was born in Minnesota, and Thelma grew up there. Though most of Myron's childhood was spent outside the state, this background played an important part in his decision to go to Pillsbury Baptist Bible College.

Hearing the stories of his father's extensive travels, Myron developed a global understanding of the world. In addition, he and Thelma lived in the Midwest and the East, and Myron in the West. So, in an age when travel was still a major event, their impression of the United States was that extensive travel was manageable. That was fortunate, for crisscrossing the length and breadth of the country was something the Cedarholms did for eighteen years on behalf of the Conservative Baptist Association and, to a lesser extent, in their college ministries at Pillsbury and Maranatha.

Both Myron and Thelma had a love for missions. At one point, they had both planned to spend their lives on a foreign mission field, but that was not in God's plans. Their love for missionaries and for their converts, however, was never lost. While they never served as missionaries, they helped prepare dozens of Pillsbury and Maranatha students who went on to serve where they could not.

The Maranatha Hymn was a testimony to their lives. Based on the Maranatha theme verse, Ephesians 1:12, the Cedarholms sought to live "To the Praise of His Glory."

THE EARLY YEARS: 1915–1932

B. Myron Cedarholm and Thelma Melford Cedarholm both came from preachers' homes. They both grew up with lives centered in church. As children and teens in their respective churches, they were both active, a trait that never changed. And they were both thoroughly Swedish. While their parents' ministries were hundreds and sometimes thousands of miles apart, the Lord brought Myron and Thelma together at just the right time of their lives so they might get acquainted, fall in love, and unite their hearts with a dedication to serve wherever the Lord might lead them. In her childhood, Thelma anticipated missionary service in China. Myron planned on missionary service in South America. The Lord, however, had something far different in mind.

Myron came from hardy Swedish roots. Peter and Ellen Cedarholm, Myron's paternal grandparents, came to Minnesota from Sweden in 1884.[1] Swan August and Mathilda Carlson, his maternal grandparents, were also from Sweden. Swan immigrated to Canada when he was 18 years old and worked for the Canadian Pacific Railroad, building railroad bridges and grain elevators. He moved south, eventually arriving in St. Paul, Minnesota, where he met Mathilda Petersdotter (the family later Americanized their name to "Peterson"). They were married in Chicago in 1883, where Swan had a brother. They lived their married lives in St. Paul, Minnesota, where Swan exercised his entrepreneurial skills, operating a small dairy and then a candy store. In partnership with an I. Jacobs, he later sold stoves, furniture, and shoes. Eventually he opened his own store near the Old Swede Hollow—the Carlson Fair Store which sold dry goods, furniture, and hardware. For a while Swan had a tin shop that made gutters and metal roofs. In

---

[1] 1900 U.S. Census.

1918, Swan sold the store, retired, and soon thereafter moved to a farm near Twin Lake, Minnesota.[2]

Myron's parents were Anton Cedarholm and Lollie Genevieve Carlson. The third of seven children, Lollie shared her childhood with Paul, David, Ethel, Marian, Ralph, and Chester. Anton had eight brothers: Axel, Henry, Emil, Peter, Reuben, Arthur, Hilbert, and Hilmore. He also had two sisters: Hannah and Helen (Helen, Hilbert and Hilmore were triplets). Peter and Arthur died as children. Anton was called "Uncle Tony" by his nieces and nephews.[3] Anton's parents, Peter and Ellen, had a stormy relationship and divorced in about 1915. Years later, when Peter lay dying, Ellen brought him to her home and asked Anton to remarry them. She did not want Peter to die a divorced man. As you might imagine, Anton found great pleasure in telling people that he had married his parents![4]

Thelma was just as Swedish as Myron! Her father, Martin Alenius Melford, was born in Sweden in 1886 or 1887 and immigrated to the United States in 1890. Her mother, Anna C. Friberg, was born in Illinois in 1893, but Anna's parents were both from Sweden. Martin and Anna were married on June 24, 1914 in Chicago.

"It's time for a story," Thelma would often say. Her "biography" was parceled out to co-workers and students one story at a time. From time to time, she would tell the ladies who worked in her office, "That's enough for a while; let's sit and I'll tell you a story." Madrigal choir members recall sitting in church basements listening to Mrs. Cedarholm talk about mission trips and her childhood, while her husband was

---

[2] Eliz and Glenn Carlson, "The Glenn Carlsons," unpublished family history.

[3] Audrey Weldon Johnson, "Time and Chance Happen to Us All," 31. This is a self-published story of some of the families related to the Cedarholms. Johnson is the daughter of Helen Cedarholm, a niece of Anton. She states, "Vivid memories of my Grandma Cedarholm are of a strong Christian woman with unwavering faith in her Lord and Saviour, Jesus Christ. She was strict, loved her Bible and never ceased to pray for her family."

[4] Johnson, "Time and Chance."

finishing the service upstairs. Everyone recalls being enthralled, but no one can recite the stories like she told them! There was just something about her style of story-telling that left any attempts to retell the same story flat and lifeless. Without her, it was just words; with her, it was a vibrant, poignant, engaging adventure. This is one of those stories.

He was a simple country boy, born and bred in the old country where life was simple, food was wholesome but scarce, comforts few. He had a longing for a home and a life that promised hope for tomorrow. The wonders that his eyes beheld as he gazed across the wide, wide world before him led to a land that offered prosperity and fulfillment of desires. His name was Karl [Friberg, who would become the father of Thelma's mother], or as sometimes called by his buddies, Charlie. "Why don't you save your money?" said his friends. "And then you could make the trip to the far away land." So, he saved all he could until one day he was able to purchase a ticket that took him to this far away land.

The tests and embarrassments of Ellis Island were difficult, but one day he found his way to the big city of Chicago, and there he found employment as a fine carpenter. This was a trade which he dearly loved, and so he was diligent in his daily duties and learned much that helped him to improve his fine art. One day a young man said to him, "Charles, you know you could make more money if you went down to the railroad and asked them for a job." "I could? How do you know that?" "Well, I don't know, but I hear the fellows talking about it, and there are many of them who have gone to the railroad. Why don't you try and see if you can find employment there?" One day he went to the railroad yard down below the Loop in Chicago, and sure enough, there was a job for young Charles. The only condition was that he would be willing to move to a little town south of Chicago. This place was named Putnam. There he became station manager and the postmaster and took up his abode at a home not far from some friends whom he met by the name of Carlson. Now these people were also Swedish, and oftentimes they invited him for a meal even if he was by himself. The evenings oftentimes passed slowly. On Sunday, he attended the little church on the hillside along with the

Carlsons and often went home to dinner with them. On this particular Sunday, the Carlsons had entertained a friend who came down from Chicago. She was Mrs. Carlson's cousin. Both of the women had been named Anna. After the service was over, they had dinner together at the Carlson home, and as usual, the Carlsons began to tease Charlie and Anna Swenson. He was rather reticent, and she was very bashful. But their visits continued until about four o'clock when it was time for the train to leave for Chicago. She indicated to the folks that it was time for her to leave, and Charlie immediately piped up by saying, "I could take you to the train, because I could carry your grip." So, she went to the bedroom where they kept their clothing and packed her suitcase. He took her to the train, said goodbye, and then walked back alone to the Carlsons'. They served him a cup of coffee, and then he decided that he should go to his home. He went to the bedroom to get his clothes, but had difficulty finding his vest; he looked behind the bed, under the bed, behind the dresser, in the closet, and then finally went out to Anna Carlson and said to her, "Mrs. Carlson, I cannot find my vest. Did you put it someplace?" "Oh no," she said, "Perhaps I can help you look for it." So, she promptly went into the bedroom, too, to look for that vest. Neither one of them could find it, and then she suggested, "You know, Charlie, Anna probably got it in her suitcase by mistake." "Oh, do you think so?" said he. "No woman would put a piece of man's clothing in her suitcase." "Well, you never can tell," said Anna. "Why don't you sit down and write a letter to her and ask her if she has the vest?" "Well," said he, "I suppose I could do that, but I still don't understand how she could have the vest in her suitcase."

That evening as he sat in his little room by himself, he took up a pen and began to write. "Dear Anna, When it came time for me to go home today from the Carlsons' I went to get my vest and I couldn't find it. We looked all over for it and began to wonder if maybe, by chance, you happened to get it in your suitcase by mistake. If you did, I could come to Chicago to get it because, you see, I ride free on the train since I am an employee of the railroad. And then, since I would be coming to Chicago anyway, perhaps at the same time we could get married. Thank you. Sincerely, Charles."

"Why?" said the other girls at the house where Anna worked, "Why would a man say something like that? You don't suppose you'd marry him, do you, Anna?" "Well," she said, "I'll think about it." One day she announced to them she was answering his letter and they were going to be married. She had no idea how it got in her suitcase, but she had the vest. She wrote to him something like this, "I do have the vest. I did not put it in my suitcase. I don't know who did it. But, anyway it will be fine if you would like to come to Chicago to get the vest and then perhaps we could get married at the same time. Yes, I would be glad to accept your proposal." It was just three weeks from the time that they had first met, and he was in Chicago for his wedding to Anna.

Now, you may say, "How did that happen?" Well, it was that tricky Anna Carlson that put the vest in the suitcase. You might know, she was full of tricks all her life. Anyway, that's how I happen to be here.

This quick romance and wedding in 1889 resulted in the birth of Thelma's mother, Anna Friberg.

Anton and Lollie were people of faith. These young people were married in 1914, a year before Anton graduated from the Boone Biblical College. Lollie also graduated from Boone, but the date is not known.[5] Founded by Rev. J. C. Crawford in 1891 in Boone, Iowa, the Boone Biblical College began as a Christian ministry training school, but it eventually developed into a complex of ministries: elementary school, high school, orphanage, retirement home,

Lollie and Anton

---

[5] "Blaine Myron Cedarholm Biography," an official vita on Maranatha Baptist Bible College letterhead.

and radio station. These ministries were supported by a cafeteria, grocery, laundry, print shop, and a 160-acre farm. When the Cedarholms were there, there were about 300 residents "on what could be called a Christian commune, or (during its period of decline) a Christian poor farm."[6]

Because Anton was looking forward to an itinerant ministry, he and Lollie moved into the third-floor apartment of her parents' huge house at 802 Sims Avenue, Saint Paul, Minnesota. He is listed as living there in 1916 and working briefly as the Vice President of the Fair Cash Store.[7]

Anton spent a year after graduation in evangelism. He then accepted a pastorate at Burlington, Iowa, where he served for a year. He moved his family back to St. Paul and became the song leader for the Union Gospel Mission and choir leader at the First Swedish Baptist Church. In a biographical newspaper piece, Anton expressed his excitement for this ministry: "I also had great opportunity to follow the musical phase of Christian work. I think every pastor ought to have a good musical knowledge, particularly along the lines of hymnology." This church in a larger city provided him with many singing opportunities. Furthermore, he accepted an invitation to take charge of music classes in one of the colleges in the state, although which college is not stated. Next, he committed himself once again to evangelistic campaign work, "and it has taken me all over our great nation and Canada and many other parts of the world."[8]

By 1920 Anton's family was living in Lomita, California,[9] so that Anton could work with R. A. Torrey in his evangelistic ministry. Anton was said to have a "winsome personality,"[10] and he was a striking figure, often dressed in an all-white

---

[6] "Remembering Donald Hustad," https://www.garbc.org/ garbcnews/remembering-donald-hustad-1918-2013/.

[7] St. Paul, Minnesota, *City Directory*, 1916.

[8] Full page newspaper advertisement with biographical article, October 11, 1928. Hibbing Minnesota.

[9] 1920 U.S. Census.

[10] Rev. George W. Arms, pastor First Presbyterian Church, Duluth, Minnesota, letter of reference, Spring, 1928.

suit with flashy cufflinks. He served God faithfully with his magnanimous personality. He worked for twenty years as a song leader and a soloist with some of America's foremost evangelists, including Dr. J. C. Massee, pastor of Tremont Temple of Boston; Dr. W. B. Riley, president of the Northwestern Bible Institute and pastor of the First Baptist Church of Minneapolis; L. B. Compton, a North Carolina evangelist; and Dr. R. A. Torrey.

Anton Cedarholm, early 1920's

Torrey was a graduate of Yale University and Divinity School and had studied in Germany. He joined D. L. Moody in 1889 and was for thirteen years the Superintendent of the Bible Institute of the Chicago Evangelization Society (now Moody Bible Institute). From 1902 to 1912, he held evangelistic meetings around the world. From 1912 to 1924 he served as Dean of the Bible Institute of Los Angeles (now Biola University), while continuing to minister in evangelism. When Torrey became ill in 1927, Anton took over his meetings; after Torrey's death in 1928, Anton finished his scheduled obligations.

In the early 1930's when Anton began to conduct his own meetings, his team included the well-known gospel pianist, Robert Harkness, and Anton's younger brother, Hilmore, who played the piano and the musical water glasses. Sometimes these tours and crusades were lengthy and far from home.

A 1928 letter of recommendation from George W. Arms, pastor of First Presbyterian church of Duluth, Minnesota, states:

> To Whom It May Concern:
>   Rev. Anton Cedarholm, together with his brother assisting at the piano and musical glasses, has completed a three weeks' evangelistic mission in our church beginning Easter Day, 1928.
>   Mr. Cedarholm not only led all the song services and sang solos but did all the preaching for two services each day. I am happy to say that Mr. Cedarholm's ability as preacher and evangelist equals his ability as song leader and soloist. In a most remarkable way, he conducts the meetings, holding his audience to the very end.
>   Our church has never had more largely attended meetings, or meetings attended with greater blessing, in its history. Overflow congregations with people standing and turned away occurred night after night. The whole city became his audience.
>   Mr. Cedarholm has a most winsome personality and particularly appeals to young people. He preaches the old-time gospel without controversy in the power of the spirit (sic). He does not do and say things which one regrets. He leaves a church on a higher spiritual level and with anew zeal to carry on its regular program.
>   I know of none better for any individual church or group of churches that are seeking a blessing in both the simplicity and power of the Gospel of the Grace of God.[11]

Promotional material for Anton often carried the following quote:

> Dr. R. A. Torrey, formerly Pastor of the Moody Memorial Church and President of the Moody Bible Institute, of Chicago, wrote, "Rev. Anton Cedarholm has for several years been my principal helper, he is a wonderful solo singer and the best choir director and song leader I have had except Charlie Alexander, but in

---

[11] Hibbing (MN) *Daily Tribune*, Thursday Evening, Oct. 11, 1928.

addition to that, he is a great preacher and many have been brought to Christ by his preaching."[12]

Another contemporary stated:

> In 1930 the Swedish Baptist evangelist, Anton Cedarholm, came to Polk county for a series of evangelistic meetings to be held in the new high school auditorium. This was a joint effort sponsored by the Covenant, Baptist, and Methodist churches. Rev. Cedarholm's campaign was more highly organized than some of the earlier visits by evangelists. He had extensive newspaper publicity pieces printed well in advance, proclaiming his ability in lofty terms. "He is an associate of R. A. Torrey" was one of the claims.

Another writer declared:

> The name Anton Cedarholm resonates with me because he was still evangelizing in 1961 when he could be heard on the Moody Bible Institute's radio station in Chicago. He had a distinctive "delivery," particularly when signing off.... "This is An–tone Cedar–holm" he would say in a drawn-out monotone. Our friend Rev. Bert Lovain's wife, Lorraine, had a story about Cedarholm. She was a student at Trinity in Chicago, about to return home after the school year, when Cedarholm made an impassioned appeal for money from listeners, "or his program would be ended." Moved by this, Lorraine sent him $10 of her last $25, which meant she would have to hitchhike the last fifteen miles on her trip home . . . the remainder of her funds would take her only that far. I hope Cedarholm appreciated that.
>
> Part of the more polished technique of the Cedarholm campaigns was to canvas the community for funds before he came, so that offerings would not be part of the meetings . . . except for a gratuity offering for the evangelist. This was duly organized and achieved.[13]

---

[12] October 7, 1944, advertisement for Anton Cedarholm preaching at Central Baptist Church (Ray Street and Shields Avenue in the Midway District, unspecified city).

[13] Folkets Vän 98. dalakarl.com/van8.html.

A 1931 newspaper article reflected on Anton's early years and concluded, "He is a man marked by the most earnest and sincere motives. He has given his life to sixteen years of sacrifice away from home and family to tell the world what he considers to be the greatest news in the world and the greatest business of the church, namely, that Jesus Christ came 'to seek and save that which is lost.'"[14] As was the case with many early fundamentalists, Anton's ministry was interdenominational, but limited to Bible believing churches. In 1945 missionaries from Bolivia told Myron that they had heard his father in New Zealand some twenty-two years earlier.[15]

Thelma's father, Martin Melford, was born on May 31, 1886, in Ving Alfsborg, Sweden, and came to the United States in 1891. He graduated from Upsala College in 1911 and Augustana Seminary in Rock Island, Illinois, with his Bachelor of Divinity (what is today called the Master of Divinity) in 1914 and was immediately ordained. His first ministry was at the Lutheran Church of Titusville, Pennsylvania, from 1914 to 1918.[16] The church was part of the Swedish Augustana Lutheran Synod.[17] This Lutheran group had been strongly influenced by the revivals of the late 1800's in Sweden and was marked by an emphasis on the need for faith to be personal, inwardly experienced, and demonstrated in one's daily life.[18] The Synod was absorbed into the Lutheran Church in America in 1962. At the time of the merger, the Augustana Synod consisted of nearly 600,000 baptized members, 1,300 congregations and 1,400

---

[14] Alhambra Post-Advocate, January 16 or 17, 1931, clipping in a scrapbook compiled by Lollie.

[15] Myron Cedarholm Journal, November 18, 1945.

[16] Conrad Bergendoff, *The Augustana Ministerium: A Study of the Careers of the 2,504 Pastors of the Augustana Evangelical Lutheran Synod/Church 1850-1962* (Rock Island, IL: Augustana Historical Society, 1980), 93.

[17] Cedarholm correspondence, 01/05/81 to Roxanne Keating, Minneapolis, MN.

[18] The following information is from "Swedish Contributions to American Lutheranism," *Grace Note*, January 2003.

Martin Melford family—Thelma is in the middle

ordained ministers, although by this time the majority of the membership was not of Swedish descent.

Two chief characteristics of these Lutherans were a concern for good order and theological orthodoxy but with a warm pietism. Thelma records an example of this warm pietism in her journal's description of 5:00 am Christmas Day church services. This group's intention to be genuine, confessional Lutherans is most clearly seen in the choice of a name for the Swedish church body—the Augustana Synod, "Augustana" being the Latin form of the Lutheran Church's chief confession, the Augsburg Confession.

The Swedish respect for "good order" can be demonstrated in the use of the Church's official liturgy on Sunday mornings—a liturgy with an unbroken continuity from the 16th Century Reformation and even the pre-Reformation Church. On the other hand, Augustana characteristically offered its congregations much opportunity for informal worship and fellowship as well. Respect for the pastoral office was balanced by a democratic polity and an emphasis upon lay participation and responsibility.

Myron and Thelma were both born in 1915, but that year was significant for more than just their births. The year was marked by great political uncertainty. Europe had been plunged into a continental war. The sinking of the Lusitania just six weeks before Myron's birth put neutral America on guard. The world was shaken with frightful new weapons such as mustard gas and armored tanks. Eighteen months later, when Myron's only brother, Jason, was born, America was sending boys "over there" in the war that was supposed to end all wars.

The year 1915 also marked the last year of publication of *The Fundamentals*, a series of twelve books published to defend orthodox Christianity against the liberalism of the day. The initial editor was R. A. Torrey. The major denominations had slid into liberalism. The national influence of evangelists and revivals had dimmed, battles to purify mainline denominations were faltering, and early in the year on February 12, the little blind poetess and songwriter, Fanny Crosby, passed away at the age of 95, bringing something of an end to an era.

Still, the Lord had his remnant. Scattered among the Presbyterians, Methodists, Baptists, and Lutherans were those who rejected the new liberalism. Today, few, if any, of those mainline denominations could be considered sound, but at that time, Biblicists were found in all of them. From such groups connections began to develop between those who were loyal Biblicists first and denominationalists second.

The connections shaped the lives, training, and ministry of the Cedarholms and Melfords and, ultimately, brought Myron and Thelma to the conviction that the label "independent Baptist" stood closest to the biblical mandate for genuine faith.

When Anton graduated from the Boone Biblical College, Lollie was expecting their first child. She was hoping for a girl, but the Lord sent Blaine Myron Cedarholm on June 20, 1915. Anton was on an evangelistic trip, so he was not present for Myron's birth.

Lollie was a woman of prayer.[19] It was not unusual to find her on her knees, praying for her boys. She always seemed to be the first of the congregation to extend an invitation of hospitality to the visiting missionary or

---

[19] The following two pages are from "A Prince of a Man," Fall Festival presentation, Fall 1970.

preacher.

Some of Myron's earliest recollections were those of being bounced on a missionary's knee or sitting at the feet of some preacher, listening with keen interest to his experiences. Sunday afternoons were spent in singing hymns and reading Bible stories and accounts of missionaries. When Myron was quite young, Lollie gave him the two-volume biography of Hudson Taylor to read. A longstanding family story was that once while attending a missionary service, Lollie was so moved by the appeal, she slipped off her wedding band and dropped it into the offering plate.

Lollie and Myron

Lollie was a wonderful musician and loved playing the piano. Music was always coming from their home. In fact, years later, when the Cedarholms moved her to Watertown to care for her in her final years, music still came from her apartment on Maranatha's campus. Staff members living in the bottom half of the duplex where Lollie lived recall her playing the piano late into the night.

Those who met Myron in his ministry years realized that he was usually in a hurry. That hurriedness started early in his life. At ten months, he gave up crawling for walking. Before he was two years old, he was on a boat ride at his grandfather Carlson's farm. Without warning he jumped from the boat into the water and did the natural thing—he began swimming. It is little surprise then that he became well known for his love of surfing, boating, and water skiing.

Jason and Myron

Since Anton was often absent, Uncle Paul, Lollie's bachelor brother, spent hours entertaining the young brothers. He decided that the boys should learn how to tell time. No one had ever explained to Paul that pre-schoolers were too young for such a lesson, but Myron and Jason learned to tell time. This seemed to prefigure Myron who would go on to accomplish numerous feats that "could not" be done.

Anton moved his family to Orange Street, St. Paul, to share a house with another evangelist couple, Eric and Hueldah Anderson. Hueldah played the harp, from which came the most magnificent music Myron's young ears had ever heard. He determined that one day, he would have a harp in his own home, an ambition realized once the Cedarholms were finally settled at Maranatha.

Sports were an early part of Myron's life. Although he still sported his long blond curls at the age of four, he could also handle a ball, any kind of ball. His youth was marked by the ball seasons: football, basketball, and baseball. In the summer swimming was thrown in for variety. There are even reports of boxing matches taking place on the family's back porch. He participated in five sports in high school: football, track, water polo, tennis and baseball. "Moss," as he was called, could play any sport. His love for sports was present his entire life.

Myron was involved in more than sports, however. On one occasion Anton boarded a train to travel to another evangelistic campaign. Myron and Jason were there. They pressed their faces against the window to watch their father settle into his seat for the trip. After the train pulled away from the station, Anton saw the hand-prints of the boys on the window. He already missed his boys. A few days later he made a long-distance phone call

Myron and Jason

home just to talk to his sons, a difficult and expensive act in those days. Myron answered the phone, but quickly said, "Hi, Dad. Sorry I can't talk to you right now. I'm balancing the books for my paper route."

Several states away, in Titusville, Pennsylvania, on August 3, 1915, a baby girl, Thelma Elvera, was born into the home of Martin and Anna Melford. Thelma was the first of five children; Eunice, her only sister, was the youngest. In between were her brothers, Wendel, Ralph, and Leslie. The family spoke only Swedish in the home. Thelma had to learn English to go to school. To the end of her life, she often sang hymns in Swedish, especially one of her favorites, "How Great Thou Art."

In 1918, her father left his church in Pennsylvania for one in West Sveadahl, Minnesota, a small town southwest of

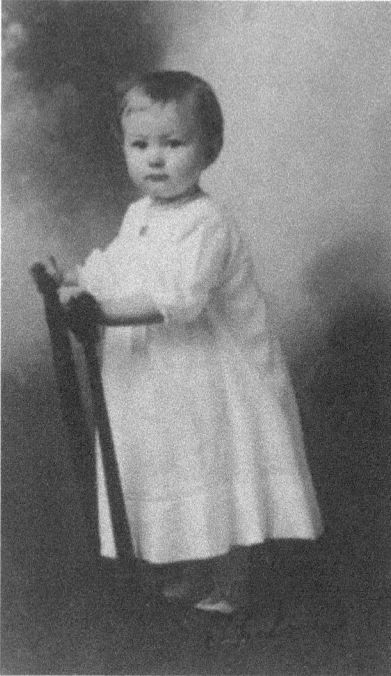

Thelma

Minneapolis. The family would make Minnesota home, where God would bring Myron, the young man born in Minnesota, and Thelma, the young lady brought to Minnesota at a young age, together for a life of service—as Baptists, of all things!

So, how did these denominationally diverse young people end up as career fundamental Baptists? To learn the why and wherefore, one must trek back to 1814, a little more than a century before Myron and Thelma were born, when the first Baptist service organization in America was formed. The General Missionary Convention of the Baptist Denomination in the United States for Foreign Missions was organized to support Adoniram Judson, America's first Baptist missionary. The name was later changed to the American Baptist Missionary Union and then to the American Baptist Foreign Mission Society (ABFMS). In 1824, the Baptist General Tract Society was started; it later became the American Baptist Publication Society. Then in 1832 the American Baptist Home Mission Society was begun. A plan to unite these societies, along with various state conventions, into a national organization began in 1896; in 1907, these

independent organizations joined forces to form the Northern Baptist Convention (NBC) to coordinate the functions of the agencies and better unite the Baptists of the north. Although the majority of Baptists at that time were theologically conservative, the leadership of this new Convention consisted mainly of theological liberals. This created an immediate division in the NBC.

For some time, American Biblicists had been casting an increasingly wary eye on the German higher criticism present in the denominational seminaries and colleges. In reaction, schools like Boone Bible College that trained Myron's parents, Nyack College, Moody Bible Institute, and a host of others provided Bible training that would not destroy faith while training ministerial students. Between 1909 and 1915, Lyman and Milton Stewart financed, and A. C. Dixon (a graduate of Southern Baptist Theological Seminary and pastor of Moody Church from 1906 to 1911), Louis Meyer (a Jewish Christian and evangelist to the Jews), and R. A. Torrey spearheaded the publication of twelve books containing articles written by sixty-four conservative believers from the United States, Great Britain, and Canada. Stewart's vision was to finance the sending of these books to "every Protestant minister, evangelist, missionary, theological professor, Bible student, Sunday School superintendent, YMCA and YWCA secretary in the English-speaking world, whose address they could obtain."[20] The series was called *The Fundamentals* and articulated a defense of the historic, literal interpretation of Scripture.

Across the nation the Methodist, Baptist, and Presbyterian denominations all felt the encroachments of liberal-minded men moving into positions of prominence, influence, and power. The situation was especially disturbing because those who had changed their beliefs from the historic, biblical norm refused to abandon the historic, biblical denominations and establish their own movements. Instead, the modernists seemed to be counting on the fact that the financial backbone of the church, the man in the

---

[20] *The Fundamentals: A Testimony to the Truth* (Chicago: Testimony Publishing Company, 1909), 1: 4.

pew, did not really know what he believed and would prove quite elastic in what he would support with his offerings. He could be loyal to whomever disturbed him the least. Those who did know were distressed by the political subtlety of the one group and the spiritual complacency of the other. Congregations that had been unified now faced the unsettling circumstance of not really knowing what others across the aisle might think. Following one's conscience began to cost friends, finances, and security. Many felt that if those who purposed to stand for the truth of Scripture could just get organized and unified, they could effectively rout those who were stealing their ecclesiastical church bodies.

From May 21 to May 27, 1919, when Thelma and Myron were but three years old, the NBC held its annual convention in Denver. The main speaker was Harry Emerson Fosdick, who would later become the popular voice of liberal theology. The Convention voted at this meeting to participate in the Interchurch World Movement, an interdenominational effort to raise funds for all member denominations; conservatives were disturbed at its lack of doctrinal convictions. Curtis Lee Laws declared, "Because it represented everybody, it was under obligation to offend nobody."[21]

In 1920, 156 pastors and laymen signed a "call" (an open letter of invitation) for a meeting before the NBC annual meeting began. The call was aimed toward those who were alarmed by the havoc that rationalism was causing in their churches and the rejection of the autonomy of local Baptist churches in favor of a strong, centralized system of authority over the churches and institutions aligned with the Convention.

> To all Baptists Within the Bounds of the Northern Convention.
> Greeting: We view with increasing alarm the havoc which rationalism is working in our churches as evidenced by the drift upon the part of many of our ministers from the fundamentals of our holy faith. The

---

[21] Curtis Lee Laws, "Introduction," *Baptist Fundamentals* (Philadelphia: Judson, 1920).

teaching in many of our educational institutions is proving disastrous to the faith of the young men and women who are to be the leaders of the future. A widespread and growing worldliness has crept into the churches, a worldliness which has robbed us of power and brought upon us open shame. We believe that there rests upon us as Baptists an immediate and urgent duty to restate, reaffirm, and re-emphasize the fundamentals of our New Testament faith. Beyond all doubt the vast majority of our Baptist people are as loyal as were our fathers to our Baptist principles and our Baptist polity, but this loyalty will not long continue unless something is done to stay the rising tide of liberalism and rationalism, and to preserve our principles in their simplicity and purity. Therefore, acting upon our own initiative as your brethren, we issue this call for a conference on "The Fundamentals of Our Baptist Faith," to be held in the Delaware Avenue Church, Buffalo, from seven P.M. Monday, June 21, to 9:30 P.M. Tuesday, June 22. These dates immediately precede the meeting of the Northern Baptist Convention. All Baptists within the bounds of the Northern Convention are invited to attend this conference. Let increasing prayer be made for the guidance and favor of God.

Adopted April 21, 1920.

Your brethren in Christ.

Three thousand responded to the call, necessitating a move from the original church location to a public auditorium for the second night. The thirteen messages preached in the hours between 7 pm Monday and 9:30 pm Tuesday were compiled into a book entitled, *Baptist Fundamentals*.[22]

When both the pre-convention and the national convention concluded, Curtis Lee Laws went to prepare his thoughts about the convention for his paper, *The Watchman-Examiner*, the leading Baptist magazine in the North. His editorial, "Convention Side Lights," issued something of its own call. Those committed to driving out the modernists from

---

[22] *Baptist Fundamentals: Being Addresses Delivered at the Pre-Convention Conference at Buffalo June 21 and June 22, 1920* (Philadelphia: Judson, 1920).

the established group needed their own defining label, a rallying point, a single word that would mark a man as standing for the inspiration of Scripture, the virgin birth, the deity of Christ, the atonement, and the place of evangelism and world-wide missions in fulfilling the cause of Christ. Laws recommended a term that would come to mark both a movement and the entire adult ministries of the Cedarholms:

> We here and now move that a new word be adopted to describe the men among us who insist that the landmarks shall not be removed. "Conservatives" is too closely allied with reactionary forces in all walks of life. "Premillennialists" is too closely allied with a single doctrine and not sufficiently inclusive. "Landmarkers" has a historical disadvantage and connotes a particular group of radical conservatives.
>
> We suggest that those who still cling to the great fundamentals and who mean to do battle royal for the fundamentals shall be called "Fundamentalists."[23]

The conservatives who attended this pre-convention conference wanted to ensure that their voice against modernism within the NBC would be a compelling one, and to this end they organized the National Federation of Fundamentalists of the Northern Baptist Convention[24] or as it was also called, The Fundamentalist Federation of the Northern Baptist Convention.[25] The Fellowship was not organically related to the Convention. "Its purpose was to oppose centralized ecclesiastical authority, to oppose theological modernism and to contend for the Baptist faith as based upon the Scriptures."[26] The primary goal of this

---

[23] Curtis Lee Laws, "Convention Side Lights," *Watchman-Examiner* (July 1, 1920), 834.

[24] James Leo Garrett, *Baptist Theology: A Four-Century Study* (Macon, GA: Mercer University Press, 2009), 331.

[25] Richard V. Clearwaters, "Forty Years of History Look Down upon Conservative Baptists," *Central Bible Quarterly*, 05.1 (Spring 1962), 17.

[26] "THE CONSERVATIVE BAPTIST FELLOWSHIP, Its History and Present Position," *Conservative Baptist Fellowship Information Bulletin* 8.6 (December 1962), 5.

Federation was to take back control of the leadership of the Convention. Each year a pre-convention conference was held to encourage the conservatives just before the national NBC convention and to make plans to deal with the liberal leadership of the NBC. And almost every year the liberal leadership thwarted the fundamentalist attempts to purge the Convention of those liberals.

After the 1920 NBC convention, a group of fundamentalists organized the General Council of Cooperating Baptist Missions of North America (now called Baptist Mid-Missions) at the First Baptist Church in Elyria, Ohio. The first missionaries focused their attention on Africa. This was the first of what would become a series of churches and individuals who would abandon the NBC and build new fundamentalist agencies and associations. These new organizations would play a significant role in the lives of Myron and Thelma in the coming years.

On June 20, 1920, Myron celebrated his fifth birthday. While much was happening in the religious world, all that is known of Myron's life in that year is that the most important decision he would ever make was sealed at his mother's knees. On July 1, he received Christ as Savior. That same year Martin Melford moved his family to Comfrey, a small town not many miles from West Sveadahl. He served as pastor of the Lutheran churches in both cities.

In Indianapolis in 1922, the conservatives attempted to have the NBC endorse the New Hampshire Confession of Faith as the standard of doctrine, but the liberals turned back the effort. Cornelius Woelfkin, a popular New York preacher, offered a substitute motion "that the Northern Baptist Convention affirm that the New Testament is an all-sufficient ground for Baptist faith and practice, and they need no other statement." It was hard for a Baptist to vote against the Bible, and this motion won by a vote of 1,264 to 637.[27] This rejection was significant because earlier in the

---

[27] Bruce L. Shelley, *A History of Conservative Baptists* (Wheaton: Conservative Baptist Press, 1971), 12.

year representatives (including the presidents) of the NBC and the Southern Baptist Convention (SBC) met to determine if they could create a single doctrinal statement that both Conventions could adopt.[28]

Little of this theological turmoil affected Myron and Thelma. Their elementary years were in the decade of the twenties, but both lived in homes that sheltered them from much of the changing culture. History buffs know the era for the Roaring Twenties, prohibition, gangsters, and the aftermath of the Great War. Biblicists recognize these years as some of the most turbulent in the modernist/literalist struggles for influence in the schools and churches of the country. In the midst of all this, Myron and Thelma lived fairly normal childhoods.

Thelma loved school. One of her stories is about her school days.

It was a sunny September morning when Papa took me by the hand and led me down the narrow street to the

Thelma – Back Row, 4th from Left

---

[28] *Watchman-Examiner*, Feb 2, 1922, 137-38, and Feb 16, 1922, 208.

big brick building I had so often longed to visit. There at the top of the stairs stood the teacher, welcoming one and all to her classroom. Papa introduced me to Miss Dahl, and at once I loved her. She led me into the classroom and when all the others had gathered in the classroom, she had us speak our names, one by one very clearly so that she would not forget and then she assigned us to our seats. At her return to go down the aisle, the little boy who stood before me made an abrupt turn to look at me, and his long, yellow pencil punctured my right hand, and there was imbedded the lead that I carried all my life as I remembered my first day at school. I always loved learning, and it was a joy to compete one with the other in the classroom all the way through grade school.

When I came as far as the third and fourth grade room, for several weeks I sat on one side of the room, but I was always interested in what was going on on the other side, the fourth-grade side.

When it came to the late spring and I received my report card for the fourth time, I carried it home, but across the top of the card was written, "Fourth Grade." I could not understand what my teacher meant by that and she never did really explain it to me until the end of the year. The card carried these words across the top, "Promoted to Fifth Grade." It was then that I realized that I had spent four six-week periods in the third and two six-week periods in the fourth grade. Thus, I left my class-mates and learned to know a new group of young people in the next grade.

In the seventh grade, I had a lovely teacher. Everyone loved her, but somehow it seemed like she was absent quite a bit during the last part of the year, and we wondered why, until one day the announcement came to us, "Miss Tholhorn is no longer with us and she will not be back." She had passed away, and we all cried. And then we had to become accustomed to a new teacher. I do not even remember her name.

When I was about in the fourth grade or the fifth perhaps, it was Papa who took me downtown to buy me a pair of ice skates. I had an early pair, the kind that you clamp on the sides of your feet, but he thought I was old enough now to be able to wear real shoe skates, and so I tried them on. Papa bought them, and we went directly to the ice rink. There I donned the shoe skates and I had the time of my life. Papa was interested that we should become accustomed to the cold and to all the sports that were associated with the cold, so we often went sledding and skiing, but I loved skating the most. And this skating was a joy throughout my life.

It was Papa who took me fishing. I can't say that I loved fishing very much, and after I spent a day with Papa in the little row boat, I loved it less. I sat all day with my pole in the water and not even a bite. Papa caught several, but the lake didn't have any fish for me, so I never learned to love fishing. My brothers all loved fishing because they caught fish all the time, but I think there must have been something wrong with my bait, or even with me since I didn't catch any fish.

Hermosa Beach Baptist Church

In 1922, Myron's father, Anton, left on a lengthy evangelistic trip to Hawaii, New Zealand, Australia, China, Japan, India, Germany, France, Britain, and Sweden.[29] Toward the end of this tour, Myron and Jason wrote a letter to him. They said that they missed him, they needed him, and they asked him to please come home to spend time with his sons, while there was still time. The letter must have been quite persuasive, for when Anton returned home, he left his evangelistic travels and took up pastoral ministry. In 1923, Anton moved his family to Hermosa Beach, California, where he became the pastor of the Hermosa Beach Baptist Church.

---

[29] Anton Cedarholm, passport application.

This was Anton's second pastoral ministry. Earlier in his life, he had served as the "Associate Pastor" of New York City's Gospel Tabernacle Church, established by A. B. Simpson, founder of the Christian and Missionary Alliance. After the death of Simpson, no one was given the title of "Pastor" of the church, but only "Associate Pastor."[30]

While the Cedarholms were enjoying the California sunshine, the American Baptist Foreign Mission Society was implementing what was called the "Inclusive Policy." The policy stated:

> Our denomination, our Society, and our churches have always given to officers, missionaries, and pastors a considerable degree of liberty of theological opinion. To be sure, we have always insisted on a living Christian experience, on a passion for the salvation of men, on loyalty to our Lord Jesus and His gospel, and on belief in the vital teachings of our religion, but it has not been our Baptist custom to limit too explicitly the form in which these doctrines must be held and expressed....
>
> The Board, composed like our churches of men and women of diverse opinions, has heretofore included and should include among its officers and missionaries representatives of various elements among our people. [31]

The losses of the fundamentalists led many to leave the Convention and start a more militant organization. The Baptist Bible Union[32] was formed in 1923, under the leadership of fundamentalists W. B. Riley, J. Frank Norris (pastor of First Baptist Church, Dallas, Texas, who had been

---

[30] Mary H. Spencer, "New Associate Pastor of Gospel Tabernacle Church Reiterates Belief of Its Founder in the Inerrancy and Infallibility of the Scriptures." This is an undated newspaper article. Anton Cedarholm refers to being a pastor in New York in *My Nervous Background,* so this took place before 1932. This writer has been unable to discover any dates for this ministry.

[31] *Watchman-Examiner* (15 Nov 1923), 1468.

[32] The definitive history of the Baptist Bible Union is Robert George Delnay, *A History of the Baptist Bible Union* (Winston-Salem: Piedmont, 1974).

evicted from the Southern Baptist Convention), T. T. Shields (a Canadian Baptist), and A. C. Dixon. Their first meeting was held on May 11–15, 1923. This organization was broader than the NBC, for it included churches in the South and Canada, as well as the North. Dr. T. T. Shields of Canada was elected President. Dr. W. B. Riley of Minneapolis was chosen as Northern Vice President, and J. Frank Norris as Southern Vice President. Because this organization separated (for the most part) from the NBC, it became a positive alternative to the Fundamentalist Fellowship. Nine years later the BBU held its last meeting, and from its ashes came the General Association of Regular Baptist Churches.[33]

The events in the NBC had little impact on Thelma. Her family was in the Swedish Lutheran church and did not go through the various battles of the Baptists. Her family moved often, so her closest friendships in her earlier life were her family. One of Thelma's stories was about her youngest brother, Ralph, who was born in 1923, when Thelma was eight years old.

> I was not happy with the message that Papa brought. "You have a new baby brother." But I wanted a sister, not another brother. I already had two of those, and besides, nobody told me that there would be any kind of a baby in the house. I ran into the bedroom, threw myself across the covers, buried my head in the pillow, and sobbed out my grief. "Lord, I wanted a sister." Well, what a sorry welcome I gave the little preacher boy. Interestingly enough, when this little boy grew up, he did become a preacher.

In 1924, when Myron was nine, the fundamentalists managed to get the NBC to create a Committee of Investigation to examine the problem of liberalism on the mission field. While the investigation discovered clear evidence of theological liberalism and inter-denominational cooperation, after it gave its report in 1926, the Convention chose to do nothing. Also in 1926, the Convention decided to

---

[33] See Kevin Bauder and Robert Delnay, *One in Hope and Doctrine* (Arlington Heights, IL: Regular Baptist Press, 2014) for a thorough introduction to the formation of the General Association of Regular Baptists.

allow churches with non-immersed members into the Convention.

Numerous sources indicate that Myron was baptized by his father on his tenth birthday, June 20, 1925. However, that was a Saturday. There is no indication as to whether he was baptized at a Saturday service or on the following Sunday.

At about this same time, Thelma was becoming quite the musician.

It was Papa who saw in me a love for music, and when I was young, he thought perhaps I would enjoy a guitar. So, he bought me a Hawaiian guitar, and I learned to play it quickly. Then he began to write verses and would put them to tunes that were familiar. When the parent-teacher association met at school, it seemed like I was always there to play a number. Papa wrote verses that included the names of the various people in the community, the postmaster, the pharmacist, the blacksmith, the doctor, the storekeeper. I don't know how many people were there, but they were all in the song by name. And I would sing them lustily to the melodies that were familiar and the people clapped, and I supposed they liked the numbers; I'm not sure. As I think of it now, it's rather interesting that that should be the beginning of my musical career.

He bought me a little mandolin, too, and I played it for a time.

I'll never forget the time that Mother and Dad were talking together in the kitchen, and I heard him say to her, "Mama, you know if that girl is going to play on those old pump organs in everybody's house, we might just as well give her piano lessons so she can play right." And so, they engaged a local teacher by the name of Professor Askeling. Now Professor Askeling was quite an old gent. He had somewhat of a suggestion of a beard and a mustache, and I'm not so sure he could always walk straight when he came to our house. I really was afraid of him, because I didn't like the way he walked. It was not too long after that that Papa said, "I think we better let him go, he's not a good influence around here." He was dismissed, but before he left, he gave me his picture, so I have that to this day.

Arlene was a young lady in our church who had gone to music school. She had learned to become a piano teacher, and she was engaged to teach me, and I loved her. I wasn't always as, well, shall I say, ardent a student as I might have been, because I didn't appreciate practicing very much. I always liked to put the clock on the piano and set the alarm. Then I knew the time would go by faster, and I could go to my other duties instead of having to play the piano.

We had another organist who came to our church, and he stopped by our place often and wanted me to play for him as I progressed, and I did. He brought me music, some of which he had himself composed, and I enjoyed all of that.

As I grew older and approached high school, I didn't like to practice, and towards the latter years of my high school days, my Father said to me one day, "Well, if you're not going to practice, you might just as well not have any lessons, so I don't think we'll have any lessons for you anymore." I rejoiced on the outside, but on the inside my heart felt badly to think that I had given up an opportunity to learn.

In my senior year of high school, I was elected to take the place of the accompanist in the school and also to become the organist in our church, for Olive (that's the name of the organist) was graduating and she was going off to college. I loved being the organist at the church. My younger brother sat at the side of the organ and he pumped it up and down, up and down, as I played. That was a strange combination we had there at the church anyway. My Father was the pastor. I was the organist, and my brother pumped the organ and also pulled the bell. He was the janitor. He rode up and down on the rope that pulled the bell, so he had a great time.

Well, since Olive had graduated, I took her place at the church and also at the school. The music teacher at the school was very interested in me for some reason. When she went to Minneapolis to take a lesson in voice and conducting, she took me along so that I could have a lesson in accompaniment. I appreciated that as it has stood me in good stead all these years.

In July of 1925, when Myron was ten and Thelma was still nine, the Scopes Monkey trial was held. John T. Scopes, a high school biology teacher, had been enlisted by the ACLU to teach evolution in a public school classroom in violation of the laws of Tennessee. When the ACLU hired Dudley Field Malone and Clarence Darrow as defense attorneys (well-known and high powered attorneys), W. B. Riley arranged for William Jennings Bryan to assist the District Attorney in the trial. The trial attracted national attention, especially because H. L. Mencken, one of the leading literary figures in America in his time, covered the trial. He was the one who coined the term "Monkey Trial" as he wrote articles mocking fundamentalism for the *Baltimore Sun* and *American Mercury*.

In 1926, the NBC adopted a resolution which allowed churches that practiced open membership (there is no requirement for believer's baptism to join this type of church) to have delegates seated in the NBC. This was representative of the breakdown of the Baptist distinctives in the NBC.

During the following year, while Myron and Thelma were in junior high school, the Association of Baptists for World Evangelism was organized in reaction to the modernism of the American Baptist Foreign Mission Society. Also in 1927, the California Regular Baptist Association organized the Los Angeles Baptist Theological Seminary. In that same year the Melfords moved to Amery, Wisconsin, a town northeast of Minneapolis. The following year, thirteen-year-old Thelma accepted the Lord Jesus Christ as her Savior at a Lutheran youth conference.

The Melfords were a loving family, and Thelma remembers Christmas as the perfect time to share gifts of love with the rest of the family. Since Thelma was the eldest child, she was usually the one left in charge while her parents were on church business or away for an evening. Many of her childhood stories centered around the events that took place while her parents were gone.

It was almost Christmas. Any day now the packages would arrive from Mama's church. Aunt Hilda always shopped at Marshall Fields, and that meant that every package was elegantly and carefully wrapped in the most beautiful paper we had ever seen. The day came. Among all the bundles was a huge wooden box. How could that be a Christmas present? Papa quickly rescued it and carried it up the back stairs and into Mama's closet. We were heartbroken. Why couldn't we open the box now? "No," he explained. "It's not Christmas yet." The boys were so overcome with curiosity, they quickly called a private committee meeting to decide if we could somehow open that box and if we could do it now. Since I was the *barnsjuksköterska* (which means child nurse) entrusted with the care of the other siblings when Papa and Mama were away tending to matters at one of the other churches, I decided that now would be the time for action.

The evening came and time was a premium. We all crept up the stairs with hammers, screwdrivers and chisels and with all the strength that we could muster we worked feverishly to pry open the cover of that box. We pulled out all the crinkled paper and the padding and carefully uncovered it, the most beautiful face of a doll almost as tall as I. Its big, blue eyes peeked out from beneath eyelids moving up and down and smiling lips and moving pink tongue and pearly white teeth looked just like those of our baby sister. The ruffled powder blue dress covered with dainty white lace brought "OOOHHHSSS" and "AAAHHHSSS" from all of us. "Hurry up, Papa might be coming." Hastily we closed the precious treasure and scurried down the stairs. No one would ever know. Christmas had come!

The Great Depression began in October 1929, when Myron and Thelma were in high school. There is nothing to indicate that the Melfords or Cedarholms suffered any excessive hardship in their families. Whether that is because they were somewhat immune from the depression because of their parents' ministries or because they were already used to living on a small income, neither made any reference to the depression. In fact, Martin had grown up in Rhode Island and was able to afford to take the family back there frequently to visit relatives.

It was Papa who gave us a start all through life and we learned many, many things from him. It was Papa who gave us a love to travel. Since Papa had spent his entire childhood in the state of Rhode Island, we often made trips by car to the East where we could visit Grandma Swanson and all of our cousins on my father's side. As we traveled through the various states, he pointed out the places of interest. When we came to particular cities, he would relate them to history and explain how that in the years past, the pioneers of our country had built a nation which we would now call "The United States." We often wanted to travel to the West, but he said, "No, we will travel in the East where history is made, and when you are older, you can travel to the mountains of the West." To this day we take great interest in Philadelphia, New York, and Niagara Falls, the Cumberland Mountains, Gettysburg, Boston, Washington, D.C., and Chicago.

Martin moved the Melfords in 1931 to Almelund, Minnesota, northeast of Minneapolis and just across the border from their former church in Wisconsin. This would be his last pastorate.

In 1932 Myron graduated from Redondo Union High School, Redondo Beach, California. He participated in track, basketball, and tennis. The family home was just across the street from the Pacific Ocean. As soon as school and practices were over, Myron would rush home, get his surfboard, and hit the waves. Sports were not his sole interest, however.

Cederholm, Myron
"Swede"
Hobby: Track; Latin Club
'29, '30; R Club '29, '30,
'31, '32; Basketball '28,
'29; Track '31, '32; Tennis
'29, '30.

He was also part of the Latin Club and the Fisherman's Club, a club at his high school for those who wanted to witness and win souls to Christ.While Myron was in high school, Admiral Richard Byrd, who had flown to the North Pole in 1926 and the South Pole in 1929, made an

CLA// C BA/KET BALL

Myron—first row, far right

Myron—second row, fourth from the right

appearance in California. Myron was not about to miss that event, so he rode his bicycle fifteen miles to see him.

Myron was not the only athlete. Thelma enjoyed sports as well.

It was also Papa who taught us to swim. At least he challenged us. You see, he had learned to swim in the East, near an old mill where the boys oftentimes played on the logs and as they did so, sometimes they had some experiences that almost would have led them to their death. He fell off the log one time and he had to swim. He

was just a little fellow, about four years of age, and since
he learned to swim that way, he just figured the rest of us
should learn to swim the same way. One day he
announced that it was time to learn to swim. So, we
scurried about back in the dressing room, donned our
bathing suits and ran down to the lake about a block
away. We threw ourselves into the water and were
determined that we should learn to swim before Papa
came down. He oftentimes walked beside the lake
swinging a little cane behind him. It probably was a willow
stick. We waited for him to come, but were so anxious to
show him that we could swim. Yes, we could swim, and
when he rounded the corner and came down by the little
park, my brother called out to him, "Look, Papa, we can
already swim, all of us, all of us can swim." Papa stood
and watched for a time and was satisfied. So, he returned
home and eventually we did, too, but we were frightened
at the first, for we feared that if we had not known how to
swim, he would have thrown us in.

Sometime later he told us that it was the day we were
going to learn to dive. Well, how could we learn to dive; we
really didn't have a diving board. But it seems that
somebody had begun to build a diving board, or else had
built some sort of a platform so that there were fenceposts
in the water, and some of them stood above the water,
maybe a foot or two, and they could serve as diving
boards, we thought. So, when the day came and he made
that announcement, we dashed into the lake, and before
he came down, sure enough, we all could dive. My little
brother dived with his nose shut, pinching it with his
fingers. My older brother and I both learned to go in head
first, and we thought that was some accomplishment.
Swimming became fun for us, and we were glad we all
learned, and we all learned to dive eventually. But it was
Papa who gave us the start.

It was Papa who taught me to love sports. He taught
me to run and to jump, and I loved both so much that I
continued to enter into competitive sports all through my
childhood and even into college. I participated in all the
sports the girls did, softball, high jumping, pole vaulting,
and throwing the shot. I even kept score for baseball
games for Papa when each Thursday he had to go over to
the Ladies Aid meeting to carry out the devotional time.
He gave me the scoreboard and explained to me how to

mark the various plays. At first, we just had a little crystal set and then a little later a battery radio, so I would sit down in his big chair, put on the headphones, and then mark the score.

In 1932, Anton moved the Cedarholms to Waterloo, Iowa. He had come earlier to the Burton Avenue Baptist Church for an evangelistic meeting. "This campaign was greatly owned of God. The church could not accommodate all those who wanted to hear the Word of God. Many people came to a saving knowledge of Jesus Christ during these special services."[34] Shortly after this meeting, the pastor resigned, and the church called Anton as their pastor. He began his ministry on September 1. While in Waterloo, Anton started a radio ministry called "The Family Altar Broadcast." The motto was "God willing, 'on' the air until Jesus comes 'in' the air." The broadcast was later taken over by Hilmore Cedarholm, Anton's brother.

That same year one group of fundamentalists left the NBC and started the General Association of Regular Baptist Churches (GARBC). This association rose from the ashes of the Baptist Bible Union. While the BBU allowed both churches and individuals in its membership, basically equating individuals with churches, the GARBC allowed only churches into its membership. In its first ten years, it attracted about five hundred churches. A sizable number of fundamentalists, however, remained in the NBC. It was with this remaining group that Myron and Thelma would eventually cast their lot.

In 1933, in reaction to the fundamentalists, the ABFMS adopted the "Evangelical Policy," which had been first promoted by the Bible believers in 1924: "We will appoint only suitable evangelical men and women; we will appoint evangelicals and we will not appoint non-evangelicals."[35] The problem was that "evangelical" had different meanings to the

---

[34] Anton Cedarholm, *My Nervous Breakdown: The Conquest of Fear* (Waterloo, Iowa: Cedar Publishing, 1945), 15.

[35] *Watchman-Examiner* (25 May 1925), 1468.

modernists and fundamentalists. While the evangelical policy sounded better, in reality the inclusive policy was the actual practice of the Board. The goal of the inclusive policy was for the various mission boards of the NBC to include representatives of all the theological positions present within the NBC.[36] This required the mission societies to appoint liberals to the mission field so that there was an appropriate "balance" of truth and error. This was one of the foremost sticking points for the fundamentalists.

Thelma grew up looking forward to what God had in store for her. "In my early days, I wanted to be a missionary to the heart of China. In fact, I had chosen the province and even the people and the mission with whom I would be associated. But then the door closed, and those whom I knew and loved either were captured or sent out of the country. Some fled for their lives, and now it all reads like a story book. I still love the Chinese people. I am glad the Lord has sent some of them to Maranatha."[37] She maintained her lifelong love for all things oriental, and though she never lived in China as a missionary, the Lord made it possible for her to visit Hong Kong, Taiwan, Japan, Korea, and, finally, in 1985, fulfilling that lifelong desire, mainland China.

One of Thelma's stories tells of her desire to be a missionary:

> Once there was a little girl whose daddy was a pastor. One day a missionary from China came to her daddy's church and spoke about the far away land of China and of the strange habits of the Chinese. One seemed almost too appalling to believe. Little girls' feet were bound in bandages to stunt the growth of their feet. The feet were compressed into delicate and beautiful shoes, but at what a cost of deformed and misshapen feet that could not do what the Lord intended feet to do. When the missionaries came, and the Truth was shed abroad in the hearts of the

---

[36] Chester E. Tulga, *The Story of the Inclusive Policy of the American Baptist Foreign Mission Society 1923-1944* (Chicago: Conservative Baptist Fellowship of Northern Baptists, n.d.), 3-7.

[37] Thelma Cedarholm personal correspondence to a former Chinese missionary, April 22, 1982.

Chinese people, Chinese believers rejected the practice of foot binding. One young Chinese girl who wanted children in the faraway United States to see and understand, gave her binding shoes to the missionary who had unbound her heart with the gospel. That missionary was much impressed with the pastor's daughter and her serious desire to go to China as a missionary. He left her with one of the little shoes. I was that little girl.[38]

Charlotte Cedarholm still has that shoe.

Thelma would tell stories of household pranks. "One night Mother and Father had gone out, and we opened up the piano just like the piano tuner and put papers in all the strings, just like the piano tuner, and then we played and played and played with the papers fluttering in the strings. Then we put all the papers away, and everyone was tucked in bed before Mother and Father came home."

In another story, she told of the time when, "Mother and Father had gone out, and the big Christmas tree stood in the room, full of tinsel and balls and little candles, waiting to be lit. We carefully lit all the candles, but somehow the tree fell over and suddenly the little flames were dancing all over the tree and the carpet. Quickly, the children put out the flames, righted the tree, repaired the decorations, and were all tucked in bed before Mother and Father came home."

---

[38] Many children know of that story from the account, *Beautiful Feet,* written by a Maranatha graduate for the BJU Press third grade reader. See Appendix A.

Another evening when Mother and Father had gone out, and Wendel was chasing Ralph with the toilet plunger, through the hall, up front steps, down the back steps, and back through the hall again. On one pass, while speeding through the hallway, the plunger stuck onto the wall, and when Wendel pulled it away, it made such a pretty shape on the wall where the wallpaper pulled off, that Wendel just had to stab the wall once more to see what would happen when the plunger was pulled away. The marks were so interesting, he had to try it again, and again, and again. Because Thelma was in charge when Mother and Father were gone, she went up to the attic, found the extra wallpaper, brought it down, and carefully cut and tore new pieces to fit every one of the "plunger pox" scattered along the hallway. All the spots were repaired, everything was cleaned up, and everyone was tucked in bed before Mother and Father came home.

Years later, when Thelma told her mother what had happened that night, her mother said, "Oh, Thelma, you could never have done that."

COLLEGE AND COURTING YEARS:
1932–1941

Myron and Thelma both graduated from high school in 1932. In the coming years, God would bring their families together in His plan for their lives.

After Myron's graduation from high school in California and the family's relocation that summer to Iowa, Myron entered Iowa State Teachers College in Cedar Falls, Iowa (renamed as Northern Iowa University in 1967), completing his freshman and sophomore years (1932–1934). He declared a commercial education major, with minors in French and history. He was active in football, basketball, and track. His goal was to play professional football for as long as he could and then coach or go into business.

Myron made quite the impression on the gridiron at State Teachers College for the *Panther Cubs* that fall.

Myron and one of his famous 60-yard kicks

A California-bronzed, high school prep star made his way onto the campus last fall and reported to Coach Melvin Fritzel along with some forty other freshman grid candidates. Before the season was many days under way, "My" Cedarholm had made for himself a place in the yearling backfield because of his battering-ram-like drives into the line and exceptionally fine punting.

Possessor of a wonderful physique which is molded into six feet of 180 pounds, Cedarholm was without a doubt one of the outstanding members of the 1932 yearling football squad. A fast and shifty runner in the open field combined with exceptional driving power made him the dynamo of the frosh running attack which gave the varsity no end of trouble throughout the fall.

A four-year football man at Redondo Beach, California, high school, "My" climaxed his football career in his senior year when he was picked on the All-Southern California football team which battled a like squad from the northern part of the state for the state championship.

Along with his football activities, Cedarholm found time to win four basketball letters, two tennis monograms, and a track and water-polo award.

Although he did not report for spring football because of track work, where he sails the discus nearly 125 feet, Cedarholm is expected to cut a wide swath in Panther athletic circles during the next three years.[1]

Myron's sterling career at Iowa State would not come to be, however. Anton become too ill to support the family.[2] He had been carrying an overwhelming load. After his arrival in Waterloo, a revival broke out. The church was not big enough for the crowds, so his church people gave up their seats in the auditorium so that visitors would have a place to sit, while the church members went to the basement to pray. In the winter and spring of 1933, the church people remodeled the auditorium to provide greater seating, and they paid every bill as it came in. In the midst of the Great Depression, the church had done all the work and paid all the bills. Anton notes, "Were we not in one of the worst depressions our

---

[1] "Panther Cubs: Myron Cedarholm," in *The College Eye* (April 28, 1933), 4.

[2] See Cedarholm, *My Nervous Breakdown.*

country had ever known? There was much poverty in our midst. I do not think more than a half dozen men were working amongst our membership. Most of our people were on county relief. Waterloo is an industrial city and practically all the factories were shut down.... I cannot tell how God met our many needs, but I know He met them."[3]

In the summer of 1933, Anton held revivals and Bible conferences in the church. The Sunday School grew to nearly five hundred. He conducted a Sunday radio broadcast and a daily Morning Family Altar on the local radio station. The burden of this much work took its toll.

Sunday morning, August 27th, I was up early as usual, preparing for a long but happy day, I thought. I was to speak at a united gathering of the Bible School and again at our 11 o'clock morning worship service, as well as at my radio service in the afternoon and of course the regular evening evangelistic service. Early this Sunday morning I received a telephone message that one of our members had a sudden heart attack. An ambulance was hurriedly called, but by the time it arrived, our member had passed away. Then I hurried on my way to speak to the large gathering at our Bible School, when I received two more telephone messages, telling of two suicides outside of our church membership circle. Perhaps I should mention that much of my time was spent ministering amongst people who were not members of the Burton Avenue Baptist Church. After the morning service, I hurried to the homes of the unfortunate sorrowing families who so tragically lost their husbands and fathers. I was expected and prepared to speak at our regular Sunday afternoon radio service which meant having all the singers prepared too. As I was about to pray in the last home visited, something strange befell me. I could hardly speak, my breathing was heavy and hard, and I broke into an awful sweat which left me with an incredible weakness. I was unable to go to the radio service, but I tried to get on my feet and go to the evening gathering at the church, but all effort was futile. That was the beginning of an

---

[3] Cedarholm, *My Nervous Breakdown*, 16.

illness that lasted for eleven seemingly long years and of which I have been asked to write.[4]

The Cedarholms were not prepared for a lengthy illness. Myron completed his sophomore year of college, expecting his father to quickly recover. The doctors, however, ordered complete rest for Anton. As the elder son, Myron felt it his responsibility to care for him at home, so he did not return to school for his junior year. Though this caused an interruption in his *formal* education, the years spent with his father, and with the books in his father's library, constituted a valuable education. During this time, Isaiah 30:21 became a life-changing verse for Myron: "And thine ears shall hear a word behind thee saying, This is the way, walk ye in it, when ye turn to the right hand, and when ye turn to the left." As the years progressed, the plan for his life changed from professional football, coaching and business to, perhaps, South American missions. Regardless of the destination, by this point Myron was resolved that wherever the "way" led, he would move in concert with God's direction.

Thelma was the valedictorian at Amery High School and was thus offered a $50 scholarship to Gustavus Adolphus College in St. Peter, Minnesota.[5] In the fall of 1932 she entered Gustavus and thus began her four years of college education. Her father, Martin, had become sick with a heart condition and realized that there was little hope of recovery. Understanding that his time on earth was limited, he had instructed Thelma to go to college so that she, the oldest, could help support the family. To be sure that she had the best possible education, he selected Thelma's classes each semester. She took some classes that were not part of her major (such as learning to run a business meeting), but these additional courses taught her much that would prove invaluable in her later ministry. It was under his guidance that she took additional graduate courses at the University of Minnesota in Library Science, preparing her for the library work at Maranatha that she would begin some thirty years

---

[4] Cedarholm, *My Nervous Breakdown*, 17–18.

[5] Gustavus Adolpus College letter to Thelma, May 28, 1932.

later. Pastor Melford believed that God would use a servant only as much as he (or she in this case) was prepared, and he was determined that his daughter would be well prepared.

Thelma's college years were quite typical. She wrote in her journal of her love for some classes and dread of others (such as biology). Her athleticism was seen in her references to "gym" and "swimming" classes and playing volleyball and "kittenball." She enjoyed watching the men play football and basketball. She joined the Sigma Delta sorority. She looked forward to her afternoon *a capella* choir practices and performances and her frequent trips to the Music Hall for her piano and organ practice. The college choir traveled to the eastern US in 1933 and to the West in 1934, singing in churches, staying in peoples' homes, visiting places she had never been, a precursor to her Pillsbury and Maranatha days. She spoke of some glorious concerts and some not-so-great concerts. She even mentioned that their director, Mrs. Nelson, was furious when they left their robes in the previous church on their 1933 concert tour! Her love for music is seen in a quote in her journal for May 23, 1937: "We should have more singing young people in order that we might have fewer sinning young people."

Thelma was an English major. Her love for literature and writing went back to her father.

> My father introduced me to literature, good literature. He introduced me to several classics, but my first gift was a copy of *Uncle Tom's Cabin*, which I dearly treasured. It was a little green book, and I always kept that little green book close by. The boys wanted their hands on it too, but it was mine, and I read it all the way through and thoroughly enjoyed the whole book. Other books were given to us as children, and we read a good deal in our home, so that we learned to love literature.
>
> The most important book that I received in my lifetime was the Bible that I received when I was thirteen years old. I had never had my own Bible up to that time, and so when I received that Bible, I kept it in the box in which it was given to me. Somebody had told us that if we read three chapters of the Bible every day and five chapters on Sunday, we could finish reading the Bible in one year. So, the first day I received that Bible, I read five chapters and

then six, and seven, until I found that the book of Genesis was so interesting, I read ten whole chapters, and I thought that was a great accomplishment. The second day I read ten chapters and the third another ten chapters and the fourth and fifth, so that I finished the whole book of Genesis in five days. The same was true of Exodus. I loved to read my Bible. I kept it very carefully enclosed in the box in which it had come, and each morning I left it on my pillow. I never did want to mark or underline in the Bible, for I felt that it was too precious, and I wanted to keep it clean, but as time went on that surely changed, and so did the reading. After Genesis was Exodus and then Leviticus, but then came Numbers, Deuteronomy, Joshua and Judges. Oh my, it became a chore to read so much each day, until finally it came to the point that I was reading only one or two verses. Then, of course, there had to be something read every day, because I felt that it was not right to forsake the reading of the Word of God. So, my diary recorded the exact amount that I had read each day until some days there were only one or two verses. I was ashamed. I was not able to finish the Bible in one year. It took two years, but at the end when I came to Revelation, I was very careful to record each bit that was read. Now I have read the Bible through many times, and I am so grateful for those precious promises that the Lord gave to me and the verses that have kept me in times of trouble and trial and heartache, the times of rejoicing, as well. I thank Him for the best Book in all the world. I am glad Papa taught me to love to read that Word of God.

Thelma related her experiences of serving in area churches, attending the Swedish services, Bible studies and prayer meetings on campus, wonderful chapel services, coming down with the mumps in April of 1935 at the ripe old age of 20, heart-to-heart talks with roommates and friends long into the night, sleeping through classes in the morning, enjoying shopping trips, looking forward to breaks when she could return home, mourning the loss of a fellow student who died suddenly, and frequently sharing what Jesus meant to her. While in college, Thelma ("Zephyr" as she was known on the track and field team) broke her ankle. During a high jump, she hit a wooden rail while landing. She had problems with that ankle for the rest of her life. School was more than classes, music and sports, however. On May 18, 1935, Thelma was elected as Corresponding Secretary for the Minnesota Student Volunteers.

For the Melford family, 1936 started with one of the greatest challenges a family can face, the death of a husband and father. Pastor Melford died in the hospital in Minneapolis on January 17[6] and was buried in frigid sub-zero degree weather five days later. It was one of coldest days ever.[7] The men in the church had to use pickaxes to dig the grave. On the day of her father's funeral, Thelma dedicated herself completely to the Lord's service. The officiating minister's challenge was that one of God's servants had fallen, and who was going to take his place? In her heart, Thelma Melford vowed to be the one, knowing full well that her first step meant obeying her father's dying request, and that meant becoming a teacher.

Thelma said of the funeral,

> Unreal—he who was my father but a few days ago. He has left us now—a mother—five children—alone—to Jesus' care. Oh, how we miss him—now that he is gone! There is none to take his place—how I cherish memories. "Watch and Pray." But regret—oh, all that I have done—oh, I have sinned—Jesus, forgive. I cannot say more. The funeral—we did not know we would see his mortal remains no more. "Han har öppnat pärleporten"[8] was so impressive—Rev. Burke, Slatt, Johnson, and Peterson sang it. Oh, they've all been so wonderful to us. And now he is gone—Jesus grant us life with thee—reunion. How blessed.[9]

One of Thelma's stories focused on the death of her father, the most important person in her life at that time.

> I pressed my nose against the cold windowpane on the Greyhound bus that was carrying me back home. The

---

[6] Thelma Melford journal, 1936.

[7] Thelma Melford journal, 1942, reminiscing of her father's funeral: "coldest day in U.S. history."

[8] "He the Pearly Gates Will Open" was written by the Swede Fredrick Blom in 1917, just two years after Thelma's birth.

[9] Thelma Melford journal, 1936.

dean had called me into his office that day to give me the message. He said, "Your father is gone. He passed away in the hospital. You need to get home." The tears flowed down my cheeks when I thought about what might be facing me when I arrived in St. Paul. Papa seemed so well the last time I was with him. What he told me that day I have never forgotten, because he made a proposal to a gentleman who was visiting him concerning his daughter. I sat on the chair and simply listened. But when he said, "She'll have to be a teacher," I almost jumped in my chair. A teacher, no, I would never be a teacher. I didn't want to be a teacher. Every teacher I knew never got married. Everyone was a cranky old teacher. But this might change things I thought. Shall I begin to make plans for our family? Papa had entrusted me with so many respon- sibilities. It seemed as though he anticipated something like this. He was at Bethesda Hospital, St. Paul, when it all happened. The nurse brought him his dinner, left it on the little bedside table and came back for the tray later, but he had not touched it. He had stepped for a moment into the bathroom alongside his bed and did not come out. He fell and went into the presence of the Lord.

Now when I came home I faced mother and many folks at the church. I had three brothers and my little nine-year-old sister. It was decided that I should go along with some of the men to choose a casket at the mortician's place. This I did until the deacons of the church decided the choice was not adequate. They wanted him to have a metal burying box, so they updated what I had chosen. There was a choice of a funeral plot, flowers, articles to be written for the newspaper, folks to be notified, and the usual arrangements to be made at home. I was overwhelmed, and that evening, cold as it was outside, I pulled a stool up beside the cook stove and I just sat there. The others went to bed. I took up my pen and began to write. I wrote the feelings of my heart, and how much I missed Papa and what he had meant to me. When finally I had finished the letter, I sealed it and sent it off to my college roommates. Days passed slowly, messages began to arrive, flowers came, and it seemed like the winter bore down upon us with a much greater intensity than ever we had known it. The thermometer dropped to 10 below, and then 15 below, then 20 below, and 25 below, until the day of the funeral, the people came in sleighs drawn by horses.

Men wore their fur coats, farmers also who could afford them.

The church was packed. The music was beautiful, and then the preacher began to preach, and he spoke from Isaiah, "Lord, whom shall I send? And who will go for us?" There we sat, those first two or three rows, three little boys, and two girls. I was the eldest, and the Lord spoke to my heart. I said to myself and to the Lord, "I heard the message, and I would love to go, Lord, but I am only a girl, and a girl can't be a preacher. She'd have to be a preacher's wife, and where would I find a preacher? But whatever you have, Lord, that's what I want. I want to serve you." And the preacher said, "One servant of the Lord is gone. Who is going to take his place?" And I said in my heart, "I will, Lord. I'll go."

The service concluded and announcement was made asking that those farmers who had fur coats please lend them to the preachers who were serving as pall bearers so that they could carry the casket out to the back of the church and to the graveside. How the young men were ever able to dig that frozen ground I will never know. They had to use a pick axe and finally got down as deep as they needed. As the men carried the body out the back door of the church and around to the side, my mother stood in a little window in Papa's study in the church and watched the burial. They carefully lowered the casket, and then brought the flowers out and put them on the grave. They sat there for six weeks and kept their beautiful colors, because it was no warmer than 25 below zero that entire time. The one bouquet of flowers that we carried to the parsonage just across the lot was covered with newspaper so they would not freeze, but when we got them to the house, they all drooped and died.

When nightfall came, Papa's sister arrived. She had come from Rhode Island to be with the family. We did not rehearse the events of the day; we just sat in silence. I went up to my room and closed the door, put my head on the pillow, and fell asleep trusting that the Lord would take care of us, provide for us, lead us, and give us joy.

The widowed minister's wife had to find someplace other than the Almelund parsonage to live. Consequently, on July 3 of that year, nearly six months after her husband's passing, Anna Melford and her five children, ranging from ages 8 to

21, moved into a home they could afford in the town of Forest Lake.

On June 7, 1936, in what was a bittersweet moment, Thelma graduated from Gustavus Adolphus College with a degree in music and English. Martin's legacy to Thelma included more than just an unusual college education. It also included a dying request. Before her father died, he told Thelma that she would have to take care of the family by taking a teaching position to support them. Thelma admitted that as she prepared to become what she never wanted to be—a teacher— she felt she was also condemning herself to becoming an old maid (because at that time these were almost synonymous). But obey she did. Her "Teacher's Application Blank" indicates that she began to look for a teaching position that focused on dramatics, glee club, or chorus. She could play the piano, pipe organ, and clarinet. She also indicated that she could teach declamatory work, gymnastics, girls' basketball, and orchestra.

That fall she began five years of high school teaching in three Minnesota towns. In the year after her graduation, she taught English and physical education, directed plays, and was the school librarian in Badger, Minnesota (far northern Minnesota near the Canadian and North Dakota borders). For one semester she taught at Big Lake,

Minnesota (only fifty miles from Forest Lake). For three and one-half years, she taught music in Benson, Minnesota (one hundred and seventy miles from home), for about $1,100 a

year.[10] Having put her future completely in the Lord's hands, she believed that serving the Lord included teaching high school far from her family, coming home only during school vacations and the occasional weekend.

As the Melfords moved south, however, the Cedarholms moved north; clearly, the Lord was bringing to the same location two families who needed to meet each other![11] The Cedarholms eventually sold their home in Iowa in 1936 to pay their bills and moved to Forest Lake, Minnesota.[12] This brought them closer to family members who could provide the support they needed while Anton continued his recovery.[13] When the Cedarholms moved to Lake Forest, however, they retained their membership in Burton Avenue Baptist Church, because there was no Baptist church close enough for them to attend. Myron and Jason began to attend the Lutheran church in Lake Forest. When Myron applied to Eastern Seminary in 1942, he listed his address as Lake Forest, Minnesota, and his church membership as Burton Avenue Baptist Church.

While in Forest Lake, Myron had a lot of free time on his hands. He frequently helped at the football practices of the Forest Lake High School team. The team was amazed when at one of the early practices Myron kicked the football sixty-

---

[10] 1940 Federal Census.

[11] Unless otherwise indicated, the following pages are from "A Prince of a Man."

[12] One article in the Maranatha Archives indicates that in 1938 Anton's health was improved enough for him to accept the pastorate of Groveland Baptist Church, Groveland, Minnesota. Groveland, however, was a Methodist campground from 1902 until 1941 when lots were leased for home ownership, but only to Methodists. It was not until 1953 that leases were made available to families who were not Methodists (see www.grovelandmn.com). This writer is not sure when or even if Anton and Lollie moved to Groveland.

[13] There were dozens of Cedarholms in Minnesota. There is even a Cedarholm Golf Course in Roseville, Minnesota, that was named after Emil Cedarholm. Emil was the mayor of Roseville from 1958-61 and again from 1964-67.

Myron in 1936

five yards in the air. He also set about to make Christ known by witnessing to folks all around Forest Lake, "at work, on the street, wherever he met them," his future brother-in-law Ralph would recall years later.

Myron and Jason became active at the Faith Evangelical Lutheran Church, not far from their home. While not a Baptist church, it maintained an unusual emphasis on soul-winning and an active youth program. Myron sang in the choir, sang in numerous duets and quartets, played trombone, preached for the Gospel Team, prepared Luther League meetings, went calling for the pastor, taught Sunday School, and even filled nut cups for a church banquet. The boy had become a man, and the man was willing to go where God might choose. His abilities now were in line with God's priorities, and his helpmeet was on the horizon.

Years later when writing to another family who faced a similar hardship with a debilitated father and two boys facing their college years, Dr. Cedarholm wrote:

> When my brother and I were in high school,[14] our father took sick, and it was ten years before he recovered. It did something for our home that I could not describe. We were all as close to the Lord and as active in our church as we knew how to be, but the Lord used this to

---

[14] Cedarholm must have meant that his father became ill while he and Jason were in college, not in high school. There is no indication anywhere that Anton's illness began before 1934.

speak to my brother and me about full-time service for the Lord. We both went off to college to prepare to be preachers. They were hard days financially on my dear mother with doctor and hospital bills, etc. But the Lord saw us through—not only four years of college for my brother and me, but each of us spent another three years in seminary. We worked at everything we could find. This taught us wonderful lessons on how God will take care of a dedicated heart. My brother and I made up our minds, by God's grace, to trust the Lord for every dollar.[15]

On January 10, 1933, Thelma recorded her expectations for the ideal husband: "My ideal would be a true example of Christian living; one who loves music as an expression of the soul; one who seeks the best qualities in his fellowman; and one who strives for the highest standards in all he does." In September of 1936, Thelma noted in her journal that "Peter asked me to go out, but Percy, Berg, and Lillian came over 'just in time.'"[16] A few months later Thelma wrote concerning her teaching career, "I really wonder at times whether or not I am cut out for this work.... All in preparation for something greater—that is, more direct service which is to come."[17] Little did she know what the Lord had in store for her in the very near future.

Thelma looked forward to school-year breaks when she could spend time back in Forest Lake with her family. The first of those vacations came during Christmas 1936. When Thelma arrived home for the holidays, her friend, Adelyn Berg, was full of stories about the two new "basses in the church choir," who, according to Adelyn, were also "women-haters." A few nights later, Thelma met the women-haters for herself at a caroling activity, and Myron met the vacationing schoolteacher and heard her play the piano. They saw in each other someone who had, for the sake of parents, surrendered dreams of the future. Perhaps something stirred in the woman-hater's heart, because shortly after that,

---

[15] Cedarholm correspondence to McElroy family, December 1, 1970.

[16] Thelma's journal, September 20, 1936.

[17] Thelma's journal, November 9. 1936

Myron began bringing music to Thelma for her to arrange. Christmas break was soon over, and to all outward appearances, nothing more came from their meeting.

During the summer of 1937, both Myron and Thelma worked for ten weeks at the Mount Carmel Lutheran Camp in Alexandria, Minnesota. While Myron was responsible only for the boys' cabins, he seemed to take charge of the entire camp: the waterfront, the athletic program, and even the kitchen. Thelma remembered that he loved to splash water on the dishwashers in general and on a certain Thelma Melford in particular.

One night after the evening campfire, the campers were returning to their cabins. Along the trail was a spot where the trees cleared, offering a remarkable view of a spectacular full moon. The girls squealed in delight, only to be rebuffed by the self-appointed director of the camp. "Oh, you girls are silly. All this nonsense about a moon." The girls protested,

which only brought further upbraiding "for being silly about an old moon." Defending her young charges, Thelma turned and faced the tall Swede. "Now you listen to me. One of these days you'll be smitten by the moon—and you'll be a goner!" She had already turned briskly away when a big hand reached out and caught her by the shoulder. "Young lady, I want to see you tomorrow at 5:00 down by the lake."

"Who?" she asked.

"You," he answered.

That 5:00 meeting by the lake marked the first official "date" of Myron and Thelma, although Myron did not need to concern himself with any silly moon at 5:00 on a summer afternoon!

Once the summer ended, Thelma returned to her teaching. Occasionally, letters would arrive from Forest Lake, Minnesota. One thick letter contained some snapshots from the summer—and it included a bill for the cost of developing, even though Thelma claimed she never remembered ordering any pictures. The total bill for the four pictures was 12¢, according to Myron's journal.

Christmas vacation, 1937, was filled with toboggan rides and ice skating. Most of the girls in the youth group did not know how to skate, and Myron patiently tried to teach them. When he would grow tired of limping along with the beginners, he would relax by taking a spin around the lake with Thelma, already an adept skater. During a figure eight, she asked his advice on whether she should wait for an opening on the China mission field. "China!" he exclaimed. "You're not going to China! You're coming to South America with me." Later, Thelma asked her mother, "Now what do you think he meant by that remark?"

Myron kept a journal[18] for much of his adult life. He began his journals in 1938. His first one opens with a list of the books he read that year:

---

[18] There are numerous references to the journals of both Myron and Thelma. Myron's handwriting is difficult to read, so please excuse any misspelled names or places.

Jan: *Mystical Life of Jesus*, Rosy; *Questions and Answers*, Rosy; *Pleasures and Profit in Bible Study*, Moody; *Quest for Souls*, Truett

Feb: *Psychology of Religion*, pamphlet; *Xtian's Secret of a Happy Life*

Mar: *Three-fold Secret of Holy Spirit* (McCarkey); *Virtuous Woman*, Parry (?); *How Far Can You See*, Anderson; *Victory*, Legters

Apr: *Lectures on Attainment*, Riddell; *Victorious Life Studies*, McQuilken; *Mystery of Suffering*, Talbot (pamphlet)

May: *Praying*, Hyde; *Husband and Wife* (?); *Prayer*, Allen; *Rightly Dividing the Word of Truth*, Scofield

Jun: *Salvation Sermons*, Simpson

Jul: *Knowing the Scriptures*, Pierson; *Weighed and Wanting*, Moody

Aug: ?, Couré; *South America, Land of the Future*, K. C. Grubb; *Getting Things from God*, Blanchard

Sep: *How to Pray*, Torrey; *Called unto Holiness*, Paxson; *Growth of a Soul*, Taylor

These journals later began to reveal his interest in Thelma, and vice versa. Thelma rejoiced in the "interest of Myron."[19] She related, "We skated so long we actually skated long after the others left us." That same evening a missionary who had spoken at her church asked, "Myron, do you think [you] would ever be able to get along without a wife? — We did have a time at that!! God bless him."[20]

Easter was late in 1938, occurring on April 17, and the start of Thelma's Easter vacation coincided with a spring concert by the famous St. Olaf Choir and the Minneapolis Symphony on April 8. Myron invited Thelma to dinner and the concert, their first formal date. They had known each other for more than a year, but had never really dated. Thelma later stated, "We knew from the beginning that this was to be a permanent relationship."[21] The special evening began with dinner at the Sir Francis Drake Hotel followed by

---

[19] Thelma Melford journal, January 28, 1938.

[20] Thelma Melford journal, January 29, 1938.

[21] "The Fiftieth Wedding Anniversary" booklet of Myron and Thelma Cedarholm.

the choir concert for which Myron had purchased two tickets. Thelma relates that she was too embarrassed even to mention the event to any of her friends in Benson, but she was clearly excited enough to purchase a new raspberry coat for the occasion. Interested parties in Forest Lake had assumed that Myron was taking his mother to the concert, but they were soon to learn otherwise. When Myron and Thelma arrived at the auditorium after dinner, if there had been any hope of a secret rendezvous, it melted away. One of Thelma's colleagues, a notorious gossip in her school system, was in the audience. To make matters worse, as they scanned the concert hall after taking their seats, they spotted even more familiar faces: Pastor Burke (pastor of the Lutheran church in Forest Lake) and his wife, and Thelma's friend, Adelyn, who was also the pastor's sister-in-law! Myron's account of the day is far more cryptic than Thelma's:

> 04.08.38 Clear windy cool 40°
> Morn[ing]. Town. Haircut-clip. Shopped. Worked on talk. Aft cleaned car a little. Talk.
> Mpls at 7:30. Bus depot. Francis Drake for supper. Finished at 8:20, got to Aud[itorium] while 1st symphony number in progress. Auditorium plenty big. Acoustics perfect. Choir perfect & same symphony. Over at 11:00. Home & bed 12:30.[22]

Incidentally, the reason "Founder's Day" at Maranatha was held in early April for a number of years was not because of any special event at Maranatha, but because of this first date!

During that Easter week, the church held special meetings every evening. Each night Myron sat alone in the front of the church, and Thelma sat with the girls. However, on Friday night, Myron took Thelma for a walk after the service to his house which was about a mile from the church. His journal entry is typically terse:

> Got Thel (10:00). Home. Sat around fire & gen'l conversation. Bed 12:30.[23]

---

[22] Myron Cedarholm journal, April 8, 1938.
[23] Myron Cedarholm journal, April 15, 1938.

Thelma's version in *Prince of a Man* elaborated a bit more. When Myron's father met Thelma for the first time that night, he took her by both hands and said with a smile, "So this is Thelma! Now I understand why he ran so light-heartedly to the mail box; now I understand why he has broken so many dishes. Come, sit down. I have a few things to tell you about my son."

Myron recorded some of the events of that Easter Sunday:

> 04.17.38, Sunday Easter. Spasmodic showers 70° cloudy & cleared at 10:30 & beautiful. Cloudy & showers in aft & even.
> Was going to get S. T. [Sweet Thelma?!?] in aft but felt a ck.
> Dad & mom both said nice & o.k. but I felt going too fast to have her out for a meal.
> Planned to canoe in aft. Was going & then rained so God closed the door.
> Even to church. Went up at 6:30 to talk to Vickner [a Lutheran missionary to China on furlough after his third term]. Talked till 7:45. Gen'l. wonderful & evangelistic man. Uses altar call in meetings. His pictures fine. 1 hr. long.
> Dad took car back & brot Noreens up & all went home.
> Back & got T. Canoed from 10:15–12:00. Cloudy when started, cleared off. Beautiful & moon bright as could be. Bed 1:45.[24]

Had she known what Myron wrote that night before going to bed, no doubt "Sweet Thelma" would have felt a tender victory that the tall Swede was finally smitten by that moon!

During the summer of 1938, Myron and Thelma found many things in common. They canoed on and swam in the St. Croix River, played chess, and enjoyed their time together. They found they both had a strong interest in missions in general, if not the exact fields of service.

---

[24] Myron Cedarholm journal, April 17, 1938.

Though Thelma was an accomplished athlete, one thing she had never done was ride a bike. One of Mrs. Cedarholm's famous stories was about a time when their date was going on a bike ride. Not wanting to admit she did not know how to ride, she summoned her natural athletic skill and did the best she could. Myron rode ahead of her, and she got a bit wobbly. Within short order she found herself in a gully along the bike trail, ruining the clothes she was wearing. Thelma's

It must be noted that the "Sweet Myron!" was written by Lollie, not by Thelma.

version says, "I could go up and hit a car. I could go down and through a gully. I chose the latter and ruined my new dress and hosiery. Myron was well in front—he turned and laughed." Myron's journal does indicate that Thelma "took a spill," but he was mercifully silent about the rest of the event! Myron also tried to teach Thelma golf and tennis, but she never developed an interest in those sports.

On the last night at church before Thelma's return to Benson, Myron gathered up several of his favorite missionary books and left them for her on the front pew. It was a tall stack, topped by the heavy two-volume biography of Hudson Taylor, all tightly secured with a cord. Much later, Thelma wondered how she had managed to carry all her luggage, as well as that great pile of books, all the way to the bus for Minneapolis, then to the train for Benson, and, finally, on the long six-block walk from the station to her house.

Myron's schooling had been interrupted for four years because of his father's illness. He was finally able to resume in the fall of 1938, but this time at the University of Minnesota in Minneapolis. He stayed in town with his grandparents, participating in football and track and field, witnessing to teachers and students alike, and meeting expenses by driving other students to school. He played football under legendary coach Bernie Bierman. Bierman accumulated a 93–35–6 record, five national championships, seven Big Ten Conference titles, and five undefeated seasons. While Myron could punt the football sixty-five yards, he was named honorable mention All-American for his play as a tackle.[25] He also served two years as the president of the Inter-Varsity Fellowship on campus.

Whether Myron's father told Thelma anything about his son's sense of humor is unknown, but on April Fool's Day, 1939, she surely got the message—or at least her landlady did. Thelma received a lovely box of chocolates from an "anonymous" admirer. Although she loved chocolates, she never ate wrapped ones, so she left those in her landlady's candy dish before she left for Forest Lake and Easter vacation. When she returned, her landlady asked if Thelma was the one who had left the candies in the dish, which, of course, she had. Her landlady then proceeded to explain that her niece had taken one of the candies, unwrapped it, and had it pop open right in her face. Myron's journal solves the mystery of the "anonymous" admirer:

[25] The All-American reward was frequently referred to in later years, but neither Charlotte Cedarholm nor this author has been able to verify this.

I shopped downtown. Got some fake candy for April. Home. 5:30.[26]

Stories of the salvation of anyone, but especially that of a family member, are joyful. Thelma's story of the salvation of Ralph, her younger brother, in the summer of 1939 is especially touching.

It was time for high school graduation, and Ralph was seriously ill. Mother called me at my teaching position to come at once. I was able to finish my responsibility at the high school where I was teaching, and I hurried home to his bedside. He had awakened one morning to go to school to take exams, and he could not get his feet out of the bed. They just would not go to the floor, and he was in terrible pain. Mother called the doctor who determined that he had rheumatic fever and had to be confined to his bed for some time. Since we did not want to move him to the hospital which was some fifty miles away, Mother and I took care of him by day and by night, alternating care, and helping him with every function of his body. We could not touch his body. He screamed with pain and cried day after day. Now he would miss his graduation, and he couldn't get a diploma. He said, "What will I do?" We said we'd just wait and see. The Lord would take care of that.

Well, about this time, he had a birthday. It was his 16th birthday, and I decided I would buy him an alarm clock. It was a Baby Ben, and there it ticked out the minutes and the hours and the days. Accompanying the little clock, I wrote this little verse, "I am only just a minute, only sixty seconds in it, forced upon me, did not choose it, and it's not mine to lose it. Only just a tiny minute, but eternity is in it." And I gave it to him, and he thought, "What will I do with a clock lying here in bed, it will just show the hours to me."

During this time, he listened to the radio. Dr. Murk was the preacher and the singer, and he often sang the well-beloved hymn, "No One Ever Cared for Me Like Jesus." This spoke to Ralph's heart as he sang it from day to day. And then there came to him the reminder that every Sunday in church, the portion from Psalm 51 was repeated by the congregation, "Have mercy upon me, O

---

[26] Myron Cedarholm journal, March 24, 1939.

Lord, according to thy tender mercies." And he said to me, "If I should confess my sin to the Lord, why do I have to do it Sunday after Sunday? Isn't it enough that I do it once? Doesn't that cover my sin?" We had many a discussion on this matter during those days that he was bedfast. But as the weeks swept by, he began to improve, take short walks, and finally he picked up his little gun and went squirrel hunting. He was able to go back to school in the summer and take his exams so that he could complete his work. And then it was time for me to go to camp, Bible camp, and I thought, "Oh, if only Ralph could go with me, perhaps there he could be saved." I talked to the doctor and asked for permission to bring him to camp. He said, "Oh, that would be fine for him; only be very careful that he never is in the rain so that he gets chilled and becomes ill again." The days went by at camp, and it seemed like every day we had a shower. In fact, several times he was out in a boat and he was soaked, something that should never have happened. One morning it was time for chapel, and since I played for chapel, I was there early, and I waited for him to come. I thought perhaps we could have a conversation together before classes began. Some of the folks began to come by me and say, "Have you seen your brother?" I thought, "No, I haven't seen my brother." And the boys came by me and said, "Did you see your brother?" "No, I haven't seen my brother." I began to wonder, "Why are they asking me so many times whether I have seen my brother?" I could not understand it. Then the back door opened and there he came with some of the fellows to chapel. His face looked as though it was radiant. I could not explain it. I wondered what had happened. And then I learned. All through the evening as the boys were together in the cabin, they asked him if he had the assurance of his salvation, and they discussed for a long time what it meant to have assurance of salvation. And finally, at three o'clock in the morning, he said with emphasis, "How can I have assurance of my salvation if I've never been saved in the first place?" At that point, they explained to him exactly what it meant to be saved and he was gloriously born again. That's why he had the radiant face when he came to chapel in the morning, and it made a difference in my life and in his life, as well, when he became a preacher.

On New Year's Eve 1939, Myron used his father's big Packard car for a youth activity. After the service, he managed to squeeze in everyone to take home, except Thelma. He told her to wait there and he would be back soon to get her. Fifteen minutes, thirty minutes, forty-five minutes went by. Mr. Pearson, the janitor, had stayed to keep her company, but finally said, "I don't think he's coming back, Thelma. You'd better go home." After an hour of waiting, she started for home in the bitter cold night. A long hill led up to her house, and to add insult to injury, she slipped at the top and slid all the way back to the bottom. Finally, at one in the morning, looking like the "Wreck of the Hesperus," Thelma dragged herself through the front door. Her entire family was waiting up to wish her a Happy New Year. Thelma's plump little Swedish grandmother, with one glimpse of her disheveled granddaughter, let out an uproarious laugh. "It's not funny, Grandma," she retorted. "I'll never see him again!"

Thelma's New Year's resolution was short-lived. At ten the next morning the phone rang, and a familiar voice asked, "Say, Thelma, how would you like to go for *another* walk?" Myron was well aware of her "walk" the previous night. Thelma was going to have to learn to live with his sense of humor. She agreed to meet halfway and as she left, her grandmother chuckled and said in Swedish, *"Hon springer som en tupp,"* which means, "She runs like a rooster."

On January 21, 1940, Thelma made in her journal the first reference to attendance at a Baptist church. She had known little but her Lutheran churches. Even Myron and Jason had been attending her Lutheran church in Lake Forest. As her interest in Myron grew, however, she realized that he was not going to become a Lutheran. If they were to spend their lives together, she would have to become a Baptist!

On June 15, 1940, just days before Myron's twenty-fifth birthday, he graduated with his B. A. degree from the University of Minnesota, with a major in history and a minor in geography. He had taken Latin, Spanish, and French. He had participated in football, track, baseball, tennis, and water polo while there, a demonstration of his discipline and will to excel. For his graduation present to himself, Myron asked Thelma to marry him. Thelma records on June 15, "This night we pledged our love. Jesus bless it to His glory."[27] Myron's question was, "Would a Lutheran pastor's daughter marry a Baptist preacher?" Thelma's answer was a definite yes. The couple planned for a wedding a year later.

The former professional football and business ambitions had been set aside; preparation for full-time ministry was now the priority. Therefore, Myron spent the summer after graduation working to save money for seminary. He got a job picking peas and corn for a farmer named Fred Nagel. In June he picked peas, and in July and August he picked corn. He was able to stay in the "bunkhouse" with other workers, none of whom were believers. Most of these men were German Lutherans who were convinced they were Christians, even though they were known to "smoke, chew, swear, get drunk, [and] talk about girls in a shameful way."[28] Myron did note, however, that they cleaned up their language when he was around. It was good pay, however; he made between $3 and $4 a day and paid $8 a week for room and board. In addition to the grueling, sweaty work, he read completely through the Bible that summer.

He was considering both Dallas Theological Seminary and Eastern Baptist Theological Seminary for schooling, but the final decision came down to the timely arrival of a telegram while he was picking corn.

> 08.15.40: 85° Semi. First day no rain. Began 6 to 7. By Gaylord. 10 acres. Home 7:40, ate. Showered. Nurse—no bandage, apply salve. Home, shaved & bed. No letter from Eastern so God must want me at Dallas.
>
> 08.16.40: Clear Semi 80.° Nurse again while mowing. Ate in orchard. Picked no 1 on left again. Sores better. Bed 9:15. Bob brot home my mail from office. Sent telegram to Eastern. God marvelously worked. If Bob hadn't have brot my mail I would [not] have got telegram from Eastern sent by dad & then I couldn't have let Dallas know by the deadline August 17th.

---

[27] Thelma Melford journal, June 15, 1940.

[28] Letter from Myron to Thelma, July 3, 1940.

The telegram, asking for information from the Waterloo church in order to clear his application, sealed the plan to attend Eastern Seminary in Philadelphia, Pennsylvania, that fall. He ended the summer with about $160 in his pocket. Eastern offered him a job working a few hours a week that would provide about $150 for the year. Since tuition was only $250 a year, he viewed himself in good financial shape.

Twelve Northern Baptists had founded Eastern Baptist Theological Seminary in 1925; it was one of a handful of seminaries established to counter the loss of biblical soundness in the five main Baptist seminaries in the early 1900's: Newton, Colgate, Rochester, Crozer, and the University of Chicago Divinity School. Eastern was the alternative to the increasingly liberal Crozer Theological Seminary, also in Pennsylvania.[29] As the thirties gave way to the forties, Bible adherents had many venues in which to propagate their literal view of the Scriptures and the doctrinal positions that grew from that position: Bible Conferences, Bible Colleges, publishing firms, mission agencies, and radio broadcasts (such as the one Myron's father had). All served as outlets for truth, even as the traditional seminary and denominational groups embraced more openly liberal positions and personnel.

The school term of 1940–41 found Thelma in her last year of teaching in Benson, Minnesota, and Myron studying at Eastern in Philadelphia. Just before Myron left for seminary, the happy couple spent one more evening together. Thelma wrote, "I can't explain the joy which has been mine! Myron was here at four to get me. Oh, how good to see him. Never have been so thoroughly happy. And at Lake Carlos he gave me my ring. How happy! Of course, we were both thrilled! God has blessed us richly."[30] Who could have imagined when Myron left for Philadelphia and seminary on September 27, 1940, that God's plans for the Minnesota boy—mixed with a solid dash of California—would

---

[29] In 2005 Eastern's name was changed to Palmer Theological Seminary in honor of Gordon Palmer, its longest serving president. Palmer was there when the Cedarholms attended Eastern.

[30] Thelma Melford journal, September 20, 1940.

include being the leader of one of the more important fundamentalist movements and president of two Baptist colleges? You would not have guessed it based on his journal entries:

September 27, 1940, Friday: clear 65° Left 8:25. Dad stayed in car, J & mom to train. Zephyr good crowd. Talked to young fellow going to Mass, missionary, India, Pryor & Christian business man who overheard us. Chic 2:40. Called Rapp. No answer. Got on Penn train—only two tracks away. Lucky—baggage so heavy. Long train—two engines—1½ coach rest Pullmans, etc. Electric at Harrisburg. Many got on. Excursion to Fair. Lancaster, two. ate—5, 12, & 8:00. Slept good in seat. Clothes not wrinkled.

September 28, 1940, Saturday: Clear 65° arrived 9:30. Sent cards to Minn. Taxi to school—½ mile. Unpacked trunk. Cleaned room. Slept 2 to 7, dressed, town, groceries, back & ate. Meetings & testimonies at 9:30. no faculty present. [Bernard] Ramm led. Refreshments. Talked to fellows. Up at 12:00. Wrote to Thelma clock back an hour. Bed 1:30.

September 29, 1940, Sunday: Clear, 65°. Ate in room. Morning to Presbyterian across street. Packed. Sermon good—"Our Commander's Orders"—Jas 1:

Aft: Wrote, Cath Sem across street. Bill McBride student took me thru talked till 6:00. Very profitable. Very devout boy. 7:00 to Presbyterian Y.P. Dead. Memories of Youth man of Youth work in Phil. Home 8:00 Read & Bed 9:00.

September 30, 1940, Monday: Cloudy all day, 60° ate in room. Read all morning. Kirk in & out. Aft. registered 2:30 Fees $11.50. To depot to see about books—not in yet. Back to room & read. Talked with Kirk—just getting acquainted. Read & wrote. Bed 11:30 Got meal ticket tonight.

October 1, 1940, Tuesday: cloudy—breakfast 8:00. Orientation 9:30 to 12:00 aft. same over at 3:00. Music with Dick in room. Reception 7:45. Devotional then met faculty & wives. Refreshments. Wrote & read. Bed 12:30.

October 2, 1940, Wednesday: rain all day—60° Breakfast 7:00. Read 1st class 9:00 in O.T. Test on content. Dr. Massee for chapel & good. 1:00 meeting for

"Grant" students. Books came & unpacked & hauled all
stuff dorm after supper. Study in lib. & room. Bed 12:00.

His graduate schooling had officially begun. Seminary in
those days was much like it is today. Myron could not stay
away from the athletic opportunities, however. During their
year apart, Myron and Thelma exchanged numerous letters,
and in one of them, Myron told Thelma about his PE and
fencing classes. There are no such classes on his transcript,
so he must have been doing these on the side. Myron noted
that Eastern men were "marked" because they were
fundamentalists; but he also noted that "our position is
respected." Holding to biblical convictions in spite of
academic and denominational onslaughts in the other
direction was tempering him for future stands in his ministry
years. By the 1940's Eastern itself was hiring faculty who
promoted liberal theological beliefs, indicating that
Cedarholm's stalwart beliefs were established in spite of
some of his academic training, rather than because of it.[31]
During Myron's first year, he met Bernard Ramm, a senior
who would graduate that year. Ramm would eventually
become a leading evangelical Baptist writer and theologian
who wrote prolifically on hermeneutics, science and religion,
and apologetics.

Pulling together sufficient funds to pay for school is a
frequent challenge for young people. Such was the case for
Myron. It was going to take his savings and all the money he
would earn working for the seminary plus a part-time job at
a men's clothing store to pay for his education.[32] There would
be nothing left to spare. Therefore, Thelma made him a
special loan that he used to purchase an engagement ring for
her. She wrote to him on October 24, 1940, telling him that
while home from Benson for a weekend, she had gotten his
ring. (Since he had given her a ring before he left for Eastern,
she must have just received it from the jeweler for resizing.)
All day Saturday Thelma was extremely "left-handed" hoping
that a family member would notice the diamond she was

---

[31] Beale, 175–180.

[32] He even sent his dirty laundry home for his mother to wash.

wearing, but no one did. As the evening wore on, she finally had to announce to everyone that Myron had given her an engagement ring. The people at the church a couple of days later were much more observant (or just already informed), for the ring was the center of attention.

It was a long and somewhat difficult year of engagement, with many miles separating Thelma in Benson and Myron in Philadelphia, and no trip home over Christmas break so Myron could work extra hours and save the cost of a trip. A series of letters flowed back and forth between Minnesota and Pennsylvania. These give clear indication of their deep love and commitment to each other, but more importantly to God, His will, and His plan for both of them. While Myron was content in God's will, his roommate, Dick Kirk, was another story. He was a lovesick creature who would stare at his girlfriend's picture and moan, "Oh, I wish I could just hold her hand!" Myron's straightforward stoic solution to this dilemma was: "Oh, why don't you go squeeze the door knob!"

This same roommate wrote years later:

> We have heard it said that we don't know anyone until we live with them. I had not been Myron Cedarholm's roommate very long until I recognized some most unusual things about this man of God. For example, if it was a matter of missing breakfast or his devotional time of reading the Word and prayer, breakfast was omitted in favor of his time alone with the Lord—and Myron enjoyed eating in those days as much as any person I know!
>
> I remember how he spent from 1 to 3 hours a day in the Word and on his knees in prayer. He felt most keenly that God had called him to a ministry of intercessory prayer. He prayed for the faculty and fellow students at Seminary—for missionaries all over the world—for loved ones and friends—for the Christian Colleges and Bible Schools and Seminaries of our nation—for the leaders of government—he remembered so many by name and need. Following the noble prophet, Daniel, he prayed morning, noon, and night.
>
> This same spirit of dedication revealed itself in the quality of his academic work, for he always got top grades. Cedar, as we students and close friends called him, always gave his best in all that he did. The admiration and high

regard in which he was held among his fellow students was evidenced by the fact that he was elected President of his class the first year at Seminary and elected President of the student body when he was a senior. Also, he won the oratorical contest in his senior year.

While we were students at the Seminary, I would say occasionally to some other students or faculty member, "Some day you are going to read about Myron Cedarholm in the history of the Christian church, for his life is going to count for God in an unusual way."

That year apart ended with a summer of preparation. The couple spent the summer of 1941 canoeing Minnesota's lakes and rivers, especially the St. Croix, planning their wedding and preparing to move to Pennsylvania. Finally, on his parent's anniversary, September 6, 1941, Myron and Thelma were married in a genuine Scandinavian wedding

complete with the Swedish wedding march and cream chicken and Swedish croquettes for 300 guests.

The reception included a full program including a girls' triple trio that Thelma had trained and a groom's cake she herself had baked and individually wrapped. Her unparalleled abilities, her joyful zest for life, and her complete dedication to Christ would enhance the ministry of Myron Cedarholm for the rest of his life. Thelma later noted that Myron had watched her for a year before asking her for their first date and though they dated for five years, the first date had settled the matter for them.

The newlyweds honeymooned in a lake cabin north of Aitkin, Minnesota, but not until after first enjoying an unscheduled walk, because their car ran out of gas on the way to the cabin! They did their own cooking, rowed across the lake for milk each day, and then one morning, while the new Swedish bride was washing the breakfast dishes, they heard a car pull up outside. "Why, Myron, that looks like your brother—and your father—and your mother—and my mother." In they came with chicken and Swedish rolls, but they also insisted on the newlyweds accompanying them back into town. There Myron's father surprised them with a new blue Ford, a wedding gift that had arrived at the dealership a little late for the wedding!

Belated wedding gift in front of honeymoon cabin

After a week's honeymoon, the Cedarholms returned to Forest Lake, packed up their gifts and belongings, took some pictures with Thelma's brother, Wendell (who had missed the wedding, due to his military service in Fort Lewis, Washington), and set out for Philadelphia in their new Ford.

SEMINARY AND LEHIGH YEARS: 1941–1947

With a September sixth wedding in Minnesota and the fall term beginning in far eastern Pennsylvania, the honeymoon was short; but for them, taking a semester off from their studies was not an option. They drove from Forest Lake to Chicago, stayed overnight with Thelma's Uncle Bob and Aunt Hildur, and the next morning set off on a long drive to Philadelphia. The new car ran perfectly. Little did they know that this was just the first of hundreds of trips that lay ahead of them.

The young couple spent the next two years taking classes. They had purposed that nothing should distract them from their seminary studies. This meant that every possible cent had to be saved from their summer jobs and the part-time work they did during the school year. Thelma found a job working at John Wanamaker's store; her printing was so neat and tiny that it looked like it was typed on a typewriter. During his seminary years, Myron was given many opportunities to preach and to travel with the men's chorus, singing and playing his trombone. He even managed the chorus one year, and that was the first time the group ended the year financially solvent. During his last two years of seminary, Myron served as a youth pastor at Second Baptist Church of Philadelphia.[1]

Seminary friends were careful to point out that the disciplined and competent Myron had some room for improvement. For example, during the first wedding he performed, Myron forgot to pronounce Howard Smith and his Swedish bride man and wife.

Jason Cedarholm also attended Eastern and then served as a missionary in El Salvador for thirty-two years. Eastern introduced Myron to at least one lifelong colleague, M. James Hollowood—and introduced Jim to *his* future wife. One day

---

[1] "B. Myron Cedarholm—Biographical Sketch." The Second Baptist Church of Philadelphia started in 1803 and apparently closed in 1972.

Jim had been patiently waiting outside a faculty member's office. The only other student in the hallway was a young lady. Finally, after several minutes of silence, she said warmly, "Hello, I'm Jane Piehl." He raised his eyebrows and replied, "Indeed." Later he and Jane were married. Hollowood became editor of the *North Star Baptist*, the denominational paper of the Minnesota Baptists, participated in the installation of B. Myron Cedarholm when he became president of Pillsbury, and taught at Maranatha from 1969 to 1984.

Both Myron and Thelma graduated from Eastern with honors in 1943, he with a Bachelor of Divinity (which today would be a Master of Divinity), and she with a Master of Religious Education. Thelma's MRE thesis was fitting for her: *The Antecedents and Characteristics of the Modern Gospel Chorus*. Myron's thesis was *A Study of the Philosophy of History in the Prophecy of Isaiah.*[2]

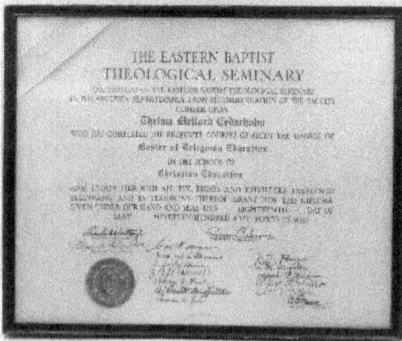

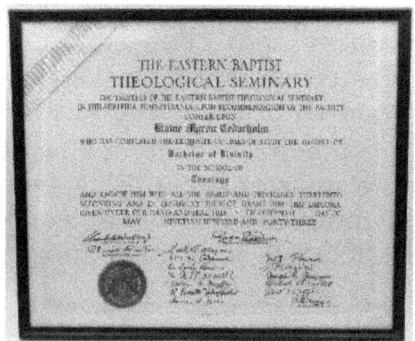

---

[2] The seminary has lost his thesis.

By 1943 fundamentalist pastors were gravely concerned with the appointment of missionaries who did not hold sound theological positions, yet were funded by sound churches. In February of that year, the Foreign Mission Board of the NBC elected Elmer Fridell as its president. Fridell was a thoroughgoing liberal. His election resulted in a wave of protests from the fundamentalists still in the NBC. Although the churches in the Convention were congregationally governed, they were co-operative in their missionary endeavors, channeling funds for missions through the NBC-approved organizations. In spite of a series of meetings and protests, the ABFMS affirmed its belief that liberals were welcome in the NBC missions family.

April 1943 found the Cedarholms in their first pastorate: Lehigh Avenue Baptist Church, Philadelphia. The church started as a mission on January 7, 1880. The cornerstone for the church building was laid on July 11, 1881, and the forty-four members organized as an independent church on June 6, 1882.[3] It had a great history, but by the time the Cedarholms arrived, there were just thirty people in an auditorium built for one thousand. Older advisors had said, "No hope for that church—Ichabod is written across the front door." Spiritual deadness permeated Pastor Cedarholm's first service there. The organist played his usual offertory, *Moonlight and Roses.* The building's roof leaked so badly that more than twenty buckets had to be strategically located around the auditorium whenever it rained, to keep the water from ruining the pews. If rain came in the middle of the night, Pastor Cedarholm had to get up, go to the church, and put out the buckets. The church was heated by coal. In typical convention church style, there was a "coal fund" that must have been underfunded. The April 1943 Easter offering was designated for this fund.[4] That soon changed, however, for

---

[3] https://lehighbaptistchurch.org/our-history.

[4] Myron Cedarholm, Easter letter to Lehigh Avenue Baptist Church, April 20, 1943.

by the fall of 1945, the coal furnace was gone, and a new, modern oil-burning furnace was installed.[5]

One of the first official functions of the new pastor was to baptize two individuals on April 25, 1943. One was Guy Melton. The other was Thelma Melford Cedarholm. Born into a Lutheran family, she had been sprinkled as a baby. Admittedly, her interest in becoming a Baptist was triggered

Myron and Thelma
at Lehigh Avenue Baptist Church

by her interest in Myron Cedarholm. But even through her years at Eastern Baptist Theological Seminary, she was still a member at her Lutheran church. To become the pastor's

----

[5] Myron Cedarholm, Easter letter to Lehigh Avenue Baptist Church, November 8, 1945.

wife she envisioned when she was just thirteen, however, she had to abandon her Lutheran heritage and become a Baptist. And become a Baptist she did.

The new pastor was ordained a month after he arrived. On May 2, 1943, an ordination council composed of 104 messengers from 26 churches met at Lehigh Avenue Baptist Church and recommended the ordination of the young pastor.

After the young couple moved all their possessions into the eight-room unfurnished parsonage, it still looked unfurnished. In the coming months, however, friends and church members graciously provided many additional furnishings. Pastor Cedarholm performed several funerals for families who could not afford to pay him; instead they gave him one or two pieces of furniture. Pastor and Mrs. Cedarholm used an accordion to provide music for the frequent church activities in their home. In fact, during the weeks after the Cedarholms first moved in, so many people came and went, the neighbors wondered if the parsonage had been turned into a hotel.

Pastor Cedarholm put a calling program into high gear, personally visiting homes in the community, day and night. People were saved, the church grew, but the roof still leaked. That is, it leaked until the Lord convincingly answered prayer for the funds needed to replace the roof. For forty-eight years the church had been waiting for an inheritance of three thousand dollars that was tied up in the courts. Suddenly it became available. Then a Mr. Wyle, a Presbyterian who lived just down the street from the church, became interested in this vibrant work and contributed the last two hundred dollars. The roof was fixed. Later, the church needed new windows and Pastor Cedarholm wanted the best. Trusting God for the finest, he suggested stained glass windows, a recommendation that received no opposition. As one deacon expressed it, "You better let pastor have his own way; he seems to have a pipeline to heaven." Stained glass windows, designed by the Cedarholms, were installed.

Thelma and Myron were a wonderful pair. Myron had focused vision, a vision that the cause of Christ was all in all. Thelma brought a balance to every aspect of his ministry and their marriage. Her gifted organizational skills put his vision into practice. As a young man, Myron was an introvert and tended to think in black and white. Thelma knew how to soften his rough edges. He was the face, the front, the voice; she was in the background, making sure everything worked properly.

On December 15, 1943, just a few months after the Cedarholms came to Lehigh Avenue, the FBF met at the Tabernacle Baptist Church of Chicago, where Dr. George Carlson served as pastor. In response to the increasing liberalism of the NBC and especially of the ABFMS, they organized a mission board that would hold to the literal interpretation of the Scriptures and the fundamentals of the faith—the Conservative Baptist Foreign Mission Society (CBFMS).[6] The purpose of this new mission society was to give Northern Baptist fundamentalists a place to send their missions giving. The CBFMS was under the control of the fundamentalists, but still a part of the NBC.

Conservatives like the Cedarholms had been critical of the American Baptist Foreign Mission Society, and they were quick to join this new organization. They wanted this new board to operate under the Northern Baptist umbrella, so they could in good conscience support this group with their church mission funds and still be considered "good members" of the NBC. The CBFMS grew rapidly because of the pent-up demand for a good foreign mission agency. With this growth came opposition from the NBC and the ABFMS. For two years, the CBFMS attempted to work with at least a quasi-official connection to the NBC, but in 1945 even this attempt at conciliation ended. In keeping with the conservatives, Pastor Cedarholm removed his church from the Northern Baptist Convention and aligned himself and his church with the new Conservative Baptist movement. Pastor Cedarholm and Lehigh Avenue Baptist Church moved quickly to support this new missions agency and the Conservative Baptist movement in general.

---

[6] Fred Mortiz, *Now is the Time: A History of Baptist World Mission* (North Fort Myers, FL: Faithful Life Publishers, 2011), 19.

While the Cedarholms were supportive of the actions of the FBF and the CBFMS, their focus was on Lehigh. One note of blessing in their early days was the improvement of the financial state of the church. In the twelve months before calling Pastor Cedarholm, the church's offerings were $4,900.92. During his first year, giving rose to $9,717.69. During his second year, offerings rose to $16,788.80. This was the result of two factors. First, the people developed a heart for giving. Second, the congregation had grown as a result of an aggressive outreach program. When the church first called the Cedarholms, they said they would pay them $25 a week, if there was enough money available. The church budget for 1947–1948 indicates that the church was by then paying Pastor Cedarholm $40 a week.

Pastor Cedarholm's plans for the church's first missionary conference demonstrated his passion for missions and amazed his congregation with its scope. Twenty-three missionaries were invited! "But, Pastor Cedarholm, where will we put all these guests? I know we don't have any extra beds in our house," asked one deacon. "Well, brother, give them your bed and you sleep on the floor," was the Pastor's can-do response. His missionary fervor and evangelistic zeal revived the old and inspired the young. Twenty-three young people from the church went into full-time Christian service. One of those young people was Margaret Scipione, better known as Skippy, who would become a close friend of the Cedarholms and eventually serve as a missionary to Italy.

Skippy and Charlotte

During their four and one-half year ministry at Lehigh, Pastor Cedarholm's energies knew no bounds. Besides keeping the vigorous church schedule, he taught Greek and psychology at Eastern Seminary for three years. He had received a scholarship to Princeton Theological Seminary and earned his Master of Theology there in 1945. The following year he completed the residence work at Princeton for his Doctor of Theology (ThD).[7]

While at Lehigh Thelma did more than serve as the pastor's wife. She prepared original material for the Philadelphia area Child Evangelism block meetings, ran the "Happy Hour," a children's club with upwards of 125 children on Friday afternoons, sponsored a children's choir, and organized a Children's Church program. Thelma's approach to Children's Church was to make it as much as possible like the adult service. Boys in suits served as ushers, they used offering plates, and the children sang from hymnals. Worshipping the Lord was as serious for the children as for the adults. Though the first offering was a "gum offering," and the preaching was on a child's level, the goal was to prepare for meaningful worship, not just to entertain.

World War II was raging while the Cedarholms were at Lehigh. Any service member at church on Sunday morning was offered lunch at the parsonage, even if lunch consisted of only a can of Spam, garnished with a little pineapple. Pieces were cut paper thin, but everyone received at least one helping and enjoyed the fellowship of the young pastor and his wife.

The Cedarholms had a heart for their people. Dick Mitchell, a local man who came to Christ while the Cedarholms were at Lehigh, struggled with the hold of liquor on his life. Every night for weeks Pastor Cedarholm would meet Dick at the bus when he came home from work and walk him home, so that he would not be tempted to visit a bar. Dick later wrote concerning the Cedarholm ministry:

> I would like to testify to Dr. Cedarholm's Christian love and understanding toward me in the early days of my Christian experience when the way seemed to be all uphill

---

[7] Undated "News Release" from Maranatha. Since the news release introduces Cedarholm as the Chancellor of Maranatha, it was probably compiled in or shortly after 1983, when Arno Q. Weniger, Jr., became President.

as I had many besetting sins, the worst of which was an addiction to alcohol. Dr. Cedarholm spent many hours praying for me and counseling with me, for which I am eternally thankful. Truly my wife and I can truthfully say with the apostle Paul that we thank God for every remembrance of him.

In 1983 Dick's wife, Martha, went to China with the Cedarholms. They visited a rug factory, and Martha told the Cedarholms to pick any rug they wanted as a thank you for caring for her husband. That rug is still at their daughter Charlotte's home.

Pastor Joe Muggleworth, pastor of Lehigh from 1950 to 1982, wrote to Dr. Cedarholm:

> Needless to say, Lehigh Baptist Church would not be the Church it is today had it not been for your vision, conviction, and ambition. Lehigh, your first and only pastorate, will be eternally grateful to you and Thelma for your sacrificial ministry.

Like hundreds of other pastors after World War II, the Cedarholms were committed to a strongly evangelistic ministry that proclaimed the fundamentals of the faith and supported missionaries who were evangelistic and Bible-believing. Some of the Baptist organizations supported by such pastors, however, continued a steady drift to interests, concerns, and religious priorities that chafed the consciences of conservative men.

While much about the NBC disturbed the conservative pastors, the organization continued to be the denominational home for many such men and their local churches, primarily because of the Fundamentalist Fellowship. The relationship between the national denominational machinery and the Fundamentalist Fellowship had not been peaceful. Virtually every Convention meeting raised questions for concerned conservatives about the spiritual vitality of the national group and produced frustration at yet another year passing with the liberals always seeming to outmaneuver the intentions of the conservatives. Any denominational votes that the conservatives considered "victories" one year seemed to be ignored or thwarted by the next convention. The conservative men pastored their churches week in and week out and met once or twice a year to try to orient their national organization to their position. Each year, however, the national organization functioned increasingly in its own orbit of in-house policies, national missions programs, and college and seminary development—an orbit funded in large measure by the offerings of the conservative churches, but with no accountability to them. Policies, positions, and personnel were promoted that bewildered and concerned the men who were truly serving Christ through their local churches.

The division between the Northern Baptists and the conservative Baptists grew. In 1946, the NBC held its annual convention in Grand Rapids, Michigan. The conservatives failed again in their efforts to override the liberals. They sought a constitutional amendment to disallow NBC employees a vote; these individuals were a sizable bloc which always voted with the liberal leadership. There was always a considerable number of employees at the annual meetings, since the NBC paid their conference expenses. The conservatives tried to adopt a confession of faith. They attempted to cut the liberal Federal Council of Churches from the NBC budget. They tried to elect a conservative slate of officers. They failed in all of these attempts. Then the Convention adopted the principle of proportional represen-tation—the number of messengers (and thus votes) a church was allowed was based on the percentage of its missionary giving which went through the NBC organizations. As conservatives increased their giving to the CBFMS, their voting strength would decline. The NBC also affirmed the use of the inclusive policy and committed its support to the Federal Council of Churches. Frustrated, the Fundamentalist Fellowship appointed a Committee of Fifteen to examine their options in light of the burgeoning problems in the NBC.

As a result, the Fundamentalist Fellowship of the Northern Baptist Convention changed its name to the Conservative Baptist Fellowship (CBF) of the Northern Baptist Convention to emphasize its connection with the Conservative Baptist movement. It also opened an office in

Chicago to help coordinate its efforts. The CBF was described as "an informal fellowship of individual Baptists of the North 'earnestly contending for the Faith once for all delivered unto the saints' within the Baptist denomination. It is the oldest of all of the Conservative Baptist societies and is the father of the other Conservative Societies, as well as the 'grandfather' of the present 20th Century reformation among Baptists."[8]

The Conservative Baptist Fellowship maintained its independence; it was never a part of any other organization. Over the years, it passed through several name changes: the Fundamentalist Fellowship, the Conservative Baptist Fellowship, the Fundamental Baptist Fellowship, the Fundamental Baptist Fellowship International, and finally the Foundations Baptist Fellowship International.[9]

In September 1946, the *Newsletter* of the Fundamentalist Fellowship sported a new name: The Conservative Baptist Fellowship (CBF). This was done to connect the old Fellowship with the new Conservative Baptist movement and to separate the Fellowship from its former identification with the NBC.[10] The next year most of the churches who identified with the CBF began to withdraw from the NBC. Some of these made a few inquiries about the possibility of merging with the General Association of Regular Baptist Churches (GARBC), but realized that they were not going to be able to do so.[11]

To this point in B. Myron Cedarholm's life, godly men had been working within the Northern Baptist structure to

---

[8] Guy Archer Weniger, "The Conservative Baptist Fellowship: A Study Outline for the Conservative Baptist Leagues," undated.

[9] This last name change occurred in 2017 and was a reaction to the negativity of the concept of "fundamentalism" (not Christian fundamentalism, but the fundamentalism of other religions), especially in the military chaplaincy.

[10] "THE CONSERVATIVE BAPTIST FELLOWSHIP, Its History and Present Position," 5.

[11] "Does the Name Change It?" *Central Conservative Baptist Theological Seminary* 6.2 (September-October 1964), 1-2.

hold it to biblical mandates. He, like others, watched the Convention continue its drift to the left. He was concerned about the liberalism in the leadership of the Convention. The Convention's rejection of the Conservative Baptist Foreign Mission Society was the last straw.

In 1947, three regional conferences were held to advance the Conservative Baptist cause. On May 17, 1947, the Conservative Baptist Association of America (CBA) was formed during the preconvention meeting of the NBC in Atlantic City, NJ.[12] Unlike the GARBC, the CBA membership consisted of both churches and individuals and allowed member churches to remain in the NBC. The CBF continued its existence as a fellowship of individuals.[13]

The organization of the CBA called for the nation to be divided into three regions, East, Central, and West, with one man responsible for each region. As a result, Lehigh Avenue Baptist Church was about to lose its young, dynamic pastor, and the was going to gain a tireless worker. B. Myron Cedarholm was asked to be the first missionary-evangelist hired by the CBA. And thus, Myron was on his way to becoming a national leader, and the Lord was continuing to do all things in His time.

---

[12] *1968 Directory, Conservative Baptist Association of America* (Wheaton: CBA of A, 1968), 2-8.

[13] Over the years, the original fundamentalist organization passed through several name changes: from the Fundamentalist Fellowship, to the Conservative Baptist Fellowship, and to the Fundamental Baptist Fellowship, with which most of the Maranatha constituency would be familiar, and on which board Dr. Cedarholm served for many years. The FBF became the Foundations Baptist Fellowship International in 2017. This name change was a reaction to the negativity of the concept of "fundamentalism" (not Christian fundamentalism, but the fundamentalism of other religions), especially in the military chaplaincy. It is significant to note that these Fellowships were related to but never organically connected with any other group. The Fundamentalist Fellowship was never a part of the NBC. The Conservative Baptist Fellowship was never a part of the CBA. And the Foundations Baptist Fellowship today has no organic connection to any other movement.

Pastor Cedarholm submitted his resignation, effective November 1947. The one goal that he had failed to accomplish at Lehigh Avenue Baptist Church was paying off the mortgage. Interestingly enough, this would be characteristic of his entire ministry and the ministries of most fundamentalists—the lack of funds to complete the task. The Cedarholms were undaunted by the lack of finances in this their first ministry, and they would be undaunted by the lack of funds in their remaining ministries.

Pastor Cedarholm wrote a final letter to his church people.

> As we look back over these past four and one-half years, our hearts overflow with grateful praise to our Heavenly Father for the miracles and blessings that He has wrought before our very eyes. Souls have been saved, homes have been blessed, and God has caused to prosper our work. Truly, the Lord hath fulfilled His promise which declares that He is able to do "exceedingly abundantly above all that we ask or think" (Eph. 3:20). We proclaim with the Psalmist, "Oh, give thinks unto the Lord; for He is good" (Ps. 118:1). At times, our faith was so small and weak. We wondered if it were possible for the obstacles and difficulties to be overcome. We often heard the rebuke of the Lord, "O ye of little faith" (Matt. 6:30). But God's grace and providence overruled, and there was "a performance of those things" (Lk. 1:45).
>
> This will be our last letter to you. The Lord has called us to another field of service. Next Sunday, November 2, will be our last with you. These past four and one-half years have been blessed years. The Lord has favoured us as people and Pastor with a relationship that has been a very happy one in our work together at the Church. The thought of severing our tie is indeed not a pleasant one. Yet, we sense the hand of the Lord in it all and rest in the Lord who "worketh all things after the counsel of His own will" (Eph. 1:11).
>
> We believe that the Lord has a great ministry ahead for our Church. There are many in our community to be won to Christ. The regions beyond need the Gospel. Our Father has been pleased to call from our congregation young people to carry the Gospel to foreign lands and has called others to prepare for full-time Christian service. To

train and send forth youth is one of the greatest blessings God can bestow upon a Church. Let us never lose the vision for preparing and sending our labourers for the Lord.[14]

This desire to train young people and send them into the harvest field remained with the Cedarholms through the rest of their earthly lives.

[14] B. Myron Cedarholm, letter to Lehigh Avenue Baptist Church, October 28, 1948.

THE CBA YEARS: 1947–1965

In 1947, B. Myron Cedarholm, with Thelma at his side, became the Central Area Evangelist for the CBA under the leadership of the first General Director, I. Cedric Peterson. His co-workers, Albert S. Taylor and Clyde Paul White, were the missionary-evangelists for the East and West, respectively. They were each charged with encouraging churches to join the CBA, planting churches, and helping local assemblies any way they could. The other field directors soon fell by the wayside, as did Peterson, leaving Cedarholm to do a national work. "As a consequence, the bulk of the work fell to Cedarholm, an indefatigable workman who traveled thousands and thousands of miles each year in the interests of the associations, counseling pastors, doing whatever seemed necessary for the Conservative cause."[1] From 1947 until the fall of 1965, over 1,000 churches were established or assisted by the ministry of this team of committed servants of Christ.

The Cedarholms' last services with their Lehigh church family were on November 2, 1947. On Tuesday, November 4 they arrived in Chicago, and Cedarholm went immediately to a meeting to discuss the great needs within the Conservative Baptist Association. When the Cedarholms went to work with the CBA, there were only two Conservative Baptist organizations (in addition to the ongoing CBF): the CBA, an association of churches, and the CBFMS, the foreign mission society. In 1948, the CBA formed the Conservative Baptist Home Mission Society (CBHMS) at its annual conference in Milwaukee.

The CBA wrote a Declaration of Purpose to establish its philosophy and guide its activities. It reads:

> The Conservative Baptist Association of America has been brought into existence:

---

[1] Shelley, *A History of Conservative Baptists*, 62.

To provide a fellowship of churches and individuals upon a thoroughly Biblical and historically Baptistic basis, unmixed with liberalism and those who are content to walk in fellowship with unbelief and inclusivism;

To encourage the spiritual interest of local churches in sound and Biblical Baptist institutions and projects both at home and abroad;

To encourage the creation of agencies and institutions wherever necessary and advisable to fulfill the commission of our Lord in the face of rising apostasy;

To provide mutual assistance among conservative Baptist churches for the encouragement of the local churches' activities, such as evangelism, missions, and Bible teaching; and

To present a positive testimony to the New Testament faith and historic Baptist principles as a body of churches before the world, religious and otherwise; and to oppose departure and deviation from the great foundational truths of the Word of God.

The CBA brought together two streams of religious thought. One was traditional Baptist thinking. They accepted the historic Baptist distinctives, and they employed traditional Baptist methods in their church life. The second stream was that of fundamentalism and particularly the parachurch ministries that had grown up at about the time of the beginning of the CBA: Youth for Christ, Inter-Varsity Christian Fellowship, city-wide evangelism, and more.[2]

After five years as the CBA General Director, Cedarholm identified the "fundamental principles"[3] of the CBA. It was first a confessional body. The NBC had refused to adopt a theological standard. Baptists have historically written and subscribed to various confessions of faith, and it was appropriate for the CBA to do so as well.

Second, the CBA was a fellowship of independent churches. The Association could make no decisions for the churches and could not force any church to participate in a program which they did not accept. "There rightly exists

[2] Shelley, *A History of Conservative Baptists*, 2.

[3] *National Voice* (January 1953), 2 and (September 1953), 9.

among the churches an interdependency, because the causes that Conservative Baptists love can prosper only under the hand of the Lord as the churches unite and cooperate together.... The Association is not a denomination. It is only a part of the true, historic Baptist family which perpetuates the New Testament faith. It has no desire to become a denomination with centralized authority, ecclesiastical connectionism, or dependent organizations which the churches must support." The NBC had violated the autonomy of the local churches. The CBA sought to retain that autonomy, while at the same time restricting their fellowship to churches that could agree with a basic theological position. This balance between theological purity and local church autonomy has always been a problem. Cedarholm and the CBA adopted the most common solution to the problem: "The Association has the constitutional right to disfranchise any church which departs from the doctrinal statement and the principles as expressed in the Conservative Baptist Association of America Preamble and Constitution." The question would later become: At what point has a church departed? As the CBA drifted away from fundamentalism, the definition of theological departure changed.

The third fundamental principle of the CBA identified by Cedarholm was that the Association had no "organic relationship to the organizations which its churches supported." Each of the Conservative Baptist agencies (the CBFMS, CBHMS, and the CBA) were independent of each other. A church did not have to support each agency to be a true Conservative Baptist. In opposition to the NBC, the Conservative Baptists did not believe that the views of one individual or even one agency could represent the views of the movement as a whole.

In addition to these three Fundamental Principles, the CBA developed two practices which demonstrated its rejection of NBC principles. First, contributions were not a prerequisite for membership or for voting privileges. The linkage of donations to voting incorporated at the NBC meeting in Grand Rapids was all too vividly remembered. Second, monies given to church plants were viewed as outright gifts; there were no strings or legal ties upon the churches. Organizational ownership had been a sore point during the turbulent years of the break between the Northern Baptists and the Conservative Baptists. There were instances when a congregation discovered that the "help" they received from the NBC to build a building was not an outright gift. Certain congregations, when they voted to withdraw from the Convention, found that they consequently lost their church building or had to make an additional monetary settlement to keep their own building. The Conservative Baptists keenly felt that the NBC had violated the longstanding Baptist distinctive of local church autonomy when they operated as if the national or state conventions owned local churches. No doubt the injustice was particularly galling when the very same Convention would loudly uphold another longstanding Baptist distinctive against creeds as a political maneuver to keep liberal leadership protected within the Convention. The NBC employed the typical tactic of choosing to uphold a principle when it suited a personal or institutional purpose and ignoring another principle when it did not. The Conservative Baptists would not be stung by such behavior a second time. From the initial constitutional discussions, gifts from the national association to help a local church would be true gifts, no strings attached. Using the name

FIRST BAPTIST CHURCH

Walnut and Williams Streets—Danville, Illinois

INVITES YOU . . . .

BIBLE CONFERENCE

—WED., NOV. 24, THRU SUN., DEC. 5, 1948—

7:30 NIGHTLY!

REV. AND MRS. MYRON CEDARHOLM

Music Galore—Vibraharp, Trombone, Vocal

GOSPEL MESSAGE

REV. MITCHELL S. SEIDLER, Pastor

Listen Every Tuesday, 9:30 P. M., "MOMENTS OF MELODY," WDAN

"Conservative Baptist" as part of a church or school name meant more of "being of the same mind and heart as what that group stands for" than any binding obligations.

The CBA got more than just Myron when they signed him on. During these years of service, Thelma was as significant as Myron in the ministry. She worked in the Chicago CBA offices and served on the CBHMS Board. In addition, Thelma, renowned for her story-telling that delighted even adults, was regularly asked to speak in church meetings, summer camps, and vacation Bible schools as the "story lady," and speak to ladies' and missions groups. They frequently maintained individual itineraries and sometimes passed each other in an airport.

There was much to do to accomplish the goals of this new Conservative Baptist movement. The CBHMS held its first meeting on June 24, 1948.[4] In 1949, the CBA began the Minute Man program, a church planting organization. Each month when the "call" came, the minute-men (pastors and laymen alike) responded by donating at least one dollar to aid the selected new church work. Though the program fell short of its goal of 5,000 contributors "on call" for any given project, it did stimulate concern for national church planting.[5]

In May 1949, the Board invited Cedarholm to assume the role of General Director; this was confirmed at the 1950 annual meeting which was held at the historic Park Street Church in Boston. Cedarholm became known as "Mr. Conservative Baptist."[6] G. Archer Weniger nominated him for the position of national General Director of the CBA,[7] the title he would hold until he left the Association, though the work would remain the same: traversing the nation, planting new

---

[4] Bauder and Delnay, *One in Hope and Doctrine*, 364.

[5] Shelley, *A History of Conservative Baptists*, 61.

[6] "The Sure Return of a Convention," 5.

[7] There is also a statement in the minutes of the May 19, 1955, session of the CBA Board meeting: "It was moved and seconded that we call B. Myron Cedarholm as General Director of the Conservative Baptist Association of America. Concurred."

churches, encouraging churches to join the CBA, and helping local assemblies any way he and his wife could. Cedarholm notes that his salary that year was $4,800.

On their way home from the Boston meeting, they planned to stop in Titusville, Pennsylvania, but they had to continue on to Chicago because of the death of a church member. Myron's journal speaks of this and then declares, "This Thelma's dad's first church. Thelma born here—Still many friends here."

Often, especially in the early years, Cedarholm was called upon to help a church sever its ties with the NBC or after it changed its name to the American Baptist Convention (ABC) in 1950 and later to the American Baptist Churches. Changing the name did not change the leanings of the organization, however. The agenda was still liberal, and many churches could no longer support the Convention. Informing congregations about the differences between the ABC and the CBA, helping churches solve legal issues with the ABC, and debating the issues with those still in the ABC were also part of the Cedarholm job description. He recalled a 1950 debate that happened in Menomonie, Wisconsin:

> We have had wonderful fellowship down through the years at Immanuel—revivals, conferences, etc. Yes, and I can never forget about twenty years ago when I was there debating with Dr. Ezra Roth, the ABC State Secretary. Brother Sanasac was the pastor. It was quite an evening. I will never forget brother Sanasac's courage and determination. The Lord blessed, and the church voted out of the ABC and into the CBA. That was quite a feat in those days. It took the resolution of a lion! Dr. Roth was about fit to be tied. He was a fundamentalist turned modernist—born and raised of godly, missionary parents in China and educated at Wheaton and Northern in the good old days. Excuse me for being reminiscent. But, I can never forget that evening.[8]

In 1951, another Bible-believing Wisconsin church demonstrated the need for a man like Myron Cedarholm to help navigate these tumultuous times. Rev. William Shaline

---

[8] Cedarholm correspondence to Hanson, December 24, 1970.

was the pastor of the First Baptist Church, Richland Center, Wisconsin. He was a gospel preacher and deeply interested in reaching the lost. Some of his congregation, however, were loyal to the NBC. They accused him of not being a loyal Baptist because he did not support the Wisconsin Baptist Convention or the NBC, even though the church contributed to both organizations. Another complaint was that he encouraged the church to support CBFMS missionaries. In late 1950, the NBC loyalists asked Pastor Shaline to call in Dr. Ezra Roth, the same man Cedarholm had debated earlier that year at Pastor Sanasac's church, also in Wisconsin. In true Baptistic fashion, Shaline called for a special business meeting of the church to vote upon the request. The convention element brought in enough irregular attendees and persuaded enough of the regular attendees to produce a tie vote, which was insufficient to pass the motion. Undaunted, the NBC supporters insisted that Roth come anyway. He came, there was a meeting, but the conclusion was simply Roth encouraging the pastor to support the Convention faithfully. The opposition continued to stir the pot, however, until things finally boiled over on January 31, 1951, at the regular quarterly business meeting. Behind Shaline's back, the contentious element had invited Roth back to the church. With their numbers bolstered by their dissenting cronies, Roth was elected moderator of the meeting. The pastor refused to be a part of the unscriptural and unconstitutional procedure and left the building. Roth allowed all present at the meeting to vote, members or not, and the pastor was voted out.[9] This was all too typical of the politics of the NBC, and the reason many churches chose to ally themselves with the Conservative Baptist Association. Part of the ministry of the CBA would be to assist so many who were threatened with these kinds of actions.

Just as they were beginning their CBA ministry, the Cedarholms fulfilled a family dream—building their own retreat in Northern Wisconsin. They purchased a lot at 7344

---

[9] "How Wisconsin Votes a Pastor Out," *Information Bulletin of the Conservative Baptist Fellowship* (May 1951), 1.

S. Maranatha Road, on Maranatha Bay, a segment of Lake Nebagamon for $200.

They were among the last to build a cabin on the bay. The early owners were unable to build traditional cabins, because lumber was scarce and expensive after World War II, so they purchased surplus Army barracks that came in 16x16-foot pre-framed sections. Since the Cedarholms built a few years later, they were able to build a traditional wooden cabin some 44 by 26 feet in size.

Maranatha Bay was an association of thirteen property owners who built summer cabins on the picturesque lake shore. George Carlson and Herbert Lockyer, Jr. organized this wonderful summer retreat for Christian leaders and

their families. Lockyer was the son of the writer Herbert Lockyer. George Carlson was a pastor and theologian, with an earned Th.D. degree from the Northern Baptist Seminary in Chicago. Initially he was assistant pastor and then pastor of the Tabernacle Baptist Church of Chicago, where the organizing meeting for the Conservative Baptist Foreign Mission Society was held in 1943. In 1946, he moved to Minneapolis to become pastor of the Lake Harriet Baptist Church. He also served under Dr. Richard V. Clearwaters at

Northwestern, when Clearwaters was the Dean of the seminary.[10] Carlson became a leader in the Conservative Baptist movement alongside Drs. Clearwaters and Cedarholm. He was the president of the Minnesota Baptist Convention for three years and a Vice-President of the CBA. He returned to Chicago to pastor the Marquette Manor Baptist Church from 1953 to 1957, when he was killed in a private plane crash; he and the chairman of the deacons were on their way to a hunting trip in Ontario, Canada. Mrs. Cedarholm was tasked with telling Mrs. Carlson that her husband had died in the crash. Dr. Cedarholm preached his funeral service.

There were other key leaders who owned property there. Cedric Peterson was the first CBA general director and the pastor of Lorimer Baptist Church, the Cedarholms' church home in Chicago. Don Hustad was the well-known musician and chairman of the Music Department at Moody Bible Institute. His parents had graduated from Boone Bible Institute, in Boone, Iowa, the same school from which Anton and Lollie Cedarholm graduated. He was born near Echo, Minnesota, but moved to Chicago after he graduated from college. He met his wife at Lorimer Baptist Church. Chester Tulga was the research director for the CBF and wrote a series of "Case" books arguing for fundamental theological positions and against the liberalism of the NBC. Henry Lovik was an immigrant from Norway and a graduate of Northern Baptist Seminary. He came out of the NBC and was general director of the Conservative Baptist Association of Illinois. Lovik was a separatist hero, and the father of Gordon Lovik, who was on the faculties at Central Baptist Theological Seminary, Minneapolis, and Calvary Baptist Theological Seminary, Lansdale, Pennsylvania. Other property owners were Mitchell Seidler (a pastor active in the CBA), Alton Turner (pastor of First Baptist Church, Streator, Illinois, and later First Baptist Church, Pekin, Illinois), Owen Miller (pastor of First Baptist Church, Hammond, Indiana from 1947–1958 and board member at Denver Seminary), and

---

[10] Gerry Carlson, "Doc and Cedar," a personal recollection, 4-5.

Larry Pearson. Most of the men were strong pre-millennialists, one of the positions that became a significant point of division within the CBA. The name Maranatha signaled not just a hope, but a position. When the Cedarholms named their new school Maranatha, they were not choosing some obscure biblical word just for the sake of its novelty. They were drawing into the name firm convictions

L to R Top Row: Don Hustad, John Mostert, Esther Pearson, Thelma Cedarholm, Shirley Seidler, Ruth Hustad, Eleanor Gotaas, Francis Lovik, Margaret Mostert (in front) Evelyn Carlson, Gladys Lockyer (in front)
L to R Bottom Row: Herbert Lockyer, Henry Lovik, George Carlson, Mitch Seidler, Herb Gotaas, Myron Cedarholm, Larry Pearson

about the pre-millennial, pre-tribulational return of Christ, as well as the deep love they held for their lake retreat. On Sundays, those in the Bay would fellowship at Lake Nebagamon Baptist Church, a Swedish Baptist church in the area. Thelma would play the piano, and Hustad the organ.

The Cedarholms' property was located on a beautiful bay, lined with white birch trees, pines, and thick underbrush. While acquiring the property was a dream come true for the couple who celebrated their tenth anniversary in 1951, the boat house and cabin on the lot did not just magically appear. They were for the most part built by the Cedarholms themselves with lots of used lumber cut into ten-foot lengths. When Myron's father visited that summer, and saw the two of them turned carpenters, he shook his head in wonder and said, "What has happened to my children?"

The construction of the cabin by "an ignorant preacher and his wife," who had only a $2.98 copy of *Mr. Fix-It* as a guide, was quite a story, best told by the builder himself:

> 06.22.51, Friday
> Moderate—office all day house & ate left about 9:00 pm. Thelma & I to Lake Nebagamon, Wisc, 40 miles south 7 east of Superior to where have a lot—100' on lake & ¼ mile deep of solid trees mostly popple [poplar], some [?], few birch & pine.
>
> Took turns driving—stopped a couple of times—arrived about 8:30 & plenty of rain—got Larry Pearson's key from Vennerstrom, Ford dealer at L. N.—a fine Christian—& out to lake lot—south and east of town—about 6 miles—Pearson pastor in Chicago & he lot next to ours & his cabin built 3 years ago.
>
> Rain let up a little bit—Thelma & I used rain coats—explored around a little & picked best spot for lot—about 100' from lake & fairly level & our lot slopes to lake last 500'—used tools & cut down about 80 trees at ground & sawed in 10' lengths...
>
> 06.23.51, Saturday
> Clear in aft.
> ...and stacked at one side. Thelma helped in all operations—however did most of trimming branches off—really worked fast & furious—quit about 8:30—Thelma fixed supper at Pearson's & stayed there overnight. Rained plenty. Cleared a spot on lot about 60' X 40' for cabin.
>
> Also marked trees for our private road out to other road so bull-dozer know where to make road.
>
> a.m. over to Brule to find Olson to bull-doze road, couldn't find him—left note to come & see me at lake.
>
> Came Sunday am at 7:00 & said would do job—wonderful becuz no other work to do over here & small job just for one job—cost $32.00 & haul caterpillar way over here.
>
> a.m. heard about a lumber mill near L.N. owned by Brenig & get unfinished lumber at cheap prices—so over to see him—his mill not running yet, but will soon, told

him what I needed & promised to have it all delivered by next Saturday—Lord is good.

06.24.51, Sunday
Clear & beauty
Church at Swedish Bapt in a.m.—Myron Voth, a Xn Miss[ionar]y Alliance & doing fine job. Single fellow, expects to marry.

Went on way back to Chicago—stopped at Eau Claire, expecting to attend p.m. service a new C.B. church which started—a split from 1st Bapt—John Ashley pastor & leading church back into convention & people really upset. However, since church giving so much to CBFMS, I suggested not to split & wait for a new pastor, but folks just couldn't take it any more—meeting in city auditorium but no pm service so Thelma & I ate & on way (learned later that some folks who know us saw us on the street—so proves wherever you are that may be seen). Arrived Chicago at mid-night & bed.

06.29.51, Friday
Office all day—Witness finished & M-M [CBA periodicals].

Ate on North side & Thelma & I to Lake Nebagamon—drove all night.

Arrived Solon Springs at 7:30 & Hardware store to see Thossen who a Xin—has all mat'ls we would need—but no discount to preachers—but said would make it up some way—

To L. N. & got Pearson's key at Vennerstrom & also looked over L.N. hardware prices & found no diff. than Solon Springs which 25 miles to the south so Thelma & I thot this best since so close by—so bought a few tools, hammer etc. & asked about delivery dates, etc. for lumber—all ok. Thelma & I anxious to get out to lake & get to work, really enthused—didn't know where going to start or how, but anxious to build. Lord seemed to be leading.

06.30.51, Saturday
Praise the Lord leading every step of the way.

Beauty. Out to lake at noon. Used Pearson's road—our road all made & fine job & went just where marked on trees—Praise Lord—didn't use becuz ground still wet—much rain—no lumber & really <u>disappointed</u>. What were we going to do—& only two weeks to build & no time to waste, but God in it all. We still didn't have definite plans—I talked about a basement unit 1ˢᵗ—Thelma said, no, just a cabin—but how start it, what for foundation? So over to Gotaas, Chicago pastor, 2 lots away, & saw used cement blocks—2 or 3 high & 8' ft. apart & so this our plan—carpenter bldg. new cabin & gave us good ideas (God leading us). (Got many hints from carpenter at Gotaas' cabin—made many trips over there.)

Over to see Brenig about lumber—will not be going (never ran all summer, he lazy). God had provided—Brenig sawed lumber for a farmer last year & farmer agreed to sell at Brenigs price of $75 per 1,000 board feet delivered. Finished lumber is $125 per 1,000 so a saving —wonderful—praise God—so over to see Tom Matalik, 10 miles south of us & will be over next Monday at 5:30—Brenig free use of truck.

07.01.51, Sunday

Still no blocks—so learned of a place near-by & over & agreed to haul them tonight—praise God—a miracle—short notice. Bought only 60 blocks & came over in his pick-up & used our road—bottom dragged but made it.

Cleaned up lot—branches tree stumps that bull-dozer left—also leveled out our lot & made a turn around place for cars by cabin. Much accomplished today & the Lord's leading & provision so evident—could all be a wild-goose chase & waste time & money—as look back upon it a miracle that got all these supplies so quickly.

Staying at Pearson's $25.00 a week—(didn't think Larry charge us but did—normally he gets $100 a week).

Sunday: played trombone & sang solos. Beauty. Church all day great blessing—pastor good & folks love the Lord. Swans for dinner—told them about cabin didn't think could do it—borrowed their ladder.

afternoon: Thelma & I worked on cabin plans—got plan settled so know where going.

07.02.51, Monday
Clear—beauty

Made agreement yesterday with Bill Liljegren from church to dig well & so he out & brought all with him & he & I drove pipe in ground with a sleeve hammer plugged with wood—pushed large sleeve hammer—5" pipe & 4 ft long and let drop—had little trouble—down 25' but not good water—so didn't finish.

Thelma & I placed blocks & leveled—put 5 high & 4 rows across front 9' apart—2 high & 4 rows across center & one high & 4 rows across back—cabin 36' front & 22' sides.

Over to Gotaas & Kennedy down by lot #1 for ideas—L.N. Hdwe for supplies—to see Benig & Matalik for lumber tomorrow—4th of July coming & had us sand & gravel for fire-place & suddenly discovered have to make base 1st (poor planning; how marvelous God overruled our ignorance). Nobody said could get it now—takes a week & so we over to see gravel man at 6:00—just had come from work & said had gravel in yard.

Praise God—never would have gone to his gravel pit & so he backed up his truck & his two sons & I shoveled a load & delivered it at 7:30 pm—a real miracle—everyone marveled at it & only cost $3.00—& worth at least $10.00—hauled it 5 miles, too, to lake—used our own road—this good, packed it down with big truck—Rom 8:28—if we not bldg this for the Lord & missy's to use free when on furlough, never dared to do it.

07.03.51, Tuesday
Tuesday: up 4:30 & to Brenig, got him out of bed—he drove truck to Metalik & he loaded lumber—Tom drove truck back to our place & I drove car. Got down in yard o.k. but rained, unloaded, & couldn't get out, used chains, etc. Tom really worked in mud. I took him home—what a mess!!

To Larson at L.N. Hdwe & ordered siding & grooved flooring—need some finished lumber—also brought bags of cement home for making fire-place base. Farmer Homquist brought over his wheel-barrow. Borrowed a hoe & mixing pan from Kennedy—God good. Kennedy labor leader in Duluth.

07.04.51, Wednesday
Beauty—up at 4:00 & got busy on fire-place base—6' by 3' & 4' deep so get below frost line. Thelma out on road & put rocks in car trunk—she really worked today—looked o.k. in over-haul dungarees. Put in layer of rock, layer of cement, etc. & finished job—hauled water from lake—then

put 2" X 6" crosspieces on for joists across the cement blocks.

8:30 pm took a bath in lake. Really worked today & food good. Bed at 9:30. Some of pastors over & really marveled at what doing—inwardly, I suppose, thot never finish.

07.05.51, Thursday
Clear—beauty
Bill Liljegren back & finished pump went down 37' put a booster cylinder on pitcher, pump not enough.

Worked on 2 X 6 & also around edges to make frame—suddenly discovered that blocks 9' apart not so good, becuz joists should be 2' apart—so have to put in some extras.

Larson's boy down with lumber—tried to back in & stuck so unloaded his truck at entrance to our road—400 yards from cabin & got him out—Brenig's truck still at our place & so dry enough & used it to get siding & flooring down to cabin—backed down with each load—wasted a whole a.m. handled lumber so many times.

My folks up at 2:00. Surprised us—thot we never be able to finish—took truck over to Brenig's & got some more 2 X 6's some worm hole & so ½ price—really hot & almost overheated—I worked too fast, anxious to get going—things seem to move so slow thot would about have cabin up by now—but things take time—bath 8:30 & bed 9:30. Bath in lake really great—when finished feel as tho never worked.

07.06.51, Friday
Hot clear beauty up at 4:00. 2 X 6 joists. Thelma helping all rough lumber & 2 X 4 studs going up—braced them with 1 X 4 to stay in place.

Getting places now.

Praise the Lord!

Preachers over to see how working out—12 CB preachers own lots here in a row—only 6 up now.

07.07.51, Saturday
Beauty—hot & mosquitoes terrific—ground so damp spray clothes with DDT.

Finished studs & Holmquist over—working on Rev. Geo. Carlson's place, lot #3, just to see how doing. God led him over—having trouble getting the floor joists level &

corners square when used our level, things looked crooked & when used eye, level crooked—so Holmquist used his eye & braced things accordingly—thank God—this operation important—whole cabin would be crooked if not right now.

Aft—Thelma worked on siding—put on back 1st & then sides—about 4' high

Quit at 8:30—bath—feels great—body feels good not stiff at all.

07.08.51, Sunday
Beauty—church both services

Aft boat ride in Pearson's boat over to Owen Miller's—pastor at 1st BC Hammond—lot #4—fine fellow—he has what other have—army officer houses which bought & sent up from Alabama on flat cars—$250.00 each—he has one—some, two & his beautiful, cute & neat.

Looked at Gotaas & Kennedy for more ideas.

Had a chest of tools given to us by Frank Levening, deacon 2nd BC in Philadelphia—never thot use them to build a cabin—but God provides.

07.09.51, Monday
Up 4:15—over for more lumber—kept Brenig's truck—Tom helped load & unload all well—took truck back—got 2 X 4, 2 X 6, & 1 X 4, 1 X 6 from Tom's.

Put up front studs—Thelma now siding on 2 sides.

Put in light pole in aft. Solon Springs power—no charge & put wires to a tree so we have use of power. Praise God—things moving.

07.10.51, Tuesday
Clear Beauty. God giving good weather.

Thelma on siding I made rafters of 2 X 4s 12' X 10' X 10' so cover 26' roof. Roof extends 2' on all four sides—put rafters 2' apart—used heavy spikes—will have to put bolts thru some day.

Cedric Peterson & Stan Sammerschield [?] over & really just literally amazed what doing—all over town what doing & folks amazed that an ignorant preacher & his wife dare to build a cottage.

But the Lord doing it—all we have is a $2.98 book—"Mr. Fix-it" for help—

Made rafters on joists & lifted up with a 2 X 4 & nailed to 2 X 4s on top of studs—Thelma to Chicago for CBHMS Business, put her on train in a.m. at Solon Springs.

07.11.51, Wednesday
Beauty
Got roof rafters all up in place.
Prayer meeting—prayed till 9:30—good meeting
We attend Wed & not Fri which [is] vacationer's meetings & special speaker.

07.12.51, Thursday
Beauty—started with 1 X 4 & 1 X 6 on roof—siding on 3 sides & front braced so o.k.—braced roof temporarily with 2 X 6s & 2 X 4s.

Evelyn Peterson brought dinner to me—kind of her—mosquitoes so bad she wondered how I live—she came by motorboat.

Went to town—left pen in rain catch on side of steel top in car & still there when home—God good.

Really hot on roof—place so thick with high trees that wind can't get in.

07.13.51, Friday
Beauty. Up at 4:00. Roof boards all on & sawed edges so even & a real job—edge of roof not solid & can't get to edge—so reaching makes it difficult.

8:30 to get Thelma—train not until 10:30—misled by a station agent who going by last year's schedule—home & back on roof—lost one hour becuz 30 minutes each way.

Back at 10:30. More work on roof & Thelma on siding —some folks over to see place & really amazed—they bldg a cottage & paying for it & when saw what we able to do, they amazed.

We not thot that bldg cabin unusual—just nailing boards together & having a great time. God is in this—very evident.

Just after folks left roof supports 2 X 6 fell down. Good thing they out of cabin or would have been hurt—braced up again—I did a poor job 1st time too temporary.

07.14.51, Saturday

Worked on front siding. Put roofing paper on—didn't tack down—laid boards down—however did cement roofing paper together.

Worked on flooring. Folks came up again & Dad helped a little on flooring.

Flooring fooled us—we thot could do a room & then close it in & live in it, but discovered have to lay floor all at once to make it fit & match—

Didn't finish—we thot we would by this time & 2 weeks gone—lost so much time getting started—

07.15.51, Sunday

Beauty church in a.m. left at 3:00—all set to be gone for a week—drove to Cambridge, Wisc arrived at 10:30—Thelma to be at camp—Chicago juniors. I stayed all night.

07.16.51, Monday

Rain. Left 8:30, Chicago 1:30, office CBA correspondence.

07.20. 51, Friday

Clear, hot

Office until 2:00. To Larry Pearson's at Norwood Park & got some blankets for his cottage.

Cleaned out radiator. Left at 6:00—2 hours late. Cambridge at 8:30. Got Thelma & drove to Lake Nebagamon arrived 5:15 bed.

Staying at Pearson's.

Paying him for 2 weeks. 3rd free.

07.21.51, Saturday

Worked on flooring all day—good thing put on roofing paper so kept things dry—roofing paper wrinkled in a few spots—not bad—

Some siding work, too, on front.

Dinner at Gotaas—nice of them.

Worked on side & back window openings—used rough 2 X 4s.

4 windows south side—7 on back side & 3 on north side.

07.22.51, Sunday

Preached at Swedish Bapt church all day—good time—God blessed—much of what said new to folks & a blessing. Several preachers there.

"Elevation" sketches of cabin: north side, south side, front, back, and look-in.

07.23.51, Monday

Beauty, warm. Up at 4:30. Put tacks in roofing 2" apart really slow—put up last strip of roofing, too—on front edge—too hot to work on roof after 9 a.m.

Put up front door—never hung a door before—put it up —perfect fit—hinges exact—thank God.

Worked on front siding.

Quit at 11:00 & bath.

Joe Liljegren put in fuse box & brought wire to house & put in a few switches for us & outside light—I will do rest of wiring.

Parts cost $40 & Joe's labor only $6.00. Parts expensive.

07.24.51, Tuesday

Beauty a.m. worked on roof until 9.

Rest of lumber came—had to order 200 board ft. of siding also 1 X 6—finished, for window casement & 1 X 4 for outside of window—finished lumber & 2 X 4, finished, for front window.

So working on siding in front—also on flooring. Vennerstrom came out in 7:00 pm & helped with flooring & finished it—praise God—quit at 11:00.

07.25.51, Wednesday

Beauty—clear—4:30 worked on front living room window—used finished 2 X 4s & 9 openings of 20" X 30"—used chisel for groovings & perfect fit—God good—total opening 6'6" by 8' 3".

Finished south siding made casements for all other windows—used 1 x 6.

Prayer meeting.

Worked after prayer meetings till 11:00.

07.26.51, Thursday

Beauty clear.

Finished front siding difficult to reach up—14 ft. off ground & ladder not quite high enough.

Made back window frames—used 1" X 2"—had Larson groove them out ½" used Geo. Carlson's mitre box to get 45° angle.

Worked till 11 & bath in lake.

07.27.51, Friday
Clear. Up at 4:30.

Closed in back with 1 X 4 under roof—between rafters.

Thelma put window frames together & painted & I to town. Got glass & ¼ round & some more 1 X 6s; carried on top carrier from Matalik.

Windows not fit, too big—over to Geo. Carlson & electric saw & cut edges—still not fit—had to take some apart, nails out, etc. over to Geo again & this time enough off so fit—had to take ¼" off in some cases—windows our hardest job. Thelma's measuring not exact.

Worked till 11.

Put in 2 X 4 partitions between rooms—also help to hold up roof.

07.28.51, Saturday
Praise God for His goodness.
Up at 4:30. Little rain, no hindrance.

Finished front window by living room—used ¼ round to hold in glass—Thelma measured & I cut—(arm a little stiff at elbow with all sawing & stiff for 2–3 months after)—really felt good after finished windows. Cost $11.00 & Cedric & Evelyn liked it & asked a carpenter what cost for them to have one & said, $300.00—Herb Lockyer got itchy (2 cabins from us)—he trashed out part of front wall & put in a 40" X 60" window—all other preachers got the itch & making improvements & saw Thelma working & so made their wives help, too—really funny.

Had to go to Poplar to get more glass—some double strength, couldn't get single. Also hung side door & perfect fit.

Worked till 11:30 p.m. tired mosquitoes bad—used plenty DDT.

Closed in front between rafters with 1 X 4 & flooring.

07.29.51, Sunday

Clear, Superior in am for service—Turk, pastor Petersons for dinner at L. N.

PM Swed. Bapt at L. N.

07.30.51, Monday

Praise God for His goodness

Cloudy. Began at 4:30. Moved out of Larry's place at 8:30, some vacationers came—ate dinner & supper at Herb Lockyers, gracious of them.

Put all finishing touches—closed up fire-place hole in floor.

Put in kitchen & dining room windows—bot these 4 dining room & 2 kitchen—nailed them in—only 3 for D. R. so covered opening with tar paper—also bath room window not in & covered with tar paper & also small north side windows.

Nailed 1 X 6 on sides under roof where opening from siding.

Used Val-oil to paint doors, all front windows.

Worked till 1:30 a.m. took Swan's ladders back—really all in—couldn't drive so slept in car at Solon Springs.

God is good to allow us to close it all in—had a few falls nothing serious.

In just over a month the Cedarholms finished their dream cabin. They finished the fireplace later, using stone gathered from around the United States and even overseas. Getting done quickly was crucial, because they knew most of

Myron's time was going to be spent with a different kind of building.

The always hospitable Cedarholms did not keep the cottage to themselves. The cabin was always available to furloughed missionaries, family, friends, and tired pastors needing relaxation. When they were on the Bay, their boat became the ski boat, as they taught many of the children there how to ski. Myron also taught the area children how to hunt and fish, and even how to skin a skunk![11]

Myron could ski on his feet and on his head!

Myron's athleticism continued to be part of his ministry. In September 1951, while attending a CBA conference in Portland, Oregon, he participated in a baseball game. His journal records the results:

---

[11] Undated script for a slide presentation on the Cedarholms.

aft—ballgame—I pitched & won 10–4—a great time & arm felt good, fast ball & curve working fine. I made a terrific slide into home, came in feet first about 3 feet high & really piled into catcher (Birchwedel, pastor of Lentz BC, Portland) he took it all in fun. I was called out, but really he never touched me (later in afternoon message, Jim Mercer referred to it as a "sanctified slide"—fellows really roared). I had on my good trousers & reason I didn't come in & hit dirt.

That same year, just before the American Baptist Convention annual meeting in Buffalo, NY, the Conservative Baptist Fellowship of the American Baptist Convention became simply the Conservative Baptist Fellowship.[12] The conservatives disavowed any hope for reform in the American Baptist Convention and connected itself solely to the Conservative Baptist movement.

Cedarholm notes that he went to the Donald Smith Memorial Church in Chicago on November 26, 1951 to preach on "CB & Why." The pastor of this new small work was Richard Weeks, who would later become a leader in the New Testament Association of Independent Baptist Churches (NTA), a faculty member at Pillsbury, and the Academic Dean at Maranatha.

In 1953, Cedarholm's work and encouragement showed results. The messengers at the annual meeting at Portland that year heard reports that nearly 500 churches were then members of the national association, and an additional 240 belonged to state associations that were closely aligned with, but not officially members of, the national group.[13] The Portland annual meeting also saw the nearly unanimous adoption of the "Portland Manifesto" by all of the Conservative Baptist organizations—the CBA, CBHMS, CBFMS, and the CBF. This was an affirmation of the founding principles of the Conservative Baptist movement.

The Portland Manifesto reads as follows:

---

[12] "The Conservative Baptist Fellowship," *Conservative Baptist Fellowship Information Bulletin* (Dec 1962), 7.

[13] Shelley, *A History of Conservative Baptists*, 62.

WHEREAS, on this happy and historic celebration of Conservative Baptist advance, which gives us occasion to reflect upon God's gracious blessing in the formation and ongoing of various Conservative Baptist agencies, we desire to give a real assurance to Bible-believing Baptists everywhere of our position and direction:

THEREFORE, BE IT RESOLVED, that we re-affirm our unchanging confidence in the trustworthiness of the Scriptures and in those foundational truths as expressed in the Confessions of Faith and Constitution of our various Conservative Baptist organizations; and

BE IT FURTHER RESOLVED, that we re-affirm our unswerving opposition to the practice of the Inclusive Policy, that policy which is inclusive of belief and unbelief alike, and results in division and conflicting testimony at home and abroad, and that we acknowledge that the Conservative Baptist movement logically thereby continues to be separatist in spirit and objective; and

BE IT FURTHER RESOLVED, that it is our conviction that Conservative Baptist board members and officers be men who have openly declared themselves to stand with Conservative Baptists on the principles set forth in this declaration, to be in sympathy with the purposes of the Conservative Baptist Movement, and to be in opposition to the Inclusive Policy as shown by their personal non-cooperation with the inclusive program.

FINALLY, BE IT FURTHER RESOLVED, that we take this occasion to recommend to Conservative Baptists in assembly in Portland that a committee be authorized to study the problems inherent in our growing Conservative Baptist movement, the inter-relations of the Boards, the role of the Regional and National Conferences, and other related problems; that this committee be composed of two representatives from each of the four Boards, one representative from each of the two Seminaries, plus two members elected from each of the Regional Conferences; and that this committee report at the 1954 Annual Meeting.

THE INTENT AND PURPOSE OF THE MANIFESTO

The Intent and Nature of the Manifesto

    A. It is only an expressional instrument from messengers of churches and from Board members of our

four Societies assembled in Annual Meeting in Portland, Oregon, in June 1953.
B. The Manifesto is not binding upon any church or any Society represented in this expression.
C. The Manifesto is a purely voluntary, democratic and positive expression of a working and workable ideal to serve as a common denominator for each of our four organizations in particular and for the whole Conservative Baptist Movement in general.
D. The Manifesto as a working and workable ideal, in its very language in at least two places, makes this Manifesto self-interpreting.
   1. "Unswerving opposition to the practice of the inclusive policy"
     a. Theological form of the inclusive policy which is an admixture of belief and unbelief.
     b. Ecclesiastical form of inclusive policy which is churches and individuals being associated with unsound bodies.
     c. Financial form of inclusive policy which is giving financial support to unsound bodies, individuals, or objectives and enterprises.
     d. Practical form of the inclusive policy which is giving one's vote, voice, or volitional influence to unsoundness as expressed in the inclusive policy in its theological, ecclesiastical or financial form, <u>without protest.</u>
   2. "Separatist in spirit and objective"
     a. Separatist in spirit means: the sincere heart attitudes, motives, impulses, desires, expressions, prayers, and actions of the individual, or individuals comprising a church or organization to give with protest the least possible cooperation to all forms of the inclusive policy as named above which will be determined in degree of cooperation by the particular circumstances that prevail.
     b. Separatist in objective means: the individual, church, or organization desires as soon as possible to arrive at the place where
       (1) All disbelief can be disfellowshipped.

(2) All unsound associations can be disassociated.
(3) All unsound objectives can be met with non-support.
(4) All participation with unbelief, unsound organizations, and financial objectives can be discontinued.

Things were so positive in the Conservative Baptist movement at this time, that the Conservative Baptist Fellowship discussed the possibility of disbanding and liquidating its assets. This did not happen, although the function of the CBF moved more toward research and publication. That confidence would change, however, when ten years later the conservatives lost their motion to reaffirm the Manifesto at their 1963 Atlantic City annual meeting.

While 1953 brought good news in the CBA, it also brought sadness to the Cedarholm household. Anton passed away on December 5.

In 1954 at the annual meeting of the CBF, Dr. I. Cedric Peterson of Los Angeles presented a resolution for the dissolving of the Fellowship. After lengthy discussion, the vote was about to be taken when Peterson withdrew his motion, perhaps because he realized that it would be defeated. Peterson had been elected the first General Director of the CBA in June 1948. By the end of 1948 Peterson quit his position out of discouragement, left the new Association to Cedarholm, and declared that the CBA would never amount to anything. His church remained in the CBA, and he became the leader of the soft core and advocator of a "General Conference" form of government—the uniting of all the CBA organizations into a single body.[14]

Also in 1954, the CBA proposed an administrative change. They recommended that Cedarholm be made the "National Field Representative and Evangelist" and that a new General Director be hired. The new arrangement stated that, "Cedarholm [is] to represent CBA in the field and not to be bothered with office detail. He will be free to conduct

---

[14] "The Sure Return of a Convention," 5.

evangelistic services, CBA promotional meetings, to participate in missionary conferences without other hindrances."[15] This announcement was followed by a motion to retain Cedarholm as General Director for the time being.

In 1955, the membership of the CBA consisted of 998 churches and continued to climb throughout Cedarholm's tenure to a peak of 1,550 in 1963.[16] No doubt this information is the source for the well-known assertion that Cedarholm either started or assisted over 1000 churches during his ministry. Also in 1955, both Cedarholms were awarded honorary doctorates from Northwestern Seminary, Minneapolis, Minnesota.[17]

Each of the churches in the CBA, especially the new churches that had only recently been planted, represented the personal faith stories of the individual pastors and their congregations, and some had very interesting beginnings. In Fremont, California, one church began in a barn; in Oregon, one met in a brewery. Many started in tents, houses, and hotels. Cedarholm birthed a church in a railroad station in Miles City, Montana, and another in an old Arthur Murray Dance Studio. The *Prince of a Man* script suggested tongue-in-cheek that the story of that church could be titled, *From Dancing Slippers to Golden Shoes*. Churches opened in restaurants and in abandoned church buildings. In Orlando, Florida, Cedarholm organized a church in a Jewish synagogue. In Tomah, Wisconsin, a lodge hall became a church, and in Estherville, Iowa, a chicken coop was used.

The January 1955 meeting of the CBA saw the censuring of Dr. Chester Tulga, Research Secretary of the CBF. He was criticized for pointing out the theological drift that was taking place at Denver Seminary. He also reported a number of problems in the CBFMS. Some of its leaders were friendly to the NBC and supported the Convention or its agencies

---

[15] Albert S. Taylor, "7 Special Days," *National Voice of Conservative Baptists* (July-August 1954), 13.

[16] Association of Religion Data Archives, Conservative Baptist Association of America data archive.

[17] "C.B.A. of A. Honors General Director," 6.

(including its "inclusive policy"). The CBFMS was engaged in pastoral placement in the US, over-riding local church autonomy. The Society was moving away from being responsible to the churches and growing more independent. Theological unity was being lost as more and more post-tribulationists and amillenialists were being appointed as missionaries by the Society and as faculty at Denver Seminary. Furthermore, an anti-CBA sentiment was growing in the CBFMS. Vincent Brushwyler, General Director of the Conservative Baptist Foreign Mission Society, was part of the "soft core" of the CBA. Cedarholm, because of his role as General Director of the CBA, was barred from speaking in the chapel at Denver Seminary. As a result, the Conservative Baptist Fellowship broke its connections with the CBA in 1955.[18]

The CBA, CBFMS, and CBHMS were separate organizations with separate boards, constitutions, and practices. While they were all "Conservative Baptists," they remained autonomous organizations. In 1956, Cedarholm wrote to the president of the CBA, Arno Q. Weniger, Sr., expressing his concern over the potential of a "General Council." The NBC had brought together its various organizations under one umbrella, and the various societies lost their autonomy. The more conservative pastors of the CBA did not want to see that happen again. Thus, Cedarholm argued that the boards should never meet together for anything but prayer; otherwise, he argued, "we will have a connectionalism and the building of a Convention."[19]

In 1957, there was renewed discussion of disbanding the Conservative Baptist Fellowship. There was concern, however, about the publishing of material necessary to keep the constituency aware of current theological trends. The concern of the CBF was that the CBA would not print these

[18] Arno Q. Weniger, "Facts for Conservative Baptists to Face in 1955." Editorial, "Conservative Baptist Fellowship Withdraws from Conservative Movement," *Baptist Bulletin* (March 1955), 8.

[19] Letter from B. Myron Cedarholm to Arno Q. Weniger, June 18, 1956.

materials. As in the past, the
CBF decided to continue its
existence and focus on
communication.[20]

In recognition of the
work of both Dr. and Mrs.
Cedarholm in church
planting and promoting of
the CBA, on May 24, 1957,
Myron was awarded a Doctor
of Letters. Thelma, in
recognition of her role in
Myron's ministry, was
awarded the degree Doctor of
Letters from Baptist Bible
College, Denver, Colorado.

One of the decisions the
CBA Board made during
their meeting in May 1959,
was for the churches of
America to raise funds to
send the Cedarholms somewhere their car could not take
them. In appreciation for their twelve years of service, the
CBA churches gave them—the world. In 1960, they were
forty-five years old and had been on the road for the CBA for
thirteen years. The churches contributed over $3,000 before
the June 1960 CBA meetings, and at that meeting another
$2,000 was added. The trip was scheduled for later that year.

Mrs. Cedarholm's first flight in an airplane was in
January 1960. Sick with the flu for two days, she flew to
Mexico for the Conservative Baptist Home Missionary Society
Board meeting. Just months later, she found herself flying
thousands of miles on their world tour.[21]

The Cedarholms' world tour was lengthy and
comprehensive. They traveled to forty-two countries and
forty-eight mission fields, visiting 350 missionaries, during a

---

[20] Agenda, Publications Committee, CBA, January 1957.

[21] Myron Cedarholm journal, January 6, 1960.

Bon voyage from good friends

five-month journey that covered 52,000 miles.[22] They left August 17, 1960, after getting $300 in traveler's checks, finalizing their wills and taking out "top air insurance for $450,000" with the beneficiaries listed as "CB schools and organizations."[23] Their first stop was Mexico City, where they were hosted by the Gerbers, CBFMS missionaries who ran a Christian publication and distribution work. There the Cedarholms saw both the typical tourist sites (Mexican pyramids, the Roman Catholic cathedral, and the primitive country life) and the missions work in the area. Myron noted in his journal that in spite of the publishing ministry, as well as the success of a Christian bookstore, there was "no sense of local church."

On August 19, they flew from Mexico City to Oaxaca, site of the ministry of Morris Ruegsegger, missionary at Quixtla,

---

[22] Myron Cedarholm journal, January 03, 1961. Mrs. Cedarholm wrote a children's story based on this overseas trip. She identified actual missionaries and events in the book. Thelma Cedarholm, *With Jim and Jane by Silver Plane* (Chicago: Conservative Baptist Foreign Mission Society, n.d.).

[23] Myron Cedarholm journal, August 17, 1960.

a Zopetec village. On Saturday, August 20, they toured the Indian ruins of the Zopetecs who flourished about 1500 A.D.

They met Ciro, a wonderful trophy of God's grace. He was a mason and had fallen off a wall, breaking both legs. The bones broke through the skin and one foot was turned in

With Jim and Jane by Silver Plane

the wrong direction. He lay at home, dying, for five months, when Morris (a medical doctor as well as a missionary) came to the home and learned of the accident. He returned with penicillin, facilitated the healing of Ciro's wounds, and took him to the hospital in Pueblo, where they straightened the turned foot. Ciro was soon saved and taught Morris the Zopetec language. Ciro's family was also saved, and the ministry flourished as a result of the caring ministry of the

Oaxaca Taxi

missionary. Morris then created a Zopetec alphabet and during the next nine years, translated the Bible. On Sunday, August 21, the Cedarholms enjoyed a goat dinner with tortillas and corn soup (eaten without silverware of any kind), participated in the 4:00 pm Sunday service, and watched Morris meet many physical needs of the people.

The next morning, they flew to San Salvador and were reunited with ABFMS missionaries, Jason and Helen Cedarholm, Myron's brother and sister in-law. Helen was the only sister of Ortiz, Archer, Max, and Arno Weniger, Sr. (The Wenigers often spoke of their only sister marrying Cedarholm's only brother.) There they toured the Colegio Bautiste with its 400 students. The Principal of the school was Miss Eva McCutcheon, a "typical ABC woman," whatever that meant to Myron! The school was a high school plus one year of college. The buildings were old, but in good condition. The school had been there for thirty-five years. Most of the teachers had grown old with the work. Myron noted sadly that the "ABC does not appoint folks like this anymore, fundamental and faithful." They had dinner with an ABC missionary, Weber, who had been in Puerto Rico for twenty-five years before coming to San Salvador. The next day they toured Santa Ana, the city where Jason and his family lived.

The Cedarholms then travelled to Panama City on August 25, where they toured the city the next day. On August 27 they flew to Caracas, Venezuela, where their trip was delayed briefly because their visas were not initially accepted.

The next day they flew to Beleur, Brazil, on the 29th to Sashuiz, Brazil, and on the 31st to Teresina. The 1st of September, they traveled by jeep into the interior of Brazil.

They flew from Brazil to Madrid on September 3. This was their first ever flight on a jet airplane.[24] At that point the journal goes blank for two weeks. Their Christmas letter notes that they traveled to London and then Interlachen. The next journal entry indicates that they left Zurich on September 18 for Geneva. From there they traveled to Naples

---

[24] 1961 Christmas Letter.

on September 20, and the next day they used an admiral's boat for a picnic. On the 22nd they visited Puzzuoli (the biblical city of Puteoli) and Pompeii on the 23rd. On the 24th they traveled by train to Rome for the day and flew out that

night for Lisbon, Portugal. September 25th, they participated in four church services. The next day they drove to Leiria and the next day to Fatima. They flew to Dakar, Africa, on the night of the 27th.

September 28th found the Cedarholms in Robertsfield, Liberia, near Monrovia. Their general itinerary had been published in Archer Weniger's *Blu-print* newsletter from Foothill Boulevard Baptist Church in California. That was how the missionary in Liberia knew on which of the two planes that landed each week in Robertsfield the Cedarholms would arrive. This was providential since the letter the Cedarholms had sent to give him the specific information did not arrive until the day after they did!

On October 1, they flew to Abidjan, Ivory Coast, and on the 3rd to Ferdesselougou and Ferke. They traveled to Nielle on the 4th, and then on the 6th drove through the Ivory Coast, visiting Kortiep, Alargiones, Korhogo, and Bouidiala. After a few days in Katiola, they flew to Khartoum, Sudan, on the 14th. From there on the 16th they traveled to Entebbe, Uganda. On the 17th they went to Nbarsara, and on the 18th they flew to Ruangaba, Congo.

They drove down dusty roads into the Congo bush on October 20, and their trip was delayed by an overturned truck, blocking the way. Two soldiers demanded that they provide a ride for them (a requirement in the Congo). As it turned out, one of the soldiers was a Christian chaplain. Even though an October 24th earthquake shook the area and caused minimal damage, the Cedarholms doggedly stuck to their itinerary.

They flew to Cairo on the 25th and toured the pyramids the next day. They also rode camels; Thelma noted that a woman should never wear Dacron (a polyester fabric that does not "breathe") when riding camels![25] On the 27th they flew to Athens, Greece, where they visited Mars Hill. On the 29th they traveled to Corinth, then took a night flight to Beirut, Lebanon, where they met someone related to people Thelma knew back in Benson, Minnesota. On the 31st they traveled to Damascus. They drove to Amman, Jordan, and then to Bethlehem on November 1. The next two days were spent touring Jericho and Jerusalem. About this time, a check they wrote was rejected due to insufficient funds—the CBA secretary back in Chicago had forgotten to deposit Cedarholm's paychecks!

On November 4, they returned to Beirut. November 5th found them in Karachi, Pakistan, where they had to stay in an "expensive hotel" ($10.00 for two people for one night), "but no alternative—God had a purpose." The next day the Cedarholms took the train to Dadur, then to Larkaur the following day, and then on to Sbilzapoor on the 8th. November 9, they traveled by car to Larhana, where they learned that John Kennedy had been elected president.

---

[25] 1961 Christmas letter.

On November 10, they traveled to Shaharper, the next day back to Karachi, and then on the 12th they flew to Nagpur, India. Two days later they visited a leper hospital in Kathara. Then on the 16th Dora Johnson took them in her open-air Jeep halfway to Dharmi, where they met Della Kirkpatrick and had a noon picnic. Myron notes that it was "hard to believe that this India—so beautiful—reminds me of No. Wisc. or Congo." They arrived that evening at Dharmi, where they were met by Eileen Prickett and Nell Grubbs and four girls who were home from school. This was described as a lovely station, without electricity, but with a church in the village. They spent two days here. November 19th, they traveled to Dharia and the next day to Ellichpur, where Thelma observed an Indian woman giving birth to her son. On the 21st they traveled to Yeotrual, where they held evangelistic meetings in the Town Hall. There were about 250 present, where this modern day "Paul" reasoned from the Hindu writings to Christ. Myron indicated that it reminded him of the way the apostle Paul did it.

> The next morning the doctor, [and] nurse, Miss Muriel, took the children to visit the Leper Asylum at Kothara [India]. On their way, they stopped to see a dying woman in a nearby village. What an awful sight they found there! Two men were forcing a woman to sit up against the wall of the hut. Her face was a terrible sight—they could see that death was near. The missionaries pleaded for them to let her lie down to rest. They finally did so. One man was her husband. He begged the missionaries to help her, but she was already beyond doctor's care. Instead, they spoke to her about the Lord Jesus. The husband repeated to her very carefully, everything that the missionaries said—just to make sure that she heard. Sometime before that she had come to sing and hear with joy and interest the Gospel message. Now the visitors all sang together one of her favorite songs.
>
> Suddenly that terrible face became changed—it became beautiful—it seemed that the Lord Jesus had come to take her right into Heaven! He made the time of

sorrow into one of joy for He saved out of sin and darkness this precious Indian woman.[26]

They spent November 24 in Calcutta, visiting the Calcutta Bible College and William Carey Baptist Church, while their friends back in the States were celebrating Thanksgiving. On the 26th they visited Serampore (where Carey first came in 1800). There they watched a Ghat, the cremation of the dead. Fifty people were cremated that day. On the 27th, Myron noted that "Bill" was doing a great job at Calcutta Bible College, but the Baptists needed their own Baptist college so they "can teach all God's Word & challenge & train men to start Bapt churches." He went on to note that Luther Rice, the partner of Adoniram Judson, had recognized this problem, but had deferred to Carey's desires. Myron noted, however, that it was "inconsistent to put Bapt way into interdenominational school & can't challenge men to be Bapt pastors."

The next three days they visited Rangoon, Burma; Bangkok, Thailand; Saigon, Vietnam; and Manila, Philippines. They had been in the Philippines for a few days, when on December 3, either Myron or both Myron and Thelma "got into bathing suit—Bill Simons & Art Beals in one boat—'Banka'— 25' long and 20" wide—hollowed out & Thelma & I in other—two men in each boat—front & back to guide up river to Pagsanjan Falls." It took them 90 minutes over ten rapids (some bad enough that they had to get out and drag their boats through the rapids). This was the "most beautiful ever seen." They saw coconut trees by the thousands. Part of the river had sheer rock cliffs with 200-foot falls on both sides. The return trip was about an hour. It was "more fun going down & thru rapids—really a thrill men really knew how to manipulate boats." They also went swimming at a "beautiful pool of warm spring water ... really a wonderful day of relaxation: 1st this trip." At this time, they learned that Thelma's youngest brother, Leslie, had died.

December 6th, they flew to Hong Kong, where they went shopping. Myron noted that the prices there were great. They

---

[26] Cedarholm, *With Jim and Jane by Silver Plane*, 61.

also did a little CBA sleuthing at the colleges there, operated by the World Council of Churches and the Southern Baptist Convention.

On the 9th they flew to Taipan, Formosa. A week later they flew to Tokyo and then took a night train 300 miles north to Sendai. They spent nine days in Japan. Myron noted, "Sad to think intelligent people can be so idolatrous."

They left Tokyo on December 27th and flew to Honolulu. There they met with a group of military personnel, wanting to start a Baptist church. Out of that meeting was born a new church plant, the Oahu Baptist Church, which a year later was running about 100 attendees on Sunday mornings. The next day they flew to San Francisco, arriving on the 29th. On January 2, they flew home to Chicago. Time after time, they flew or took the train overnight, so as not to waste daytime hours. The Cedarholms summarized the trip as follows:

> 52,100 miles
> 42 countries
> 48 villages
> 220 CB missionaries visited
> 27 CB missionaries missed
> 105 missionaries on other boards visited
> 1,200 slides
> 22 ball point pens used for notes
> 500 postcards

They recalled discussing polygamy, modernism, Congolese riots, indigenous churches and interdenominationalism with missionaries, and in almost every stop they already knew the missionaries with whom they were staying. They visited radio stations, colleges, Bible institutes, and hundreds of churches. When it was all over, Dr. Cedarholm noted that Thelma had been sick only part of one day, and he "not really sick even for a day."

While the itinerary itself is legendary, Dr. Cedarholm's travel wardrobe was even more so. He made the entire trip with only one change of clothing—leaving ample room for artifacts. Whether in Zurich, Hong Kong, or Rangoon, the frugal world traveler washed his clothing nightly in a sink so it would dry overnight and be ready for the next day. Traveling out of a suitcase was nothing new for the Cedarholms, however.

As a testament to their tireless stateside ministry, the membership in the CBA came to a virtual standstill while the Cedarholms were abroad; only one church joined the Association.[27]

After his return to Chicago, his non-stop stateside travel resumed immediately; he left on January 4, 1961, for services with Chester McCullough in Tipton, Indiana. When giving his report to the Conservative Baptist Association board in mid-January, he felt that one idea that resonated with the Board was his ambition to see the CBA plant a Conservative Baptist English-speaking church in every major population center in the world. This local church foundation could then develop radio stations, colleges and institutes, servicemen's outreaches, and other ministries that were often missionary projects, but which he was now convinced should come after the establishment of a local church, rather than before or instead of it.

Probably no one associated with the Conservative Baptist movement had a more personal influence on as many Baptist preachers and laymen as the Cedarholms. Rarely have a man and wife demonstrated a more practical commitment to the primacy of the local church than the Cedarholms. He did not just speak at annual Association meetings and return to a comfortable administrative job for the rest of the year. Week after week he traveled from state to state, holding evangelistic meetings for one pastor, preaching stewardship and tithing messages for another, knocking on doors to invite people to an infant work, or helping a new work acquire its first building. Year after year, the Cedarholms were on the move, helping pastors whenever and wherever they needed help in their ministries. This was an investment that would not be forgotten.

[27] Association of Religion Data Archives, Conservative Baptist Association of America data archives.

In something of a replay of the attempt to begin the Conservative Baptist Foreign Mission Society within the Northern Baptist Convention in 1943, the Conservative Baptist Fellowship organized a new mission society in 1961, the Conservative Baptist World Mission, and appointed their first missionary, George Mensik, on January 26, 1962.[28] The CBFMS and the CBHMS were both permeated with new evangelicals and some non-Baptists. Missionaries in this new organization were expected to uphold a clear separatist, anti-new evangelical, premillennial, pre-tribulational position. Had the plan been accepted by the other Conservative Baptist societies, fundamental churches would have had yet another "approved" mission society through which to funnel their church missionary giving. The Cedarholms remained with the CBA, but the problems were growing more significant with each passing year. The contention over the new mission board brought to the forefront another outspoken conservative, Richard Weeks, who would become a colleague of the Cedarholms in their later years. Just four years later the new mission society changed its name to Baptist World Mission, because the Conservative Baptist movement was going in a direction these men rejected. This name change demonstrated that their ties with the Conservative Baptist movement were now severed.[29]

In 1964, the Cedarholms noted that they had traveled over 70,000 miles by car and more by train and plane. They visited 133 churches and met with 148 different families. One night they even stayed in a Navajo hogan near Gallup, New Mexico.

The Cedarholms realized that they needed a home closer to their office—533 West Dulles Road, Des Plaines, Illinois. It was designed according to their specifications, for like the cabin, this was meant to be a ministry center—a place for pastors, missionaries, and indeed anyone who needed a meal

[28] *Bluprint*, January 1, 1965.

[29] The reader is directed to Fred Moritz, *Now is the Time: A History of Baptist World Mission* (North Fort Myers, FL: Faithful Life Publishers, 2011) for a history of Baptist World Mission.

or a room. At one point seven missionary boys were living there while attending school in Chicago: Bill and Jack Cedarholm (nephews of Myron and Thelma), Kelsey and Tim Pietsch, Judd Sanford, Guad, and one additional boy.

Two problems developed that caused the hard core to seriously consider abandoning the Conservative Baptist movement. One was the decision of the CBA to accept into its membership a church with unbaptized members. The hard core was unable to block the CBA from seating messengers from this church. The second was the refusal of the CBA to reaffirm either its original statement of purpose or the Portland Declaration of 1953, both of which committed Conservative Baptists to a separatist direction.

In 1963, a committee of reconciliation, including both hard core and soft policy leaders, issued a report that could have stopped the conflict. That report, however, was blocked by soft policy sympathizers and never presented to the Conservative Baptist constituency. About that time calls began to come from the soft policy for the hard core to "get out and leave us alone." Then in 1964, the CBA voted to void the election of representatives from the Central Regional, which was dominated by the hard core. Clearly a division was imminent.

Mrs. Cedarholm and Mrs. Seidler
in a Haitian kitchen

In 1965, the Cedarholms, nearing the end of their ministry with the CBA, traveled to the West Indies with Dr. and Mrs. Mitchell Seidler of Cincinnati. The Seidlers had been loyal supporters of the Cedarholms during their CBA days and would continue to stand by them. They visited missionaries and churches in Jamaica and Haiti. There they met Bertha "Granny" Holdeman. At the age of 59, after the loss of her husband, she joined Wallace Turnbull and his medical missions work in Haiti. Granny visited Maranatha a few times to encourage the students to consider missionary work, no matter what their age.

On Friday, August 13, 1965, many friends of the Cedarholms gathered at the Sheraton–O'Hare Hotel in Des Plaines, Illinois, to "pay honor to a man who faithfully served the Conservative Baptist Association for eighteen years."[30] For the nearly two decades that he had served as General Director, he had traveled about 75,000 miles a year, ministered in churches, camps, association meetings, and

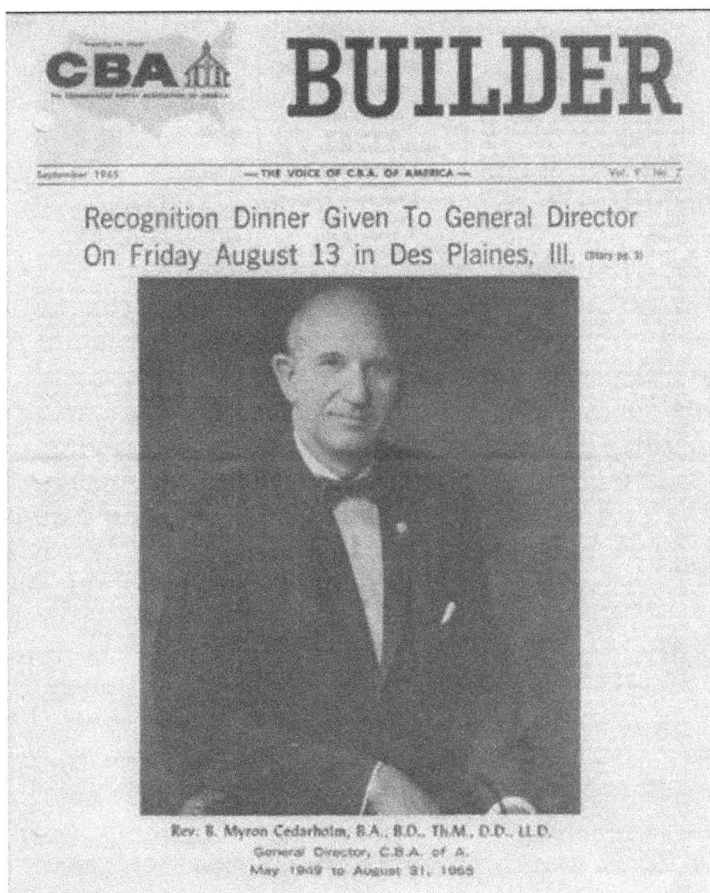

CBA BUILDER

September 1965   — THE VOICE OF C.B.A. OF AMERICA —   Vol. 9, No. 7

Recognition Dinner Given To General Director
On Friday August 13 in Des Plaines, Ill. (Story pg. 3)

Rev. B. Myron Cedarholm, B.A., B.D., Th.M., D.D., LL.D.
General Director, C.B.A. of A.
May 1949 to August 31, 1965

---

[30] "C.B.A. of A. Honors General Director," *CBA Builder* 9.7 (September 1965), 3.

schools. The CBA grew from about 100 churches in 1947 to 1,500 churches in 1965. Mrs. Cedarholm was honored for her assistance to Dr. Cedarholm. In the early days of the CBFMS, she wrote much of the missionary education materials for both children and adults. She was actively involved in the organization of the CBHMS. She worked in the office, spoke in various conferences, and served on the CBHMS Board from 1951 to 1960. This Recognition Dinner was organized as a sendoff for the Cedarholms, as they were to begin their ministry at Pillsbury Baptist Bible College.

Personal concern was a mark of the Cedarholms' ministry. Harris Steurmer, during their Recognition Dinner, said, "Another outstanding thing about the Cedarholms: they have a personal touch for their fellow ministers in the gospel. When they come to your home, they know the names and interests of every child in the home; and they enquire into their health, welfare and their doings.... Myron has a place in his heart for the humble, lowly and needy."[31] Personal attention to others was reflected in a very practical way by their fantastic ability to remember names. For the thousands of times he remembered obscure names in unusual places, one anecdote demonstrated the unfortunate result when both his memory and his adroit face-saving backup plan failed. While visiting with people at the church door, one man warmly greeted Dr. Cedarholm. Though he recognized the gentleman's face and handshake, he could not remember his name. "Now, brother, tell me again—how is your last name spelled?" The man, a bit unkindly, replied in a loud voice, "J–O–N–E–S." With rare exceptions, they knew the children's names, their ages, their favorite school subjects, and their future dreams and desires.

The years following the world trip were marked by another series of denominational struggles. Less than twenty years had passed since the conservatives left the Northern Baptist Convention and formed the Conservative Baptist Association. When they formed the CBA in 1947, the men felt they were building an organization that would hold to biblical

---

[31] *CBA Builder*, 3.

truth and escape denominational control over individual churches. They clung as well to the belief that helpful cooperation between like-minded churches was necessary to support schools and missionaries.

As the years passed, the men with whom Dr. Cedarholm shared an affinity developed growing concerns with the CBA itself. Their concern was not that the group was embracing modernism or an overt rejection of Scripture as the Word of God. Instead, they sensed that some men in the CBA had an affinity towards new evangelicalism, which was known not for blatantly rejecting biblical principles and standards, but for soft-peddling them. Men like Dr. Cedarholm were convinced that once such a drift began, the Association would eventually be willing to accept those who hold the liberal position, something they never wanted to see happen again. Those who shared these concerns became known as the "hard core" of the Association or the "militant minority," and B. Myron Cedarholm was clearly the Association Executive most sympathetic to their cause.

Fifteen differences between the hard core and the soft core were explained in a pamphlet entitled "Hard Core vs Soft Policy," produced by the Conservative Baptist Fellowship, no date given.

1. On Autonomy. The Hard Core believed that "each local church is free to support or not support any agency and make decisions without penalty or loss of standing." This was the position taken by the CBA at its Long Island annual meeting in 1964. The Soft Policy refused this, insisting that CBA churches should be required to support only CB agencies.

2. On Historic Ideology. The Hard Core favored the Portland Manifesto which was adopted by all the CB agencies and schools in 1953. The Soft Policy repudiated this document as being "separatist in spirit and objective." The Hard Core was also in favor of the "Five-Point Declaration" of the CBA which was unanimously adopted by the Board and put on every piece of literature until the Soft Policy opposed it in 1962.

3. On the Second Coming of Christ. The Hard Core were premillennial and pretribulational. The Soft Policy was a collection of post-tribulationists, amillennialists, and premillennialists.

4. On Dispensationalism. The Hard Core were dispensational premillennialists, arguing this view makes the rapture of the church the "Blessed Hope" of the church. The Soft Policy downplayed the dispensational interpretation of Scripture and took issue with the dispensationalism of the Scofield Reference Bible.

5. On New Evangelicalism. The Hard Core was totally opposed to this new movement, whether it took the form of Kierkegaardianism as at Denver Seminary, higher criticism at Fuller Seminary, or theistic evolution as at Wheaton College. The Soft Policy was friendly to this new movement.

6. On the National Council Bible. The Hard Core condemned the Revised Standard Bible and its sponsorship by the National Council of Churches. The Soft Policy took a more benevolent attitude toward the RSV.

7. On Fellowship with Unbelief. While both parties opposed this in principle, the Hard Core refused to practice any type of religious cooperation with apostate leaders and theologians. The Soft Policy was enthusiastic in its support of ecumenical evangelism, the joining of believers and unbelievers in evangelistic and missionary efforts.

8. On Fundamentalism. The Hard Core endorsed and honored those who held to the fundamentalist position. The Soft Policy not only rejected fundamentalism, but often attacked its leaders.

9. On Neo-Orthodoxy. The Hard Core was united in its opposition to Neo-Orthodoxy. The Soft Policy rejected the Hard Core concern as overdone and was generally silent on the issue.

10. On Support of Mission Agencies. The Hard Core believed they could support missionaries in and out of the CB movements. They had started the

Conservative Baptist Mission (now the Baptist World Mission) and would support any mission or missionary they deemed worthy of their support. The Soft Policy believed that supporting missionaries outside of the CBFMS and CBHMS was a betrayal of the CB position.

11. On Information and News. The Hard Core believed that all Baptists suffered from a lack of information. They supported a free religious press, unconstrained by denominational leaders. The Soft Policy desired to manage the news going to the denomination.

12. On Conservative Schools. The Hard Core was focused on supporting schools which held their positions: Pillsbury Baptist Bible College, San Francisco Baptist Seminary, Central Baptist Seminary, and Denver Baptist Bible College. The Soft Policy was in strong support of Denver Seminary, in spite of its history of bad theology and causing disunity in Colorado and the nation.

13. On "Mainstream" Position. Those holding to the Soft Policy preferred to call themselves the "Mainstream" Conservative Baptists. However, the Hard Core was quick to point out that the "Mainstreamers" were the ones moving away from the earlier positions of the CB movements.

14. On Unity and Harmony. The Soft Policy group had been calling for the expulsion of the Hard Core. The Hard Core responded that it was the Hard Core who had started the CB movements, had supported them with far more funds than the Soft Policy group, and that it was "hardly the ethical thing for those who have not built nor maintained a house to ask the builder to leave."

15. On the Word of God. The Hard Core took their positions because they believed that the Christian faith was at issue. They believed that the Bible supported local church autonomy, ecclesiastical separation, premillennialism, dispensational interpretation, freedom of information, biblically sound Bible schools. The Soft Policy promoted the spread of

New Evangelicalism and Neo-Orthodoxy and a
weakening of the authority of Scripture.

One soft core pastor defined "militant minority" for those
not familiar with the era: "An observer finds difficulty in
making sense of the events of these years unless he
understands the attitude of men who helped to shape those
events. These men were purists. Theirs was what J.B.
Phillips aptly calls 'one-hundred-per-cent Christianity.' ...
Being men of a single eye, they viewed nearly every action as
supporting or destroying faith as they accepted it and boldly
preached it."[32] This would hardly be considered an insult to
anyone sold out for Christ. But being known for such single-
mindedness carries a weighty responsibility: the smallest
deviation from the purity being championed gives ready room
for others to dismiss and discredit what may be legitimate
concerns.

In the midst of the blend of politics and purity in the CBA
during the sixties, the militant minority of the CBA pursued
a series of attempts to keep the three Association bodies (the
Association itself, the Home Mission Society and the Foreign
Mission Society) from heading down the slippery slope of
ecclesiastical compromise. They opposed a wording change
in the original statement of purpose, a change which they
believed would open the way to inclusivism. Then they
sought a wording change in the original written position
papers for both the Foreign and Home mission societies to
include a premillennial position. They attempted at various
board and association gatherings to "withdraw" the more
conservative central portion of the Association from the rest
of the body, so that it could become yet another independent
organization.

Along with all these proposals, there were also ongoing
issues with the Conservative Baptist schools. Several had
started with high hopes, but quickly gave warning signs to
the hard core men that the new evangelical persuasion was
becoming part of the teaching philosophy. A major conflict
occurred in Denver in 1962 over Denver Conservative Baptist

[32] Shelley, *A History of Conservative Baptists*, 86.

College; many Colorado churches, led by Ed Nelson, withdrew from the CBA. They were the first wave of a national exodus from the Conservative Baptist movement. From 1962 until 1967, men classified as hard core among the Conservative Baptists began withdrawing their churches. In 1964, the Pillsbury board voted to drop the word "Conservative" from their name. Central Conservative Baptist Theological Seminary and San Francisco Conservative Baptist Theological Seminary did the same.

On May 27, 1965, the CBA Board met in Denver, Colorado, ahead of the annual meeting. During that Board session, Cedarholm submitted an eight-page, thirteen-point paper he called, *Problems of the Conservative Baptist Association of America: A Solution.* He presented the paper because the organization faced the "possibility of some of its good churches leaving the fellowship." Those churches felt that the organization was taking a weaker doctrinal position and that it was no longer confronting new issues that "are seeking to destroy the Word of God and biblical practices." He reminded the Board that "The Genius of the CBA of A," one of the official documents of the association, states, "The Association longs for the day when divisions between Bible-believing Baptists, which bring reproach upon the Lord, and the faith we hold, will no longer exist. To that end, the Association is open for any proposal that will no longer make it necessary for Bible-believing Baptists to be divided."

Something of Cedarholm's last ditch effort to save the organization he had labored in for 18 years is reflected in the introduction to the paper:

> In our humble judgment, the following are some areas that CBA of A must investigate, some re-affirmations CBA of A must make, some corrections CBA of A must invoke, some changes CBA of A must institute, and some issues CBA of A must rise and meet in the present day of a compromising theological world, if CBA of A is to put its house in order, be true to the Bible and its original documents, keep itself together and continue as a biblical power for God. We related these convictions to the board orally in January 1965, in Chicago at the mid-year board meeting, but no action was taken. No price is too high or

changes too revolutionary to make CBA of A true to the Bible in faith and practice. These also were related to our president, Dr. Herbert E. Anderson, in correspondence of March 17, 1965. We plead for action now, immediately. It is now or never for CBA of A. It is our hope and prayer that the board will be led of the Lord to unanimously adopt these recommendations and present them for favorable action by the constituency at this annual meeting in Denver, 1965

He listed four steps the CBA needed to undertake.

1. CBA of A must bear in mind the teaching of the Scriptures concerning compromise and apostasy. No organization is exempt from the attempt by satanic forces to change, weaken and destroy it.
2. CBA of A must bear in mind the lessons of history. The passing of time usually makes organizations weaker and not stronger. Every organization carries the seeds of its own destruction.
3. CBA of A must bear in mind that associations, as years come and go, usually become more centralized, take to themselves more power than they had in the beginning, have a tendency to attempt to control the churches and become less receptive to constructive criticism and reform.
4. In our humble judgment, the following are some areas that CBA of A must investigate, some reaffirmations CBA of A must make, some corrections CBA of A must invoke, some changes CBA of A must institute and some issues CBA of A must rise and meet in the present day compromising theological world if CBA of A is to put its house together, be true to the Bible and its original documents, keep itself together, and continue as a Biblical power for God.

Cedarholm concluded his report with a series of recommendations he believed needed to be undertaken to preserve the founding ideals of the Conservative Baptists. His first proposal was to restore the Statement of Purpose. This was first adopted in 1948 (Cedarholm indicates that he was present at that 1948 meeting[33]) and remained in place until 1962. He argued that this document "did more to . . . attract

---

[33] B. Myron Cedarholm, letter to CBA of A Board Members, June 20, 1962.

churches into the fellowship than any other CBA of A document."

His second proposal was similar: restore the CB "Portland Manifesto" of 1953. This was a declaration that the CB movement was "separatist in spirit and objective." By 1963 the conservatives believed that the CB organizations had moved away from their separatist moorings and therefore attempted to reaffirm the Manifesto. This was defeated in 1963, but was accepted by the Board in response to Cedarholm's proposal.

His third proposal was to restore the CBA to its original position as an "independent, autonomous fellowship of churches and make it completely disconnected organizationally from all other organizations, societies, schools, institutions, projects, etc." Originally the CBA, CBFMS, and CBHMS were three separate organizations, each with its own board of trustees, constitution, and mission, and each under the authority of the churches who elected the trustees. This structure was a rejection of "conventionism." In the NBC, the autonomy of the local church had been reduced "to a shell, and the boards had become the masters of the churches." Cedarholm majored on the primacy of the local church. The CBA's growing organizational linkage between the three societies put it in a "convention" mold in the eyes of the public. In addition, the CBA was held captive to the mission boards; the mission boards could outvote the CBA two to one. The CBA was becoming more board-controlled and less church-centered.

The fourth proposal was to disallow anyone to serve on the board of more than one of the Conservative organizations or the board of any of its schools. Likewise, no person who "advocates, promotes, supports or participates in the ecumenical movement, ecumenical evangelism, or any form of religious inclusivism or activities where believers and unbelievers function or cooperate together" would be allowed to be a board member of any of the Conservative organizations.

The fifth proposal was to make the CBA a distinctly Baptist organization, by rejecting any form of interdenominationalism.

The sixth proposal called on the CBA to take a "strong, vocal, Biblical stand on theological and ecclesiastical separation." The CBA was becoming fuzzy and weak on separation.

The seventh proposal was to require the CBA to take a position in opposition to New Evangelicalism. The founding documents of the CBA had not addressed this issue, since New Evangelicalism was just beginning at the time of its founding. At this point of time, however, New Evangelicalism advocated working with unbelievers in evangelistic efforts and stressed the importance of education as a prerequisite to a proper understanding of the Bible. Cedarholm insisted that the CBA "must speak up on this subject."

The eighth proposal was for the CBA to return to a clear premillennial position. "Everyone knows what that united front was—strongly dispensational, pre-tribulation rapture, the restoration of Israel, and a literal millennial rule on this earth. That this united front is broken is no secret."

The ninth proposal was to strengthen its doctrinal statement to address the tongues movement, eternal security, the trinity and other doctrines that were under attack.

The tenth proposal was to restate the position of the CBA that a church is free to support what God leads it to support without fear of penalty or loss of standing.

The eleventh proposal was that only CBA business be allowed to be discussed. The CBA meetings were "not a place to wrangle over non-CBA of A matters."

The twelfth proposal was to restrict exhibitors at CBA meetings to those who were in agreement doctrinally.

The last proposal was to allow the staff of the CBA to speak up on issues germane to the CBA.

The board rejected his presentation and shortly after the Denver meeting, Dr. Cedarholm resigned as General Director of the CBA. "Nothing could erase the years of energetic service he had rendered. His resignation, however, was a symbol of the mounting militant despair."[34]

In 1967, Cedarholm published his arguments for a new association of churches.[35] Using the concept of a remnant (Isaiah 1:9), he compared the present situation with 1947. The CBA was organized in 1947 as a "remnant of God's people who stood for the truth." Within just twenty years, however, the CBA was "no longer standing for all of God's Word." Another remnant was ready to be formed. His first reason was that the CBA was no longer standing for all the Word of God. He referenced his 1965 report to the Board of the CBA and indicated that there were too many incidents to report in a short article. He did, however, note that the Board did not disagree with anything in that report; instead, they responded, "Brother Cedarholm, we just don't want the CBA to be what it was in the beginning."

Another argument was that the CBA had moved away from its original Statement of Purpose: "The CBA of America was to provide a fellowship of churches and individuals upon a thoroughly Biblical and historical Baptistic basis unmixed with liberals and liberalism, and those who are content to walk in fellowship with unbelief and inclusivism." Separation was necessary. He specifically identified separation from ecumenical evangelism, particularly Billy Graham's ecumenical evangelism.

An organizational argument was raised. When the CBA began, it was organized on both a national and regional level. Cedarholm was in favor of this, for the CBA was closely connected to the local churches. When the CBFMS and CBHMS saw the success of the regional organization, they modified their structure to include regional representatives and meetings. What this caused, however, because the mission societies were less conservative than the CBA itself, was a vote in each region that was routinely two to one. The

---

[34] Shelley, *A History of Conservative Baptists*, 99.

[35] B. Myron Cedarholm, "Why a New Association of Churches is Needed," *Central Testimony* 9.3 (November-December 1967), 1-4. This was originally written in 1966.

CBA was no longer able to choose its own speakers, to have its own place of meeting, and to develop programs that were true to God's Word. The mission societies had been instructing their missionaries **not** to sign the doctrinal statement sent to them by the CBA and **not** to sign any doctrinal statement from a supporting church. Cedarholm's concern was clear: "To whom do the missionaries belong? To mission societies, or do they belong to the churches where the people pray for them, sacrifice for them, and send them out? We read in Acts, chapter 13, how carefully Paul guarded this right of the churches, how the Holy Spirit spoke to the local church, and out they went."

An interesting problem developed with the CBFMS. The Constitution could be changed with a two-thirds majority vote of the messengers at an annual meeting. The Doctrinal Statement could be changed only with a 100% vote of the messengers. For Cedarholm's last few years at the CBA, conservatives attempted to add the word "premillennial" to the statement: "We believe in Jesus Christ—and His personal visible return to the world according to His promise." There was no way to obtain a 100% approval.

Cedarholm was concerned about a lack of transparency with the mission societies. The CBFMS sent a group of men around the world to shoot pictures of their missionaries. "When they got over to Italy, they found out that their Bible school had only a few students in it. So, they said, 'We can't photograph this and come back to America and show this great picture on Italy and what God is doing, and only a few students in the Bible school. So, one of the great missionary leaders stepped right out on the streets of Naples and just pushed in the men, the women and young people and said, 'Here, sit down; let's take your picture.'"

A final concern that Cedarholm noted was that the CBFMS was holding 1.2 million dollars in reserve. He acknowledged that it was appropriate to have a reserve; what concerned him was that with that much money being held by them, they continued to ask churches to send more money. He was convinced that they would eventually get to the position of the NBC: "They finally had so much of their money invested in the stock market and business enterprises, that they said to the churches, 'We don't need your money nor your suggestions for reform—just quietly leave.'"

So Cedarholm concluded that each church needed to take whatever steps necessary to stand by the Bible. He encouraged the churches to "remember God's Word and be in fellowship with that which is true to the Bible."

Describing the events of the May 1965 Denver meeting of the CBA, an article entitled, "The Sure Return of a Convention" reveals how the "soft core" was able to take control of the Association.[36] The leader of the soft core was Dr. I. Cedric Peterson, pastor of the Lorimer Memorial Baptist Church, Chicago, and Calvary Baptist Church, Whittier, California. He had been briefly the first General Director of the CBA. Peterson was opposed to Cedarholm's strong separatist position and was in favor of a "General Conference" type of convention. Unaware initially of Peterson's position, the Cedarholms had joined Lorimer Memorial Baptist Church when they moved to Chicago in 1947. Dr. Sam McDill became the pastor at Lorimer a few years after Peterson left. Peterson and McDill led the opposition to Cedarholm and helped swing the Board of the CBA from a strong, separatistic position to that of an inclusivistic one. At the CBA Board meeting on May 31, 1965, McDill presented a proposal with three alternatives: a) Cedarholm be immediately dismissed, b) Cedarholm be given a six-month notice of dismissal, c) pray about it. Peterson moved that Cedarholm be given a six-month's notice of dismissal. The vote was 7-7, with President Herbert Anderson breaking the tie with a vote against the motion. The main reason for the action was that the CBA did not have a "program." However, the Board had been seeking for years

---

[36] In "The Sure Return of a Convention" the unknown author looked at the CBA, parroting John Milton with a "Conventionism Lost" in the 1940's and "Conventionism Regained" in 1965. This was an account of the Conservative Baptist meetings in Denver, Colorado, May 1965. It was removed from a magazine of some sort; it is pages 5-11. There is no author mentioned, nor is the name of the magazine identified.

to develop a program that would appeal to the local churches, but had been unable to develop anything that would appeal to both the soft and hard cores. In spite of the lack of a formal program, under Cedarholm, the CBA had become one of the major Baptist bodies in America.

Cedarholm had taken a great deal of abuse for his position, but "in spite of mounting criticism, he had maintained a sweet, humble spirit and has never fought back when personally assaulted." He simply let his record speak for him. For several years before Cedarholm's resignation, the CBFMS and the faculty of Denver Seminary under its president, Vernon Grounds, had worked together to silence any opposition to their shift to the left. Grounds came to Denver in the 1951–52 school year. The "Neutrals" (those who were seeking to take some kind of middle position) had been reluctant to recognize that the CBFMS and Denver Seminary were moving away from a separatist position. However, there were no "Neutrals" in Chicago or Denver. "It is either compromise on the basic issues and blindly follow the agencies in that area or face complete ostracism." The President of the CBFMS, Dr. L. T. Anderson, attempted to overrule the decision of the Central Region to hold its annual meeting in Minneapolis. The CBFMS messengers who met at Lorimer Memorial Baptist Church in 1964 had voted to hold the next Central Region annual meeting in Minneapolis. Anderson was concerned that the Minnesota Baptists were too hard core. Every soft core proposal made in Minnesota had been voted down the last time the CBFMS met there (in 1958). Therefore, he led the messengers in 1965 to violate their constitution and move the meeting. L. E. Pearson, pastor of the Judson Baptist Church, Oak Park, Illinois, an American Baptist Convention church, pled with the messengers to "deliver *us* from the tyranny of the Conservative Baptist Central Regional."

Conventionism grew further as the constitution was changed to require that members of the Board must be "aggressively interested in supporting the work of the CBFMS" and that a Board member could be removed from the Board if he missed two Board meetings "without satisfactory reason." When the question was raised as to how it would be decided that someone had violated one of these two ambiguous requirements, Herbert Anderson responded by calling for the question. An additional constitutional change was made, which would require the coordination of the meetings of the CBA, CBFMS and CBHMS, so that they all met at the same time in the same place. The Time and Place Committee for the Inter-Societies' Meetings was to decide the time and place of the annual meetings, but the Board could change their decision at will.

The article includes a statement from Dr. Rufus Jones, the soft core president of the CBHMS, "I think if we can change the image of our movement and give evidence that we are ready to launch out into a new direction with a program that will be relative to the needs of the inner city and the campus, we shall be able to capture the interest and secure applications from future graduates of our evangelical seminaries." The author was concerned that this would result in a shift from the gospel to something closer to the social gospel.

The author of "The Sure Return of a Convention" notes that both the CBHMS and the CBA voted to move their 1966 meeting from Minneapolis to Indianapolis, in direct opposition to Cedarholm's recommendation. But the final accomplishments of the soft core takeover of the CBA were realized at the 1965 Denver meeting: the resignation of Cedarholm, the final softening up of the CB movement in its ecclesiastical framework (bringing all three independent organizations into one organization), and the beginning of a more rapid move toward New Evangelicalism and theological deterioration.

The end result was that between 1965 and 1968, the Conservative Baptist Association lost over 350 churches (about twenty percent of the total membership). As is often the case in church history, once those desiring a pure stand separate, the original organization rarely shrivels and dies. Instead, it normally makes adjustments, searches for an amiable constituency that supports the new direction, and continues at some adjusted level. In the case of the CBA, the group moved quickly to become more denominationally structured by consolidating all offices in Wheaton, where the Foreign Mission Society was already located.

Those who left found themselves, once again, starting over, many for the second time in their pastoral careers. They found themselves truly independent from denominational ties, if not personal loyalties. In October 1964, about 200 key leaders of the hard core of the CBA met at Marquette Manor Baptist Church, Chicago, to consider the organization of a new association. Richard Weeks was present at that meeting. In May 1965, a second meeting of representatives from about 400 hundred churches met at Beth Eden Baptist Church, Denver, to establish the New Testament Association of Baptist Churches (NTA). A constitution was presented which was clearly and definitely separatistic; it required that for a church to affiliate with the NTA, it could "not be in affiliation with any other national association of churches." Cedarholm was involved in the organization of the NTA, the one attempt after the exodus to build another church-based membership organization.

After the soft core gained control of the CBA, the Conservative Baptist Fellowship began to consider a name change.[37] It became the Fundamental Baptist Fellowship, to demonstrate its rejection of the Conservative Baptist movement. It continued as a nonbinding, voluntary fellowship for pastors and other individuals, but not churches. Regional and national meetings provided pastors the opportunity to discuss current issues and concerns. FBF resolutions provided a peer pressure measure of consensus, though no resolution was or is binding upon any pastoral participant or the church he pastors. Writing in 1984, Cedarholm said, "I am anxious to keep my relationship with FBF as long as I can ... the Lord is good to give us FBF as a uniting fellowship for fundamental, independent, separatist, Baptists."[38]

---

[37] "Conservative—What's in a Name?" *Conservative Baptist Fellowship* 11:2 (March 1966), 1-2.

[38] Cedarholm correspondence to Kirk, August 7, 1984.

In 1966, the World Conservative Baptist Mission severed its remaining ties to the Conservative Baptist movement. The re-named Baptist World Mission began operating as an independent faith mission, linked to like-minded churches by a self-perpetuating pastoral board and the voluntary giving of over 4,000 individual churches to individual missionaries or the home office.[39]

For undergraduate studies, there were a handful of schools that were distinctively Baptist. But the one that seemed most akin to the men now calling themselves independent Baptists (the word independent being used as an adjective, not a convention or association or even a fellowship label), was Pillsbury Baptist Bible College in Owatonna, Minnesota. At the end of the school term in 1965, Dr. Monroe Parker, president of Pillsbury and a genuine biblical statesman, resigned the presidency to return to full-time evangelism.

The Pillsbury Board began its search for a new president.

> At the Board meeting, June 21, 1965, after a unanimous recommendation from the Presidential Committee, a motion was made and carried unanimously to call Dr. Cedarholm as President-elect of the College. Later in the meeting, the Cedarholms, who were present in the building, were presented to the Board.
>
> Dr. Cedarholm commented on Matt. 7:1–6 and Mark 14:36 and said briefly: We feel led through our private devotions and the reading of the Scriptures to continue in the place where Dr. and Mrs. Parker leave off.
>
> Mrs. Cedarholm spoke briefly and referred to "an open door" (Rev. 3:8), which had been in her thinking and prayers for some time: I believe that this is that open door, she said.
>
> Dr. Parker commented, I am thrilled, this is of God![40]

At fifty years of age, Dr. and Mrs. Cedarholm were ready to embark on a new venture.

---

[39] Moritz, *Now is the Time.*

[40] Larry Dean Pettegrew, *The History of Pillsbury Baptist Bible College* (Owatonna, MN: Pillsbury Press, 1981), 149.

THE PILLSBURY YEARS: 1965–1968

Minnesota has a long history of Baptist involvement. In 1847, a woman named Harriet E. Bishop started the first Baptist Sunday School in the state.[1] In just seven years the Baptists had grown sufficiently to start a Baptist college. The Minnesota Baptist Convention (this is not the state convention that later took that name; at this time, it was a regional association centered in the Minneapolis-St. Paul area) wrote the charter for the Minnesota Central University. Classes began in 1859 in Hastings, Minnesota. Two years later the school was placed under the control of the Minnesota Baptist State Association. Due to financial difficulties, however, the school closed in 1867.

---

[1] Information on the background of Pillsbury Baptist Bible College is from Pettegrew, *The History of Pillsbury Baptist Bible College.*

When the Minnesota Baptist Convention opened Minnesota Central University, they started a long history of maintaining a school in the state of Minnesota. The goal of a Baptist school in Minnesota did not die with the death of Minnesota Central University. A decade later a new school, the Minnesota Academy, began offering classes in Owatonna in the fall of 1877, under the charter of the former Central University. While the school initially struggled financially, George Pillsbury, a one-time mayor of Minneapolis, a faithful member of the First Baptist Church of Minneapolis, and a successful businessman who was part of the Pillsbury Baking Company, stepped in to fund the Academy, both in an ongoing manner and in his estate. He almost single-handedly built the growing Minnesota Academy by sponsoring (directly or through his estate) the construction of eight separate structures between 1886 and 1914. Two years before his death in 1888, the school's name was changed to Pillsbury Academy.

The Great Depression left the Academy in dire condition, but it survived by borrowing from its endowment, even though George Pillsbury's will specifically restricted the use of the principle of the endowment. The liberals had taken control of the Minnesota Baptist State Convention in 1930. The fundamentalists fought back, however, and in 1936 they regained control of the Convention. In 1948, they withdrew from the Northern Baptist Convention. Pillsbury Academy, however, remained under the control of an independent liberal Board of Trustees.

In most of the states, strategically placed liberal minorities were able to control most boards and convention decisions, regardless of the desires of the majority of pastors. Minnesota was a refreshing change for biblicists. They were able to sponsor a truly representative vote which elected a majority of conservative men to convention leadership. Pillsbury, however, operated somewhat independently of the convention. The school would submit recommendations of individuals to serve on the Board of Trustees to the Minnesota Baptist Convention, and these names were routinely accepted. As the convention leadership became more liberal in the 1920's and 1930's, so also did the leadership of Pillsbury. Once the Minnesota Convention was captured by the conservatives, however, the leadership of the school went to work to try to prevent a takeover of their Board by the conservatives. The battle over the ownership of Pillsbury Academy ended up in the Minnesota courts. The question was whether the Academy belonged to its liberal Board of Trustees or to the conservative Minnesota Baptist Convention.

The case went all the way to the Minnesota Supreme Court, and on December 23, 1955, the Court unanimously ruled in favor of the Convention. The Supreme Court declared the Minnesota Baptist Convention, "the sole member of the Corporation of Pillsbury Academy, with the Minnesota Baptist Convention holding exclusive rights to the Academy." The Minnesota Baptist Convention owned the Academy from which Pillsbury Conservative Baptist Bible College would be formed.

After the favorable ruling and the subsequent changes in Board personnel, the Convention set about to reopen Pillsbury in 1957 as a Bible College, under the leadership of Cedarholm's long-time friend and advisor, Dr. Richard V. Clearwaters, a pillar among the Minnesota Baptists. He was the pastor of Fourth Baptist Church in Minneapolis and had founded Central Conservative Baptist Seminary under the church's auspices in 1956. He served as Chairman of the Board of Trustees for Pillsbury Academy and was Chairman of the Board when Pillsbury was founded as a Conservative Baptist College.

In September 1957, Pillsbury Conservative Baptist Bible College opened its doors for the first time. The opening meetings were scheduled for the beginning of September, and Cedarholm was asked to be the preacher for the week. During the week, both Paul Williams, chairman of the Presidential Committee, and Clearwaters told Cedarholm that he was the committee's unanimous choice to assume the presidency of the school. Cedarholm had no clear leading to make the change, although he did record in his journal that the idea held personal appeal. His concern was for the void that would be left in the CBA were he to leave:

Paul Williams, St. Paul chairman of Pres. Committee (RVC elected to settle situation)—but only temporary until get a pres.—Pres Comm wants me for job—unanimous choice—I have no leading to leave CBA nor desire. Very happy in CBA.

I would love to go to Pillsbury & Thelma could handle music dept & mission dept—I have never wanted any job—Lehigh nor CBA had no temptation when accepted, just an opportunity that God led clearly to—but this is something that really appeals to us. But what about CBA? God has to lead. If I leave, feel that Board would elect Claude Moffitt of Arizona & he not "strong core" man has SBC ideology & CBA would soon centralize under his leadership, was against putting Pre-mil in CBFMS, asked for a secret ballot on me in St. Paul in 1955—yet Claude good for new churches, etc.

Told Paul & RVC that would pray about it & talk to friends across the nation.[2]

His journal for the week indicates not only his discernment between personal desire and the Spirit's leading, but an interesting allegiance to the Pillsbury board:

09.07.57
Arrived Pillsbury at 10:30. Thelma & I in "prophets chamber" boys' dorm—first floor.

Pillsbury new CB college at Owatonna Minnesota—1st year & 106 students including 56 freshmen—God good—prayed for 100 students & this a miracle.

School former military academy which Minn. Convention got free—¾ million property—14 acres & several bldgs, 2 gyms, inside pool, indoor track, etc.

09.08.57, Sunday
Beauty—new CBA church at Owatonna, Grace C.B. church—no pastor—organized today.

College makes most of members. I taught adult S.S. class a.m. Rev. 12:11 Good meeting & spirit—no visible results.

Beautiful dining hall—excellent food. The Lord provided an excellent cook, too. Rested.

---

[2] Myron Cedarholm journal, September 12, 1957.

P.M. Phil Cows. Good meeting, no visible results. Several visitors present—some folks from Owatonna—most churches closed in town.

Went over house to house with ads of meetings this aft with students.

09.09.57, Monday

At Pillsbury Fall Bible conf, am chapel & pm service.

1 hr for chapel each day—gave messages on Bapt Hist, ideology, C. B. history & work, organizational, etc.

[illegible] a Bible—Evangelistic message each night.

Faculty—Dr. Ed & Dr. Frances Simpson, Rev. Oswald Morley (Morley also cook), Rev. Ernie Butler (Butler also Business mngr), Rev. & Mrs. Arthur Haik—he N. T. Greek, etc.—she speech.

Excellent spirit, students happy, some transfers from Moody, Bob Jones, Northwestern & like Pillsbury better.

One young man from Moody—in class these wouldn't say what Bible taught on Baptism, prof. said come to see me privately—this fellow not like it, wanted a school where teach whole Bible—didn't know about Pillsbury until this summer—likes Pillsbury because teach whole counsel of God....

Morley, Simpson, Butler, & Haik & [illegible] pastor really worked this past summer to get place in shape. Spent about $25,000 too & Board now disturbed. Board trusted Butler—because he did a good job of bldg. his new church & seemed economical—but somehow not too econ. here—so now Board put a limit of $100.00 on what can spend.

Board should have done this earlier—now a little friction between board & faculty. Faculty must realize they can't run school—this board's job. Can understand faculty viewpoint because they live here & have done all the work. However, can be worked out easily. Also Simpson who leads not as Baptist as ought to be & board put "conservative" in title this week.

09.11.57, Wednesday

Testimony of Pillsbury in town great. Military Academy really bad fellows & poor testimony—things better now—even 2 fewer policemen now—business men are so pleased about college & have given them much publicity. Even fire department notices difference—used to

come up often to put out fires by careless smokers at
school.

PM Services—people from town coming up—3 teachers
from high school & saved—belong to Meth. Ch (worried
fund).

Newspaper editor, a Xtian, came too.

09.12.57, Thursday
Clearwaters, Alfus, P W, down today = Bldg &
Grounds committee.

Clearwaters also elected pres. of school by board last
Saturday. (Simpson not like this too well. He wanted
presidency.) Simpson could have had it but excluded
himself—1 He made up catalog & not use word "C.B." even
once. 2 made up 1st letterhead & not use "C. B." or put
any names on letterhead, not even R V Clearwaters
president of board—hoping that he would be president. 3
wrote a tract & not even mention a CB school. A very
foolish procedure—shows he not a strong C. B. & not pres.
timber. Butler in on part of this, too. Too bad—always lose
out by failing to be strong.

09.14.57, Saturday
[Written along left margin:] faculty running school is
problem Western Sem. Lord & trustees won out & some
faculty left.

Rain today. Letters & CBA correspondence all day.
Faculty supper tonight at [Nerleys?] had planned a picnic
but rain –

Nice evening of fellowship. Good spirit & harmony.
(found out that Simpson a little disappointed when he
asked to leave Board meeting last Sat. when called exec
session. Apparently he not used to exec sessions, CBA
soon teaches one.)

Also taught some classes this week—some fine
students here. Some came on faith—yet God good & all
have jobs—several calls from town from business men,
etc.—students a good testimony & good workers. Several
married couples there & wonderful testimonies of God's
provision for work, housing, & children.

09.15.57, Sunday

S. S. class—college freshmen; a.m.—fellowship; y. p.—all college age—single; p.m.—money.

Several public decisions toward end of week & today one freshman, Dave Wagner, for salvation—fine boy, professed at 9 yrs.—never believed saved. Several kids wondered what to do about church membership—I encouraged them to join here—this is where they live most. About 60 decisions all week for various reasons—the Lord really moved. Made it as plain as the Lord enabled me—wherever sin is preached against hard, amazing what the Holy Spirit brings to light—much sin in the lives of these kids that faculty members didn't dream possible—faculty prayed with each one forward so they knew 1st hand sin of young people. The more I see of Xians, the more I see it is of great profit to preach on personal sins.

Though they had no clearance from the Lord to become a part of the school, both Cedarholms were vitally concerned for the school's success. Mrs. Cedarholm had composed the music for the college hymn, while Parker penned the words. One of the women's societies was named for her. Dr. Cedarholm was the baccalaureate speaker for the first commencement in June 1958.

In southern Minnesota, ten thousand lakes of blue
On the hills of Owatonna 'neath skies of azure hue,
There stands a mighty fortress of the truth our fathers taught
O God, we stand in awe of the work which Thou hast wrought.

In ancient ivyed halls, 'mid culture's pleasing grace
Within these hallowed walls, our Lord shall have first place.
Teach us, Lord, thine inspired Word writ by men of old
Moved by the Holy Spirit, dearer far than gold.

Ten thousand men and demons attack our Cause forsooth
We're fully panoplied, girt round the loins with truth.
Breastplate of righteousness, made ready our feet are shod,
With thorough preparation, the gospel of peace with God.

With the mighty shield of faith we quench each firey dart.
Fill us now, O Holy Spirit, and ne'er from us depart,
In helmet of salvation we wield the Spirit's sword,
A weapon never failing, God's everlasting Word.

Arise, ye sons and daughters, Pillsbury's warriors all!
From jungles far away, from town and hamlet small
Come cries of souls sin-bound and doomed to endless woe.
All your hearts aflame with love arise and to them go.

P.S. I think "Ghost" fits meter better than "Spirit"
if not Change to "Spirit".

— Monroe Parker

Clearwaters was offered the presidency by the Board, but he did not want to resign the pastorate of Fourth Baptist Church nor move to Owatonna from Minneapolis. With no one else readily available, Clearwaters was named president for the first semester of Pillsbury Conservative Baptist College. Late in 1957, the Board of Trustees asked Dr. Monroe Parker to become the resident president. Though the typical understanding of most people was that the president was the head of the college, within the context of the Minnesota Convention's thinking, he was more of a chief executive officer under the leadership of the Board of Trustees. Clearwaters as Chairman of the Board of Trustees was the significant voice of the Board. He would maintain a strong off-site presidential influence, while Parker, should he accept, would assume oversight of the day-to-day running of the College. Parker was a gracious, godly man, a proven fellow worker in the cause of Christ. He was a gifted evangelist, articulate, and engaging. He brought solid credentials from his administrative experience and leadership at Bob Jones University. Clearwaters and Parker had served together as leaders within the Conservative Baptist Fellowship and had years of camaraderie knitting them together as they endeavored to strengthen the Conservative Baptist groups.

Monroe Parker was born on June 23, 1909, six years before the Cedarholms. He came from an extensive Baptist background. His great-grandfather founded the first Baptist church in Alabama. His grandfather started the First Baptist Church of Thomasville, Alabama, Parker's birthplace. He received Christ when he was nineteen years old, in 1928, while teaching a Sunday School class. Later that week Bob Jones, Sr. spoke in his church and talked about the college he had started just the year before. Parker knew immediately that was the place for him. He was elected to the Board of Trustees of Bob Jones College in 1933 and worked in full-time evangelism until 1937. From 1937 until 1949 he worked at Bob Jones, first, as the director of religious studies, then as assistant to the president; during this time, he completed his Master of Arts degree (1943) and a Doctor of Philosophy degree (1947). In 1954, he returned to Alabama as pastor of

Grace Baptist Church of Decatur. Throughout this entire time, he maintained a schedule of ten evangelistic meetings each year and was a major voice in the Fundamental Baptist Fellowship.[3]

In 1957, Parker spoke at the Minnesota Baptist Convention's annual meeting; in November of that year Clearwaters invited him to hold meetings at Fourth Baptist Church in Minneapolis. He met with the Pillsbury Board of Trustees at that time, and as a result they extended the offer of the presidency of Pillsbury to him on December 7, 1957. He accepted their invitation and assumed the office February 5, 1958. When the official installation service for Parker was held in October 1958, Cedarholm was the speaker. Cedarholm was part of a 1959 joint summer school venture between Pillsbury and Central Seminary.[4] In his years with the CBA, Cedarholm was often on campus as a speaker for chapel and missions conferences.

During Parker's seven-and-a-half-year tenure, the college grew from 106 to 550 students. During the third year of the school (1959–1960), Pillsbury was the largest school in the Conservative Baptist orbit.[5] He brought his evangelistic zeal to the College, implemented the Student Handbook, and oversaw the building of both a new dormitory and a new gymnasium. His national reputation encouraged a wider range of student applications, and that led to the formation of a Board of Reference, comprised of pastors from across the nation, not just from Minnesota. This Board of Reference consisted of men who were willing to have their name associated with Pillsbury as a show of their support for the philosophy and direction of the school. Though the Board did not vote on school policy, it did develop a sense of ownership, concern, and involvement in the institution.

---

[3] See Monroe Parker, *Through Sunshine and Shadows: My First 77 Years* (Murfreesboro, Tennessee: Sword of the Lord Publishers, 1987).

[4] *Pillsbury Conservative Baptist College Bulletin*, January 1959, 1.

[5] Pettegrew, *History of Pillsbury*, 135.

Under Parker's presidency Pillsbury was associated with the CBA. While the CBA was being organized, the Minnesota Baptist Convention was separating from the NBC. So many of the churches in Minnesota had joined the CBA in the 1950's that the state paper, the *North Star Baptist*, adopted subtitle, "Conservative Baptist News in Minnesota." In 1957, 68 of the 100 churches in the MBC were members of the CBA. In 1960, there were eighty Minnesota churches in the CBA.

Albert G. Johnson, the president of the Western Conservative Baptist Theological Seminary, wrote in the *North Star Baptist* in March 1957:

> If Conservative Baptists are going to perpetuate their witness and fulfill the divine mission for the propagation and perpetuity of pure Biblical doctrine and polity, we cannot expect this to be accomplished effectively apart from the distinctive Conservative Baptist schools. It goes without saying that Conservative Baptist ministers and missionaries should have Baptist training. Baptist doctrines and principles and ecclesiology (basically New Testament doctrines and principles and ecclesiology) have never been more assailed than today, in an age when they are imperative. Interdenominational schools, by their very nature as such, cannot be expected to emphasize these Baptist distinctives.[6]

In 1958, the Association of Conservative Baptist Schools of Higher Education was formed. Central Baptist Theological Seminary, the Fourth Baptist Bible Institute, and Pillsbury Conservative Baptist Bible College[7] all joined. It was not long, however, before the division between the soft core and the hard core in the CBA began to affect Pillsbury.

The statement of purpose of the CBA, written in 1947, was: "to provide a fellowship of churches and individuals upon a thoroughly Biblical and historically Baptistic basis,

---

[6] *North Star Baptist*, March 1957, 10, quoted in Pettegrew, *History of Pillsbury*, 144.

[7] "Conservative" had been added to the name in 1957 by vote of the Pillsbury Board and in 1958 by unanimous vote of the Minnesota Baptist Convention.

unmixed with liberals and liberalism and those who are content to walk in fellowship with unbelief and inclusivism." But there was a contradiction in that statement: "the affiliates of the Association shall consist of ... Autonomous Baptist churches without regard to other affiliations." This opened the door for continued fellowship with churches that were still in the NBC.[8] This was part of the reason for the development of two opposing groups within the Conservative Baptist organizations. Hard core members advocated for separation from all forms of compromise, while soft core members argued that separation was over-rated, and more could be done for the cause of Christ by compromising in some areas.

The Minnesota Baptist Association was solidly hard core. A January 1965 article in the *North Star Baptist* outlines ten differences between the hard core and the soft core Baptists in the CBA.

1. The hard core believed in the autonomy of the local church. The soft core argued that CBA churches should have been required to support only CB agencies.
2. The hard core was adamantly in favor of separation from liberalism. The soft core rejected the concept of separatism.
3. The hard core was pre-tribulational and premillennial. The soft core was a mix of post-tribulationists, amillennialists, and pre-millennialists.
4. The hard core was dispensational. The soft core downplayed dispensational thought and often scoffed at the Scofield Reference Bible.
5. The hard core was completely opposed to the New Evangelicalism. The soft core was friendly to the new group.
6. The hard core was opposed to the liberal National Council of Churches' sponsored and owned Bible, the Revised Standard Version. The soft core was more accepting of the new translation.
7. The hard core was opposed to ecumenical evangelism, while the soft core supported Billy Graham and others like him who participated in evangelistic services with liberals and Catholics.

---

[8] Beale, 292.

8. The hard core was unashamedly fundamentalist. The soft core was critical of fundamentalists in general and of Dr. John R. Rice, Dr. Bob Jones, Dr. Robert Ketcham, Dr. Carl McIntire, Dr. Richard V. Clearwaters, and Dr. Chester Tulga in particular.

9. The hard core was opposed to Neo-Orthodoxy; the soft core was unconcerned about its dangers and significance.

10. The hard core believed they could support missionaries in a variety of fundamentalist agencies; the soft core, who dominated the Conservative Baptist Foreign and Home Missionary Societies, believed that CBA churches should restrict their giving to only CB missionaries.[9]

Parker, while president of Pillsbury, became critical of the CBA, CBFMS, and CBHMS, because many of the member churches were not fundamentalist, and some were still in the American Baptist Convention.[10] Even as the prospects for Pillsbury prospered under the leadership of Parker, the confidence in the Conservative Baptists withered. On October 10, 1964, the Pillsbury Board of Trustees voted to remove the word "Conservative" from the college name, not because the school was no longer conservative, but because "Conservative Baptist" indicated a new-evangelical mindset antithetic to Parker, Clearwaters, the Board of Trustees, and the Minnesota Baptist Association. The change was effective immediately, though the new name was not officially registered with the state of Minnesota until 1967. The school would serve those churches who were now truly independent of any associational ties.

On April 30, 1965, Parker resigned, though he agreed to stay until August 31 to ease the transition for a new President.

> Dr. Monroe Parker "rocked" the Conservative Baptist movement with his announcement last week before Pillsbury Chapel of his resignation as president of Pillsbury College, a position he had held with distinction

---

[9] *North Star Baptist* (January 1965), 23-24.

[10] The Northern Baptist Convention changed its name to the American Baptist Convention in 1950 and then to the American Baptist Churches in 1972.

since 1958. The Board voted to refuse his resignation last Friday, but he insisted that the pressure of evangelistic meetings all over the nation had forced him to this action. Dr. Parker has built Pillsbury from 104 students in 1958 to 500 students and he merits the gratitude of multitudes of Bible-believing people. Pray earnestly for the Board's selection of his successor. We wish him the best as he launches out in an intensive series of evangelistic meetings that may well help restore evangelism to its Biblical position in America. He is one of the best.[11]

When Parker resigned, he wanted to find someone who would work harmoniously with the leadership at Pillsbury to recommend for the Presidency. He thought of Cedarholm because Cedarholm had often said that he looked on Clearwaters as his spiritual father. Also, though he had not yet left the Conservative Baptist movement, Cedarholm was identified with the hard core element. In addition, Cedarholm had already taught at Central Baptist Theological Seminary. In the spring semester of 1958 he began teaching a one-credit module in church planting that consisted of some Monday morning sessions, a series of chapel services, and assigned field work.[12] He taught this class later in various formats. For these and other reasons, Parker and others suggested Cedarholm to the Board of Trustees.[13]

Parker returned to Decatur, Alabama, to resume his ministry of full time evangelism. In 1969, the still young Baptist World Mission asked him to become its general director which he agreed to do with the stipulation that the operation move from Chicago to Decatur. Baptist World grew steadily throughout the years of his leadership. In 1981 Fred Moritz began assisting Parker, and he in turn was named Executive Director in 1984. Parker continued to serve as able until his death in 1994. At that time, Moritz assumed

---

[11] *Blu-print*, May 4, 1965.

[12] Michael H. Windsor, *Valiant for Truth: The Ministry of Richard Volley Clearwaters* (ThD Dissertation, 1991), 196. This is a sympathetic biography of Clearwaters. The Pillsbury episode is a very small portion of the work.

[13] Pettegrew, *History of Pillsbury*, 149.

Parker's position, but retained his title of Executive Director. This gave Parker the distinction of being the only *General Director* of Baptist World Mission.

Cedarholm wrote a letter to John Pereira in Orlando on May 9, 1984, summarizing his view of what had happened in the CBA and why he was more than ready to leave the CBA.

> I was one of the founders of CBA in May of 1947, when I pastored the Lehigh Avenue Baptist Church in Philadelphia, Pa. I had graduated from Eastern Baptist Seminary in 1943 and also taught there for three years. Eastern was a good fundamental seminary in those days. It is so sad to see what has happened to Eastern now.
>
> I was the first man that CBA employed in September of 1947, and resigned my church and moved to the Chicago office. In 1949, I became the General Director of the organization. Even though my leadership was thought too strong by some, I had the majority of the board and constituency to the end and had the privilege of resigning. I gave almost 20 years of my life to CBA, helped to organize hundreds of new Baptist churches, lived out of a suitcase 10½ months out of the year, and traveled over 100,000 miles each year. My wife and I were so happy in the work. My wife worked in the office in Chicago.
>
> What wrecked the CBA was pastors coming into the churches from new evangelical and neo-orthodox schools. How the churches could be so blind is beyond me! These pastors soon had control, swayed the messengers at annual meetings, and were successful to vote out the separation laws in the CBA constitution, which stated we would not fellowship with liberals or fundamentalists who fellowshipped with liberals or compromisers. One leading pastor, Robert Duggan, who is now Executive Secretary of NAE, stood and said to the entire assembly that this means we cannot support Billy Graham! This was the magic word! A political trick, indeed! For who, thought uninformed messengers, could be against Billy Graham? The vote carried by only 12 votes among 800+ messengers after considerable discussion. An attempt was made the following year to re-instate the separation clause, and the vote was lost by over a 300 majority! The handwriting was on the wall that the CBA was captured by the compromisers and who were not present at the founding of CBA. So, most of us soon left the CBA. The Lord gave

us almost 20 years of wonderful blessing and tremendous growth. Soon over 1,000 churches left the CBA and most of its founders.

If the present CB periodicals are carefully read and compared with the Scriptures and CB founding principles, one can readily detect a tremendous drift from CBA, CBFMS and HMS beginnings, and I was a part of all three beginnings.

Concerning Denver CB Seminary, no one was any more active than I in its beginnings in the spring and summer of 1950. I made 12 trips to Denver at that time, took all the pictures of the building inside and out, prepared the advertising, had a big part in selecting the faculty, and suggested to the chairman of the board all the trustees who were soon elected. I probably did more to raise the first student body than anyone else. This was not unusual since I traveled more than anyone else, visited more churches than anyone else, and had the opportunity to know so many people and prospective students across the nation.

However, when Vernon Grounds came on the faculty, things changed overnight almost—leading trustees and faculty resigned. Dr. Grounds had a way of deeply ingratiating himself into the favor of new evangelicals in the CBA who strongly defended him. Dr. Grounds was employed as a strong GARB fundamentalist from Johnson City, New York, where the GARB college and seminary were located—now at Clarks Summit, Pa. We all thought we were headed for great days with a tremendous Baptist, separatist, fundamental scholar. However, it soon was evident that Dr. Grounds had fooled us all—his strong Kierkegaardian views. The GARB's at Johnson City claimed that Dr. Grounds had never showed these strong views when he was there. It turned out that Dr. Grounds was a good fundamentalist when he went to teach at Johnson City, but getting his Ph.D. at Drew—a liberal Methodist school at Madison, New Jersey, completely turned him around. Dr. Grounds, no doubt, has a brilliant mind, but he certainly turned that seminary in the wrong direction after such a wonderful beginning! Dr. Grounds' influence affected the entire CB movement from what it started out to be. D.D.'s were given out by the seminary to leading pastors, and they in turn became strong defenders of Dr. Grounds and the seminary. I personally believe that Dr. Grounds was more responsible than any individual for the CB downfall.

Parker firmly established the educational philosophy of Pillsbury before he left. He brought Richard Weeks, a longtime friend of the Cedarholms, to the faculty during the summer before he left. Weeks had been the Vice-President of the CBF and the editor of the *Information Bulletin.* Parker also agreed to speak at the opening meetings in September.

The Cedarholms' time at Pillsbury opened with high promise. Dr. Cedarholm's national reputation greatly aided the college. The student numbers at Pillsbury grew by 192 students in the Cedarholms' first year to a total of 605, with 290 new freshmen. The next year the student body was over 700.[14] An appeal went out to the constituency to enable Pillsbury to expand their musical opportunities. "Pillsbury Baptist College needs good musical instruments for their band and orchestra. Far more students are reporting than available equipment. Anyone wishing to give a good instrument to the college is asked to write Dr. B. Myron Cedarholm, PBBC, Owatonna, Minnesota 55060."[15]

Clearwaters   Parker   Cedarholm

---

[14] Pettegrew, *History of Pillsbury*, 150.

[15] *Blu-print*, October 12, 1965.

The ministry of the Cedarholms focused on building lives, but as the ministry grew, Pillsbury needed to construct buildings as well. Cedarholm oversaw construction of a women's dorm for 300 in 1967, and another for men for the start of the 1968 school year. Myron's Christmas present to Thelma in 1967 was a set of handbells so that Thelma could begin a handbell choir.

Mrs. Cedarholm rejoiced in two special blessings at Pillsbury. First, she was able to teach Christian Education and Music, and with the gift of the bells she was able to begin and direct the Madrigal and Handbell Choir. Second, God answered a prayer she had prayed for many years. Early in their marriage, Mrs. Cedarholm suffered a miscarriage; God chose to never give them another biological child. She took comfort in the confidence that this was God's will for her. That did not, however, stop Mrs. Cedarholm from praying for a little girl—but not just any little girl. She wanted one who was already potty trained and could feed herself! She just did not see how they could take the time to care for an infant.

Eunice & Charlotte – 1961

Just before they went to Pillsbury, the Lord answered that prayer by giving to them a little girl named Charlotte. Mrs. Cedarholm's sister, Eunice, had recently learned that she had only months to live; she asked the Cedarholms if they would be willing to take Charlotte.

While their hearts were broken at the thought of losing Eunice, they were thrilled with the prospect of having a child in their home! Eunice passed away about the time the Cedarholms were moving to Minnesota, so Charlotte stayed with another aunt and uncle briefly until the Cedarholms were settled at Pillsbury. Charlotte recalls being brought to her new home by two pastor friends late one night, with all her earthly belongings in one paper sack. She stepped into a room with new rosebud wallpaper, white frilly curtains and bedspread, and gifts from the college students. Charlotte watched as her new Mom and Dad knelt beside her new bed and prayed for her. Charlotte was a delightful, although sometimes mischievous, addition to the campus at Owatonna. She was five years old and fit every one of Thelma's requirements. The new mother knew this child was a special gift from the Lord to their family.

Dr. Cedarholm was fully committed to Christian education and had faithfully heralded the truths surrounding the need for a biblically based education: (1) God's Word demands it, (2) logic demands it, (3) conditions demand it, (4) our youth demand it, (5) our homes demand it, (6) our nation demands it, (7) the church demands it, and (8) God's work demands it.

The Cedarholms quickly came to be loved and appreciated by the Pillsbury family. The 1967 *Northern Light*, the college yearbook, was dedicated to Dr. Cedarholm:

Dedication of the 1967 Northern Light of
Pillsbury Baptist Bible College

"The man of God whom thou didst send..." Judges 13:8. Dr. Cedarholm was sent from God to us out of a rich background of experience which has so admirably fitted him for this work. A star athlete at the University of Minnesota in undergraduate days, a B.D. graduate from Eastern Baptist Seminary, and a Th.M. degree from Princeton combined to prepare him for a spectacularly successful pastorate in Philadelphia. From this he was called to become the General Director of the infant, struggling Conservative Baptist Association of America, and through an unparalleled prodigious work of eighteen years all across America became the one man most responsible for the phenomenal growth of that association, earning the title, "Mr. CBA." Providentially arranged, at the same time Pillsbury was seeking a leader, God's prepared man was found in the person of Dr. Cedarholm whose previous work had included a youth ministry to many thousands in churches and colleges all over this nation.

Dr. Cedarholm has proven himself again these two years as an educator and administrator par excellence. His evangelistic zeal, missionary vision, local church emphasis, and strong doctrinal preaching together with a carefully and consistently cultivated walk with God have combined to endear him to the students, faculty, and staff alike as a leader both born and made and worthy of implicit trust.

We salute Dr. Myron Cedarholm, this "God-sent" man, thank God for him, assure him of our prayers; and believe that, should Christ's return still encompass a number of years, under his leadership Pillsbury will thrust increasing hundreds of prepared soldiers of the Cross into the conflict's final hour as we anticipate His appearance. With great appreciation and love, we dedicate the Northern Light of 1967 to our "God-sent" leader and President.

The tension that would rise between Cedarholm and the Board, however, was anticipated. "The one dark note sounded in 1965 was an observation that Cedarholm might not be an easy man for the board to work with as Cedarholm had never been under the authority and supervision of a governing body in his past ministries."[16]

---

[16] Windsor, 226.

In the next three years, Cedarholm made decisions he believed were within the purview of the president, but which the Board saw as theirs alone to make. One example of such an independant decision was Cedarholm's authorization of the use of $200,000 of Pillsbury's assets as additional collateral for dormitory construction (the loan for the dormitory construction and the collateral for that loan had been approved by the Board, but the bank wanted more collateral). He also spent $2,000 for building improvements in Old Main that were not approved by the Board. In March 1966, Cedarholm invited two missionaries to speak in chapel who were still associated with the CBFMS, the most liberal of the CBA organizations. This led to a public rebuke by the Fundamental Baptist Fellowship and forced the Board to offer an apology on the part of the Board and Cedarholm.

Regardless of his fondness for Clearwaters and his respect for the strong stand the Minnesota Baptist Convention had demonstrated throughout Northern and Conservative Baptist struggles, Cedarholm was discovering his administrative style was too free-wheeling to work amicably with the Board of the College. While the Board saw a clear line of authority from the Minnesota Baptist Convention through themselves to the President and out into the college, Cedarholm saw a two-headed authority that constrained his ability to operate. Over his three years of service to Pillsbury, several situations arose that were never fully resolved. Each event laid down another layer of concern and distrust on each side, until a discipline issue arose in the spring of 1968, where Dr. Cedarholm's biblical principle of spiritual leaders ruling without partiality ran directly into the Board's biblical principle of requiring obedience to them that have the rule.

A discipline decision was made in the normal process of the college administration. A Board member had a personal interest in the discipline, and the Board requested the decision be reconsidered. The college administration reviewed the circumstances, but made no change. With that the Board stepped in, removed some administrators from the college Discipline Committee, and had the decision reversed. The Dean of Students resigned immediately, and the Cedarholms resigned soon thereafter. Cedarholm announced his resignation to the students in their daily chapel and explained the reason for his sudden departure. Clearwaters came to the chapel the next day, giving the Board's side of the story.

Cedarholm took his case to the public in a letter to the Pillsbury constituency.

> 325 East Main
> Owatonna, Minnesota 55060
> April 30, 1968

Dear Friends,

At the regularly scheduled meeting of the Board of Trustees of Pillsbury Baptist Bible College held yesterday at the Fourth Baptist Church of Minneapolis, Minnesota, I submitted my resignation as president of Pillsbury College. It would not be possible to go into all the background that led to our resignation, but, since you are vitally concerned, let me give you a little history.

About four months ago, three of our students were disciplined by "campusing" (75 demerits) which meant that they would not be permitted to leave campus without special permission. This disciplinary action was meted out for serious infraction of the rules and, after careful investigation, was, in our judgement, just and fair.

Ever since coming to Pillsbury, I have always had a part in hearing special and more serious cases of discipline. Dr. Parker as president before me always considered this his responsibility, and I have followed his example. When Mr. Barnes, Dean of Students and head of the Discipline Committee, reviewed these cases with me, I agreed with him and members of the Discipline Committee that the discipline administered was just and fair.

The three students involved were so disturbed by the discipline measures taken that they wrote their parents, complaining that they had been treated unjustly and too severely. This was wrong on their part. The Student Regulations make it very clear that the college will not tolerate complaining and especially when it concerns the discipline system. Any student who feels that he has been dealt with unfairly or too severely may always see the Dean of Students for further consideration.

Upon receipt of letters from the students, the parents wrote the chairman of the Board of Trustees, Dr. R. V. Clearwaters. (I read the correspondence.) The parents did not support the college in the matter of the discipline. At an earlier board meeting, Dr. Clearwaters stated to the board that he had received several such letters and that he was concerned that the college was about to lose a number of students over what parents and students called "unjust" discipline.

We live very close to the students on campus. The Lord has given us one of the best years we have ever had. We certainly are not aware of any great number of students contemplating leaving. Our enrollment has been the highest in the eleven-year history of the college—719 in the fall and 712 in the second semester. We matriculated the largest entering class in the history of the school last fall—326. In January, we enrolled the largest second semester class in the history of the school—58. Between the semesters, we had the smallest number of dropouts. It would appear to us that the students are comparatively happy here on campus.

It is true that the contemplated entering class for next fall is down about 45 as compared to one year ago. We do have, however, more women students enrolled for the fall term than at this time last year, but there are fewer men. In checking with other Bible College and Institute presidents and deans, we find that the situation is virtually the same all over, but the experience of others seems to be to a greater degree than here at Pillsbury. Perhaps some of the decrease could be attributed to the war in Viet Nam.

In all matters we have sought to be fair and objective. We do not find any dissatisfaction to a major degree here among the students. The Lord has given us a great year. As far as finances are concerned, we have the largest bank balance we have ever had at this time of the year—over three times the amount we had last year at this time. The Lord has surely blessed.

At the suggestion of Dr. Clearwaters, the Board felt some time ago that the three cases of discipline should be reviewed by the Discipline Committee, with power to sustain or reverse the previous action. The Discipline Committee was unanimous that the previous action should stand. I felt that the matter was a settled one.

At a later date, Dr. Clearwaters brought the matter to the attention of the Board once more with a motion to change the personnel of the Discipline Committee. Mr. Barnes, Dean of Students, had been relieved of all responsibilities and replaced by Mr. Pratt. The Dean of Women, Mrs. Cedarholm, was replaced by Dr. Frans, Dean of the College. (Our established regulations state that the Discipline Committee is to be comprised of the Dean of Students, Personnel Deans—Dean of Men and Dean of Women—and Student Body President.) Why should the personnel be changed during the course of consideration of any one case? As directed, the "new" Discipline Committee reviewed the case, voted two to one to reverse the previous action. This we did not like to see since the first action was just and fair. Furthermore, it was not in respect to the office of the president, since he had a part in confirming the first decision.

The Board also voted to remove me, as president, from any voice in the matters of discipline. This, I felt, was unfortunate, since I have always had, and Dr. Parker before me, a voice in the discipline if I deemed it necessary.

With all this in mind, I presented to the Board yesterday, April 29, 1968, several conditions under which Mrs. Cedarholm and I felt we could remain at the college and maintain an effective ministry that would honor the Lord. These were to take effect immediately with the exception of No. 4.

1. The Discipline Committee personnel shall be as defined by the Regulations—Dean of Students, Mr. Pratt; Dean of Women, Mrs. Cedarholm; Dean of Men, (none at present); Student Body President, Mr. Lynn Howe.

2. The President of the college shall participate in matters of discipline as he would deem it wise and necessary.
3. The three cases of discipline shall be reversed to the original decision (all three students shall be "campused").
4. Dr. Richard Weeks shall be named Dean of Students, Mr. Raymond Pratt Dean of Men (effective September 1).
5. Dr. Frans shall continue to serve as Academic Dean.
6. Until apology shall have been made to the President, one faculty member's teaching contract shall be suspended. (This was a personal matter involving social misconduct.)

After lengthy deliberation in Executive Session, the Board of Trustees did not accept these six conditions. The vote was not unanimous. Two favored accepting the president's suggestions. Thus, our resignation was submitted to take effect today, April 30. It was accepted by the Board.

Naturally, our hearts are heavy. We love this institution. Perhaps the Lord may yet be pleased to work things out in order that we might remain. However, we cannot do so until the above conditions are accepted by the Board.

It is upon the strong Bible program and excellent discipline system which this school has been built. These have drawn students here. These we must maintain and defend. We cannot surrender these points. If we do, Pillsbury Baptist Bible College has lost its distinctiveness and usefulness.

May the Lord bless you. Pray for Pillsbury, the Trustees and us in these days. Romans 8:28 and Ephesians 3:20 are His promises for us.

Yours and His,
B. Myron Cedarholm
BMC/c

P.S. I want you to know that this letter is being sent at my own expense. If the Lord should lead you to write to the Board of Trustees, you may write them in care of Dr. R. V. Clearwaters, Chairman, Fourth Baptist Church, 2105

North Fremont Avenue, Minneapolis, Minnesota. We would appreciate a carbon copy of your letter. Thank you.

A week following the chapels, the May 8, 1968, *Blu-print* brought its national constituency up to date:

CEDARHOLM RESIGNS AT PILLSBURY COLLEGE

Shock waves are still being felt widely across the country over recent developments at Pillsbury College as a result of the power struggle on the campus at Owatonna, Minnesota. A nation-wide letter to the Pillsbury constituency dated April 30, 1968, reveals that Dr. B. Myron Cedarholm felt impelled to resign abruptly on April 29, 1968, effective the next day at 6 p.m. This terminates a brilliant three-year leadership which reached an enrollment higher than any other strictly Bible College in the country. Dr. Cedarholm's letter told about the crucial board meeting on April 29, at which time a majority of the trustees brought such pressures to bear and stripped him of such authority that he felt he had no honorable course but to resign and lay the matter before the constituency. He laid down a six-point set of requirements, under which he would remain as president. This was overwhelmingly rejected by the trustees who were under the influence of Dr. R. V. Clearwaters, chairman. Observers close to Pillsbury felt that the letter was only a partial explanation of the continuing problems as to who was to control policy and give leadership to the college. Disregarding President Cedarholm's recommendation, the Board then reversed several cases of discipline and removed the President from any authority in discipline. Dr. R. V. Clearwaters was then elected as Interim President "with power to act." Among his first actions was to quarantine Dr. Cedarholm and his wife, and make his house on the campus "off limits" to faculty and students. This virtual "house arrest" was not received enthusiastically by the college community nor by pastors across the country. The flood of telephone calls which students made throughout the country to their home churches soon overloaded the circuits. Dr. Cedarholm gave his farewell chapel address on April 30 involving two periods, after which he met with the faculty. Dr. Clearwaters then answered him with an address the following day. Since the same pressures forced the resignation of Dr. Monroe Parker a few years ago after eight fruitful years of leadership, it does not take much imagination to realize what a potentially explosive situation could develop. Dr. Cedarholm's influence with pastors and churches is great. With a $1½ million indebtedness, Pillsbury is in no shape to undergo another almost complete turn-over of faculty or a diminishing student body. Those pastors who have been loyal to Pillsbury through the years, both in finances and student procurement, are praying that the Board will take immediate steps to reverse the actions and allow the continuance of the blessing of God which has been so marked over these eleven years. These trustees should not provide evidence that Fundamentalists will divide over matters which have as little moral and theological justification as the present case involves. By law, Pillsbury trustees must be from Minnesota, and it is hoped the brethren there can resolve the problem. Fundamentalists need colleges free from the clutches of the ecumenical movement, neo-evangelicalism, and other unscriptural ideologies. Dr. Cedarholm is still living in the presidential residence on the campus, but his mail is received through P. O. Box 286, Owatonna, Minnesota 55060. His phone is (507) 451–5657.[17]

The Pillsbury Board prepared a letter to document their position concerning the student discipline situation. In addition, the letter presented other issues that they perceived as administrative failures: decisions made prior to board approval, an unwise choice for a chapel speaker, and authorizations that overstepped his position.

May 10, 1968

Dear Friends of Pillsbury Baptist Bible College,

This form letter is authorized by the Board of Trustees of Pillsbury Baptist Bible College to answer some of the recent communication that have resulted from the resignation of Dr. B. Myron Cedarholm as President of the College. This is not for publication, nor to be reproduced without permission of this Board. A copy of material released by the Board for publication

---

[17] "Cedarholm Resigns at Pillsbury College," *Blu-print*, May 8, 1968.

can be obtained from our Interim President, Dr. R. V. Clearwaters.

Before the Beginning of Dr. Cedarholm's Presidency

The Committee of three Board members that went to see Dr. Cedarholm about his being considered by the College Board heard this from Dr. Cedarholm's lips "that I am no administrator,[18] and if the Lord leads in this I would have to depend much on your Committees and the Board" (there is no verbal record of this, but this is as near verbatim as the Committee recalls).

Dr. Cedarholm's Presidency

On the day Dr. Cedarholm was inaugurated on the Campus, in introducing him, Dr. Clearwaters confessed before some 1,200 people that when his name was first mentioned in the Board for President, he did not favor it. He further stated that the groundswell of the constituency represented in Denver, Colorado, manifested him as a favorite among many witnesses. His reason for this confession was Dr. Cedarholm's own statement made above, that he was no Administrator. After serving as his President in the Conservative Baptist Association for three years, he knew from that experience that he was speaking the truth with soul sincerity.

The Principle Involved

Practically all of the difficulties that Dr. Cedarholm has encountered as President have been when he has insisted on imposing his will upon his Committees and the Board of the College. Pillsbury College has always been a "Board-run school." This he knew full well, and that the first Faculty resigned in mass, demanding that it be a Faculty-run school. The Board accepted their resignations, and stood by the then President. The Board of eighteen members is elected by the messengers of the Minnesota Association of 110 Baptist Churches in annual session (six each year, serving a three-year term). By the Charter of 1854, all Trustees of the College

---

[18] What was said in this meeting cannot be ascertained. However, Clearwaters stated near the end of Cedarholm's first year at Pillsbury: "I told Cedar when he began that he was the worlds [sic] worst administrator. For this reason, we brought Weeks to the campus." Letter from Richard V. Clearwaters to Henry Lovik, March 31, 1966.

must be residents of Minnesota, and the College must be under the patronage of the Minnesota Association of Baptist Churches.

Dr. Cedarholm's Dissatisfaction with the Committees and College Board

1. The Finance Committee

a. When he began, Dr. Cedarholm asked Dr. Clearwaters what the College was thinking about in setting the faculty salaries so high. Dr. Clearwaters defended the previous administration in this. In his first year Dr. Cedarholm had faculty members talking to him about more salary. He pressed upon the Finance Committee to act upon it with raises, and was provoked, because they knew that the college had operated in the black after its first year, each year, but that the College had to borrow $10,000 almost every summer to get through lean summer months. He carried it to the Board and again was refused. (After a year's experience with our present financial obligations, the board has pledged itself to do what it can in this area.)

b. The Finance Committee recommended, and the Board approved, a First Mortgage on all of the Real Estate that the College owned. The money was to be used to pay off the Bonded indebtedness and build a $400,000 girls' dormitory (which building is now in use). When the banker came with the papers for the Board Chairman and the President to sign, the banker asked Dr. Clearwaters to sign another paper, which would have added over $400,000 of the College's liquid assets to the Real Estate already accepted by the bank for all of the loan (at this time we had a letter from the bank stating that our loan had gone through—and to now no mention had been made of these additional assets). Dr. Clearwaters refused to sign for the additional assets, and he explained that he had no such permission from the College Board. Dr. Cedarholm stood in the room when the banker stated that Dr. Clearwaters was "being difficult,"—Dr. Cedarholm had agreed to sign for the additional assets. Dr. Clearwaters promised them both that he would ask the Board, as their servant, if this was their desire. He did so, and Dr. Cedarholm agreed that he had presented it to us fairly, and we unanimously agreed that he had done right in refusing to sign away an additional sum, not authorized by the Board.

2. The Building and Grounds Committee

a. Dr. Cedarholm in 1966 when we were building the girls' dormitory pressed upon this Committee a strong recommendation of his to remodel and add to the showers, etc., in the gymnasium, especially for the girls' benefit. The Committee got preliminary estimates, and the $30,000 recommendation was refused by both the Committee and the Board (fortunately so, because when the dorm was finished, we were just able to furnish it without any balance in the treasury).

b. Without consulting this Committee or the Board, Dr. Cedarholm authorized about $2,000 for remodeling in "Old Main" and resented being asked about it.

3. The Academic Committee

a. When Dr. Cedarholm came to the Presidency, the College had already dropped the word "Conservative" out of its name. In being responsible for the College Chapel, he arranged to have and let speak the Foreign Secretary of the Conservative Baptist Foreign Mission Society, which caused an uprising among the students and the constituency.

b. Dr. Cedarholm brought recommendations to this Committee for Faculty positions which were often refused—some of these afterwards left the impression with some Board members that they were of the opinion that they were as good as employed through their communications with the President.

c. For graduation speaker for the College, Dr. Cedarholm made a recommendation and was refused three times by the Academic Committee, and then when he presented it to the Board, he was refused again. The individual named wrote a Board member a personal letter to ask what we had against him—that the President had announced in the presence of his people that he would be the speaker at Pillsbury's Graduation. The President did this before his Academic Committee or Board knew anything about it.

3. The Discipline Committee

a. The Handbook describes the Character Conduct for students, and the Board is responsible to administer, or have administered, this Handbook. The College Board is responsible to the students legally, to administer, or have administered, the legal rights of the students as regards finances, curriculum, etc., in the catalog.

b. Until Dr. Cedarholm's Administration, each student was privileged to (1) meet with this Committee if he desired, when turned in for any discipline. (2) He was allowed to have his day in court. (3) He was allowed to face his accuser, if he desired. Some accusers have been face to face with the accused and confessed that they lied. Some people think this should be a secret—who is the accuser. If the accuser is more interested in his personal popularity, then the Campus spiritual life is not "suffering for righteousness sake."

c. Under Dr. Cedarholm's Administration, students would often meet with not more than two people present, sometimes just the President and the Dean of Students, rather than meeting with the whole Committee and having the benefit of the three steps named under "b" above.

d. During our early years many criticisms came because of the faculty, but lately this has ceased and an avalanche of criticism came increasingly because of discipline.

e. Dr. Cedarholm's Administration kept adding many rules not in the Handbook, and in administering this discipline utterly disregarded the principles named above under "b." At this point the Board asked to have two cases of discipline reviewed. Dr. Cedarholm obstructed the unanimous action of the Academic Committee to review these two cases, to see if any injustice had been done. The College Board enforced the action of the Academic Committee and to get these two cases reviewed, the Board was compelled by the obstruction of Dr. Cedarholm to compose a different Committee in order that the Board learn about the justice or injustice done the students.

f. Dr. Cedarholm ordered the newly constructed Committee to leave discipline already administered stand. He threatened to resign if this was changed, and when one faculty member was threatened to be brought before the Board, he said, but I have to do what I feel is right in my heart—and Dr. Cedarholm called this insubordination to him as President. The President charged these two students with not defending the discipline system of the school—specifically they asked two other students if they had turned them in (something done very [sic] week on the Campus). For this they got half enough demerits to be expelled from the College and campused for the semester. It is reliably reported that another student lied three times to

A second letter from the Board of Trustees was much simpler, but less clear.

For public release—authorized by the College Board
May 10, 1968

A Statement by the Trustees of Pillsbury Baptist Bible College pertaining to the resignation of Dr. B. Myron Cedarholm

Discipline standards and procedures at the College will follow the same pattern that obtained at the College before Dr. Cedarholm's Administration, namely (1) that the Handbook will be followed, (2) that every student will have the privilege of meeting the Discipline Committee, (3) that every student accused will have his day in court, and (4) that every student will have the privilege, if he desires, of being faced by his accuser.

The strong doctrinal position and stand of the College remains unchanged and the discipline system insisted on by the Board strengthens the discipline of the College.

Three times the Board requested in recorded motions, Dr. Cedarholm to consider continuing with us, and furthermore Dr. Cedarholm took any further reconsideration by the College Board out of the Board's hands or power by carrying the matter to the Student Body, the public, and by his written communications to the parents of many students.

Two shaken men must have closed their doors on Wednesday night, April 30th. This issue had been developing for months. The initial discipline decision had taken place in January. Letters from the parents of the students who were disciplined were written in February. The Board took its original action, requiring the Discipline Committee to reconsider its decision, on April 6. The resignations came at the end of April. Clearwaters grieved that a private Board matter was held up for public opinion by a trusted friend, almost a spiritual son, who he felt would always support Board decisions as a matter of personal loyalty, public testimony, and legal obligation. Years of personal friendship and a shared love for Pillsbury led Clearwaters to believe that Cedarholm would be very aware of what serving as President of Pillsbury would mean, and that he would be quite comfortable with the Board-directed arrangement. Cedarholm grieved that his own spiritual mentor could not see the danger of partiality and that Clearwaters either could not or would not use his influence to convince the full Board that Cedarholm's commitment to principle gave his conscience no room for any other choice.

High emotions prevailed on both sides of the conflict. For instance, in Illinois, leading pastors such as Peter Mustric (First Baptist Church, Rockford), Henry Sorenson (Faith Baptist Church, Pekin), and Henry Lovik (the State Director of the Conservative Baptist Association of Illinois) stood with Clearwaters and Pillsbury. Arno Q. Weniger, Jr. (Calvary Baptist Church, Normal) and Wes Potter (East Park Baptist Church, Decatur) sided with Cedarholm and Maranatha. It is amazing that the Illinois association was not destroyed, for nearly every pastor in the association found himself on one side or the other of the conflict. To everyone's credit, the men worked hard to keep the conflict out of the association so they could continue to work together. Shortly after 1968, the board of the CBA of Illinois (now the Association of Independent Baptist Churches of Illinois) adopted a policy that no representative of an educational institution would speak at state association meetings. That policy prevailed for years. Stories similar to this could be repeated across the nation.

Students, faculty, and area pastors aligned themselves with one or the other of the two leaders. FBF president G. Archer Weniger, whose sister was married to Cedarholm's brother, was sympathetic to Cedarholm.[20] That May, Cedarholm went to the FBF meeting that was taking place at Calvary Baptist Church, Normal, Illinois, to answer questions regarding his resignation from Pillsbury. This was interpreted by Clearwaters' followers as a clear sign that the FBF was siding with Cedarholm. A number of pastors loyal to Clearwaters served in churches in the fledgling New

---

[20] The *FBF Information Bulletin*, July/August 1968, contains a report about the controversy.

Testament Association of Independent Baptist Churches (NTAIBC), and thus a rift developed between the FBF and the NTAIBC, even though Cedarholm had a part in the formation of the NTAIBC.

In June, Cedarholm sent out letters, announcing the new college God was leading him to begin in Watertown, Wisconsin. The founding of Maranatha Baptist Bible College added fresh fuel to the dispute, for it was seen by many Clearwaters loyalists as a spiteful action, designed to harm Pillsbury.

The events produced rancor between the "sides." The bitterness displayed (not so much by the two leaders themselves, but by their supporters) "left angry sentiments among some Baptists in the Midwest for two decades."[21] Contention and conflict between strong Christian leaders is not a new phenomenon. The book of Acts records such a conflict between good men. Barnabas, the "son of encouragement" (4:36), is described as "a good man, and full of the Holy Ghost and of faith" (11:24). It was Barnabas who sought out Paul and brought him to the apostles in Jerusalem (9:27) and brought him from Tarsus to Antioch, involving him in the church there (11:25–26). Their years of laboring together in Antioch were followed by the Holy Spirit's choosing them for a missionary journey (13:2). They preached and suffered persecution (13:46–50; 15:35), but God blessed their work. When they were considering a second missionary journey, they had a disagreement concerning John Mark. Their disagreement was so "sharp" that they separated from one another (15:36–40). The language implies that their conflict was heated; their separation was not just a parting of the ways.[22] Although the New Testament does not explicitly say that Paul and Barnabas were reconciled, their reconciliation is implied in several Scripture passages. Three passages involve Mark, the cause of the dispute between Paul and Barnabas. The best known of these is 2 Timothy 4:11, written near the end of

---

[21] Windsor, "Valiant for Truth," 232.

[22] Bob Whitmore, "The Cedarholm/Clearwaters Conflict," *Frontline* (March/April 1999), 11.

Paul's life, where Paul says, "Take Mark, and bring him with thee: for he is profitable to me for the ministry." Apparently, Mark had at some time redeemed himself with Paul. In Philemon 24, Paul refers to Mark as his fellow-laborer. In Colossians 4:10, Paul again commends Mark. In one other epistle, Paul mentions Barnabas. In 1 Corinthians 9:6, written after his separation from Barnabas, Paul implies that he and Barnabas are again co-laborers.

There is a parallel to the dispute between Cedarholm and Clearwaters. Their reconciliation is implied in several letters and events, and reconciliation is even clearer among many of their followers. Less than three years after the dispute, G. Archer Weniger wrote a kind letter to Clearwaters after hearing that he had been ill. "We think of you from time to time and rejoice in all that the Lord has done through you." Later that year Archer's brother Max was invited to sit on an ordination council with Clearwaters. In October 1974, the boards of the FBF and NTAIBC met together in Atlanta and passed "A Resolution Toward Unity and Fellowship" to promote "warm fellowship between the two organizations." Reconciliation between the two primary individuals in the dispute, however, came more slowly. "I would be delighted to have fellowship again with Central and Pillsbury," Cedarholm said in a June 21, 1979, letter to Dr. Harry Love. "I am ready any time to restore fellowship." So, in October 1980, Clearwaters and Cedarholm were both invited and appeared as speakers at the annual fellowship of the Independent Baptist Association of Michigan, an association headed by Love. In 1981, Cedarholm heard that the Pillsbury board passed a resolution, stating that they considered Maranatha a sister school. Rejoicing in the news, he wrote, "We thank the Lord that things seem to be working out real good."[23] In 1985, Pillsbury Baptist Bible College hosted the FBF's national meeting. Cedarholm and Clearwaters were

---

[23] B. Myron Cedarholm, letter to Dr. and Mrs. Harry Love, September 2, 1981. Dr. Robert Crane, later president of Pillsbury Baptist Bible College, was unable to confirm this action of the Board, although he said it could have happened and not been recorded in the minutes.

both speakers. They were obviously willing to put aside any personal differences that may have remained between them for the good of all fundamental Baptists.

Knowing the end of the story and having the long years of history to soften wrong and solidify right has given Biblicists the small comfort of saying that they were both great men in the mold of Paul and Barnabas, and that when sharp contention arose between them, the Lord used their separation to double His outreach. In this case, He built two schools.[24]

In May 1968, the Cedarholms, convinced that they had done what principle demanded, found themselves in their fifties, unemployed, reputations impugned, and ministry shattered. The take-charge man had a quiet week of soul-reflection and uncharacteristic inaction before the Lord picked him up for the ride of his life. However, just at this uncertain moment, God's timing was made evident. The buildings of the Sacred Heart Military Academy in Watertown, Wisconsin, were sitting on the market.

[24] Whitmore, Frontline, May/June, 1999

THE MARANATHA YEARS: 1968–1983

In 2007–08, Maranatha Baptist Bible College, now Maranatha Baptist University, celebrated its 40th anniversary. One project completed for that memorable event was an extensive history of the college, *Rich in Mercy*.[1] Readers are encouraged to obtain a copy of this carefully researched work to gain an understanding of the history of the school. Because the starting of the college was such a significant event in the lives of the Cedarholms, the following pages borrow heavily from *Rich in Mercy*.

---

[1] Kim Ledgerwood, *Rich in Mercy* (Watertown, WI: Maranatha Baptist Bible College, 2008).

In 1988, Dr. and Mrs. Cedarholm wrote the story of the "Miracle of Maranatha." Twenty years had passed since the miracle summer. Dr. Cedarholm had told the story in churches all over the country. Students in Madrigal or those who had traveled on gospel teams with the Cedarholms could recite the story from memory. For years, the opening convocation was primarily the retelling of the miracle story, so when the Cedarholms wrote their account, it was not to tell a story no one had ever heard. Their purpose was to leave for succeeding generations a testimony of something amazing the Lord chose to do in the war-beleaguered, riot-permeated, rebellion-wrought United States of 1968. The Cedarholms could only stand by and watch as the Lord picked up shattered dreams and made a miracle in modern America. Their exemplary character, their rare abilities, their competence, and their connections were swept along in a work the Lord chose to accomplish in their midst and which they were powerless to manipulate or contrive. Truly, it was: "What God Hath Wrought."

The Cedarholms tell their tale in the following bold print, while the annotations augment what could not be covered in their short history.

A History of the Founding of Maranatha Baptist Bible College
by
Dr. B. Myron Cedarholm
Thelma M. Cedarholm[2]

It was a quiet evening in early May, 1968. It was Wednesday, May 8, 1968, at about 9:45 p.m. according to Dr. Cedarholm's journal. They had just come home from

---

[2] Material in bold is the Cedarholms' handwritten account, undated, but probably written about 1988. The unbolded material is additional information from various sources. If no source is included, the material is from untitled documents in the Maranatha Archives.

church in Owatonna. His resignation from Pillsbury had been submitted just eight days before.

The tone of that telephone voice shall never be forgotten—"Come over to Wisconsin and start a Bible college. I've found just the place..." and then, she proceeded to tell us all about it. This phone call came from Mrs. Harold (Elayne) Senn of Watertown, Wisconsin. Her son, Dwayne, was in Mrs. Cedarholm's choir and was one of the students who sat in chapel on April 29, 1968, and heard Dr. Cedarholm explain why he resigned. Dwayne also sat in chapel on April 30, 1968, when Dr. Clearwaters explained the position of the Board and advised the students to go about their business and leave the Cedarholms to themselves in their campus house until they were able to move out. Dwayne, along with hundreds of other students, called home to share the stunning news with his family. The students had access to only a handful of payphones in the dormitories, but those phones were busy that week. A week later, Mrs. Senn stood at her kitchen window, doing dishes on Wednesday evening and began thinking about the Sacred Heart Military Academy over on Main Street. It had been on the market since November 1967.

There was good reason to start a college in Wisconsin. From the early 1900's, Wisconsin had been known as the "graveyard of evangelism."[3] Many Baptist churches, small to begin with, especially in the southern part of the state, had closed. In 1968, there were just two Bible colleges in all of Wisconsin, Illinois, Iowa, and Minnesota. There was need for another.

Troubled and torn by various circumstances, we sought some refuge with God's people, so that just the previous Sunday we decided to attend Temple Baptist Church, St. Paul, where we might be refreshed by the preaching of the Word of God. Sunday, May 5, 1968, their resignation was only five days old. They traveled the hour and twenty-minute trip north to St. Paul, to a church and pastor friend they knew well. There was already talk swirling

---

[3] "Maranatha—The Miracle School."

around about a Catholic school building that was available in St. Paul; perhaps they could start another school there. The Cedarholms had relatives and thus contacts and some measure of support throughout the Twin cities area. The clock was ticking. Things needed to be packed. They needed a new home. They needed a new church. They had to find work. But on this Sunday, they just needed the encouragement of God's Word preached among God's people.

When they arrived, Pastor William Murk was surprised. Dr. Cedarholm had a standing invitation to preach at Temple Baptist any time, but he usually got a call from Cedarholm, forewarning him. When he asked Cedarholm to preach that morning, however, he declined. It was highly unusual, but that day he came not to minister, but to be ministered to.

Pastor William Murk read the Scripture for the day:
Now the Lord had said unto Abram, Get thee out of thy country, and from thy kindred, and from thy father's house, unto a land that I will shew thee; and I will make of thee a great nation, and I will bless thee, and make thy name great; And thou shalt be a blessing. (Genesis 12: 1, 2)

It was as though the Lord were speaking to us. We wondered and trusted. Dr. Cedarholm calculated that he had some three hundred relatives living in the state of Minnesota. Though there were options with fine facilities to start another college right in Minnesota,[4] in the way only the Lord can do with the Living Word, this text planted in his heart the sense that whatever the next step was for the Cedarholm family, it would not be in Minnesota.

Since November of the previous year there had been for sale a lovely sixty-two-acre property, beautifully

---

[4] Cedarholm chapel notes, September 12, 1968. Cedarholm used the very first Maranatha chapel to outline all that happened to birth Maranatha. Both the former Bethel College site and the facilities of Temple Baptist church were options for the site of a new school in Minnesota. The multitude of counselors directing him to continue in Christian Education was a confirmation not to pursue other ministry opportunities that availed themselves at the same time.

landscaped, complete with buildings for educational purposes. Set on a hill overlooking the city of Watertown in south central Wisconsin, Old Main, an imposing structure of brick and stone, now some seventy years in age, stood tall and firm, offering its facilities to any who might find them usable. The military academy which presently occupied the premises had for some time contemplated a merger with another school in northern Indiana; in fact, the move was to take place at the close of this very year. Several had studied the possibilities and offers to purchase had been made, but, somehow, none had been accepted. Since the buildings had been consecrated for the training of young people, the present owners were not willing to allow them to be used for any other purpose than education.

Thorp Realty had appraised the land on November 21, 1967, for $285,000, $60,000 for the property and $225,000 for the buildings and landscaping. They suggested listing the property for $213,000.[5] There was a very interested buyer. The Watertown hospital had money saved for building a new facility, and, according to Cedarholm, had already offered the Catholics $400,000 for the property. The old hospital, located on East Main Street on the opposite side of the downtown area, was woefully inadequate and had to be replaced. There was nothing about the Catholic buildings that could be incorporated into a modern hospital, so they would need to be demolished. All the hospital wanted was the land in its prime location. Though offered more than the asking price, the Brothers said they would wait. Their desire was to keep the property involved somehow in education; what they did not realize was that the Lord was saving the property for something special. Cedarholm relates the conversation between himself and Mrs. Senn briefly: "Mrs. Senn called to let me know about the availability of this place. Well, I want to tell you that I never thought anything like this would be possible, but I wanted to be courteous to Mrs. Senn, so I asked a few questions. When I asked the

---

[5] Thorp appraisal, November 27, 1967.

price, $225,000, I lost my interest immediately. Did you ever know a preacher that had $225,000?"[6]

At the conclusion of the conversation with Mrs. Harold Senn of Watertown that evening, she said, "Dr. Cedarholm, you SHOULD come and buy this campus. I'm going to pray that the Lord will use you to start a Bible college here." Mrs. Senn is the mother of Carol Senn Ruffin, a long-time member of the Fine Arts faculty at Maranatha. The obvious question was whether her mother was the sort of person who called up important people she barely knew and told them what they should do. Carol said it was very much out of character for her mother to do what she did that Wednesday night!

We thanked her for her concern and laid the matter aside, but not for long. **We pondered all that we had heard—the matter was not forgotten. The very next day,** Thursday, May 9, 1968, **Dr. Don Camp, pastor of the Grace Baptist Church, Anderson, Indiana** (Grace was one of the many churches Dr. Cedarholm was instrumental in founding during his CBA days[7]), **extended an invitation to come to preach at his church the next Sunday, Mother's Day**, May 12. **That invitation was gladly accepted, not realizing how providential was its timing. Previous to this, there had been no intention to visit Watertown or the available campus. Now, however, since the Interstate highway 94 passed so near the city, we decided to stop by the next Saturday** May 11, **"just to see what the Lord might have in mind."**

The first sight of that campus brought a sense of excitement and, perhaps, fearful expectation. The entrance was bordered by flowering fruit trees. The entire property was resplendent in spring beauty. Tall evergreens shaded the sculptured shrubbery while vari-colored blossoms bordered the luscious expanse of green lawns.

---

[6] Cedarholm videotape, 1988.

[7] Cedarholm correspondence to Lindberg, November 10, 1981.

A tour of Old Main revealed most adequate facilities for a college. Everything fairly shone with careful maintenance (two ladies were the proud keepers of the entire interior) and we were impressed with the manner in which all had been so meticulously preserved. Encompassed within these walls was dormitory space for students (the first news release for Maranatha said "dormitory space will accommodate almost 300"), a large chapel, recently paneled in beautiful mahogany with gold trim (the chapel had been restored and rededicated in 1961 at a cost of $71,000), an auditorium (Room 306 or Fine Arts Hall, with no stage at that time), gymnasium (now the Student Center, Bookstore, and Post Office), dining hall (now Old Main Cafe), post office (across from the current IT Office), recreation room (now the Academy area, but then it was complete with exquisite slate-top billiard tables that Cedarholm told the brothers the college would have no need of), infirmary (Piano Pedagogy studio), tailoring shop, science laboratory, barber shop, large reception room (Financial Aid and the East Conference Room), kitchen, cold storage (an outdoor cellar between the current Development Office and the Gazebo), laundry rooms in the basement of Old Main and the current West Conference Room, some twenty faculty living quarters, and many, many administrative offices. Other buildings included a large garage (the current Development Office), maintenance shop (where the library now stands), and storage building (a barn where the Dining Commons is now located).

While speaking with the headmaster, Brother Carl Englert, that afternoon, we learned that all financial matters concerning the price and sale of the property rested with the Provincial General, whose offices were located in South Bend, Indiana. This was Don Bailer at LeMans Military Academy in Rolling Prairie, Indiana. Since we were soon to be in Indiana, we thought we just might stop by to see him and express our interest. What a "coincidence!" The invitation to go to Anderson took them past Watertown *and* put them in the path of South Bend as well. Mrs. Cedarholm mentioned in her journal that they even found a home to rent on West Road in Watertown.

Strangely moved and yet amazed at that which we had seen, neither one of us spoke a word as we drove down the highway. Later, lest we should forget the details, a hasty sketch was drawn of each floor, indicating how the rooms might be used in the event a school became a reality. The Cedarholms kept many documents important to the school, but this is one piece of paper no one has ever discovered. We wondered again, "Why did we stop here?" We could only reiterate, "We never know what the Lord might have in mind." (Those very plans were used in making room assignments later—even to the numbering of the rooms!)

Upon arrival in Anderson, Indiana, we enjoyed a good time of fellowship with the pastor and people of Grace Baptist Church. During the morning service, Dr. Camp announced that there would be a new Bible college starting right there in Anderson and that Dr. Cedarholm was available to serve as its president. Church facilities would be provided for classes, and all that would be needed in addition would be dormitories for students. What a surprise this was to us!

Monday noon, May 13, a luncheon was served to some sixty interested pastors from various churches in the central states. A report of the visit to the Watertown property was presented; picture post cards of the buildings were shown, and the men became convinced that with such available facilities there was no doubt that the Lord was leading in the starting of a new Bible college in Watertown, Wisconsin. The consensus of opinion that day was that we should go ahead and look into the matter of securing the property.

During all this time, there had been many anxious moments during which the Lord proved to be very near and precious. Peace came only in the recognition that this entire moving was in the Lord's hands, and that He was guiding in every step. We sought counsel from many close associates. Dr. Jack Hyles, pastor of the First Baptist Church of Hammond, Indiana, encouraged us by telling us to "Go ahead and start the school, and I will help you all I can." His generosity and personal kindness to us throughout these years that have followed shall never be forgotten.

It was Dr. Monroe Parker, eminent Bible scholar, evangelist, preacher, and educator, whose outline of procedure served as a guide.

When a school is to be founded, there are four points to consider:

> FIRST, one must have a FOLLOWING, that is there must be those who will stand by to help and to pray—pastors whose trust in you has already been established so that they will be willing to send their youth to your college. There must be parents who will entrust their children to your care for establishment in the faith and for training for Christian service. There must be young people who will desire to come with you and sit under your ministry. (Twenty years in the field of evangelism and work among churches all across the country led us to believe that we did, indeed, have a following.)
>
> SECONDLY, there must be a FACULTY, and Dr. Cedarholm, if the incoming student body is small at the start, never fear, you and your wife could serve as the first faculty. (Imagine that!)
>
> THIRDLY, there must be a FACILITY—a place to meet, even if it be but a log with the teacher at one end and a student at the other. This has been the case on many a mission field, you know. (We had already visited the property in Watertown. Perhaps this might be the place!)
>
> LASTLY, there must be FINANCES, but this need is not of great concern if the Lord is in the move. Whatever he orders, He will sustain.

And as Doug Jackson, the current Chairman of the Board of Trustees, later quipped, there was a fifth "F" to be considered: freshmen, of which he was one that first year.

Although these and many other words of encouragement were forthcoming, there were also those who sought to discourage. "It will never work!" said one, and another, "Why, it would take at least two years or more to start a BIBLE college!" Many queried, "Where would you find students? And teachers—at this late date?... and, where would you get the money?" One prominent pastor announced, "It will fold up in a year—they won't even have twenty-five students." But, we remembered the promises from the portion in Genesis—"I WILL.... I WILL.... I WILL" (Genesis 12:1).

Our visit with the Provincial General in South Bend the day following the pastors' meeting in Anderson proved to be very interesting. Dr. Cedarholm elsewhere recounted the great trepidation he had going into the meeting. Uppermost in his mind was a long and unpleasant history of official Catholic treatment of "heretics" like the Baptists, followed by his keen awareness of the Lord's displeasure when His people chose to trust the "Egyptians" rather than Himself: "with all due respect to our Catholic friends, only God knew the fear I had dealing with the Catholics. I never had any dealings with them. I never signed any papers with them. When people went down into Egypt they always got into trouble with the Lord. I didn't want to get into trouble with the Lord, because I knew he was a pretty good shot, and I didn't want him to shoot me." To settle these legitimate concerns of Cedarholm's heart, the Lord directed him during his 7:30 a. m. devotions on May 14th to Genesis 46:33–34: "And it shall come to pass, when Pharaoh shall call you, and shall say, What is your occupation? That ye shall say, Thy servants' trade hath been about cattle from our youth even until now, both we, and also our fathers: that ye may dwell in the land of Goshen; for every shepherd is an abomination unto the Egyptians."[8] The text challenged the Cedarholms to be forthright about their intention to use the facility to train men and women for the gospel ministry, though that might seem to be an abomination to the owners. In turn, the Lord would give them a Goshen settlement (a

---

[8] Cedarholm chapel notes, September 12, 1968; videotape from 1988.

perfect location for their "occupation") in the midst of the Egyptians.

We found the gentleman to be most congenial in every respect and, after perhaps an hour or so of discussion, even desirous of selling the Watertown property to us. When we explained to him that we had no money for a down payment, but that we did have the Lord, he seemed to understand for he said, "Well, you just try to raise what you can, and we will talk again. Perhaps if we could set a figure of $5,000, that could serve as a starting point." The expectation was that the Cedarholms were to see how much of a down payment they could raise. That accomplished, the brothers would then finance the remaining balance at 5% interest (the same interest rate as the original 1871 sale to the brothers) for ten years. Don Bailer was proposing a land contract sale with the seller holding the mortgage. A late payment or nonpayment, and the property would immediately revert back to the seller, along with any improvements or investments that had been made. It also meant that the College would need clearance from the Order before adding buildings. This requirement would have a bearing on the College in its early years. **"Meanwhile, I will do all in my power to help you get that property."** Dr. Cedarholm knew that the Brothers had spent about $250,000 in recent years to build the new stairwell on the north side of Old Main and to refurbish the chapel. The stained glass windows in the chapel had cost $5,000 each. To just walk away and leave such an investment seemed to make no human sense at all, but "My ways are not your ways … my ways are past finding out."

Returning through Watertown, an appointment was made with one of the banks in the city to meet with their board concerning the possibility of securing a loan. Dr. Cedarholm recounted his method for choosing the bank; he looked for the bank with the "newest building, largest parking lot, beautiful shrubbery, most wall-to-wall carpeting." The winner of the informal survey was the Bank of Watertown, forerunner of the current BMO Harris Bank in Watertown.

In the meantime, several Wisconsin pastors had been notified of the plan to purchase, and they were requested to meet with us and the bank board to consider the matter. Dr. Gale Schafer, pastor of Calvary Baptist Church in Jefferson, and Dr. Charles Sanders, pastor of Calvary Baptist church in Watertown, were both in Arkansas when the Cedarholms tracked them down by phone to see if they would support a new school in their area. Just a few months before, Calvary Baptist of Watertown had providentially expanded their modest auditorium to one that would seat over 600. Though Schafer was not available to meet at the bank, he did recall joking with his close pastoral friend, Sanders, that this was just what the state of Wisconsin needed: a school and the problems that would come with it like all the issues they had in Minnesota.[9]

Upon returning to Owatonna, Cedarholm met with Ed Caughill, the business manager at Pillsbury. Caughill recalled him returning from the weekend trip with the words, "You could move right in!"[10] In just a few weeks, Caughill would do just that—move his family into the second floor of Old Main and cook in the kitchen, as they made preparations for the new school.

The meeting with the Bank of Watertown **was arranged for the following week** on Monday, May 20, according to Dr. Cedarholm's handwritten account.

After prayer seeking the Lord's guidance, we [Cedarholm's undated, written account says that he, Caughill, and 12 pastors met with the board; Mrs. Cedarholm did not make the trip] **entered the bank. When they** [the bankers] **heard that we did not represent any particular denomination, that we were not underwritten by any denomination, and that we were only a group of independent Baptists who desired to start a Bible college in Watertown, the members of the board lost their interest immediately. The meeting was over, and we were dismissed. Were we disappointed!** Cedarholm said that it

---

[9] Gale Schaefer interview.

[10] Edward Caughill interview.

was easy to get the Catholics to cooperate, but they could not get the Lutherans to even listen to them. What was the Lord trying to do? How could the Lord have made the circumstances seem so confirming of this direction and then apparently close an open door? Here is the irony of the Lord. He brought these men who had struggled for years to learn what ecclesiastical independence meant, and then He put them in a place that from a human perspective showed the foolishness of such a stand. It looked as if their fine principles of independence and autonomy were not doing them any tangible good. **We all stood for a time on the parking lot, then had prayer together and committed everything to the Lord. From there we departed to our homes.**

Arriving back in Minnesota later that evening around 6:00 p.m., **we** (he and Caughill) **shared the experiences of the day** with Thelma **and rested the matter with the Lord. After a good night's sleep, morning came with peace and confidence that He would prove Himself faithful. It was not but a short time when we were startled with a telephone call from the man in charge of loans at the bank in Watertown,** Mr. Wagner, a Lutheran man. **He informed us that they had just arranged a $70,000 loan for us to be used for the down payment. Our question to him was, "Whatever happened? We met with you just yesterday and were told that no funds would be available." He explained that the bank president,** Mr. Gerald Flynn, **had called an early morning meeting of the board and that theirs was a unanimous vote to give us the $70,000 loan. We would have been happy with $5,000, but, no doubt, they decided that we ought to have at least one-third of the asking price which was $225,000. "Praise the Lord!" was our response with rejoicing.**

"What was that?" he asked. Perhaps he did not really understand that this was answered prayer. Question: When is a $70,000 loan not an answer to prayer? Answer: When God wants to provide in another way.

Many Scripture promises came to mind, but Philippians 4:19 stood out above all others—"But my God

shall supply all your need according to His riches in glory by Christ Jesus."

Immediate contact was made with the Provincial General relating to him the good news. Whether this "contact" was in person or by phone is somewhat open to question. Dr. Cedarholm did recount that he was so excited at this news that he drove 300 miles—all the way to Watertown, picked up the check, and went straight on to South Bend, without even ascertaining if the Provincial General would be available to see him. **He appeared happy to hear of the provision, but offered still another suggestion. "We have also had another meeting since you were here." (Now, what would he say? Had there been a turn of events? Had someone else made an offer and would we not be able to secure the property? We wondered.) "We have decided that since you do not have any money"** (as though we didn't already know that!) **"you will not need a down payment."** Dr. Cedarholm said of this news, "I thought, all that trouble we'd gone to, to get that $70,000 and then they didn't want it!"

We were stunned. For a moment we could say nothing. Then came to mind, Proverbs 21:1—"The king's heart is in the hand of the Lord." This was not just a pious platitude.

He continued—"Something else we will do for you, since you do not have any money. We have also decided to offer you the property for $150,000 instead of the $225,000 which we originally asked." Just keep in mind that this is the seller speaking! **"Furthermore, you may have ten years to make the payments—at 5% interest. And ... your first payment will not be due until you have occupied the campus for the first year."** Cedarholm indicated at other times that they also did not have to pay interest the first year, an additional savings of $7,500.

We could hardly believe what we had heard. We thanked him as graciously as we knew how. Who but the Lord could lay upon the heart of a man such a set of workable conditions as these! This is, of course, the most

miraculous element of all. It would have been understand-
able for Don Bailer to make his generous offer if the
Cedarholms failed to secure financing or support. But to turn
down ready money, knowing the Cedarholms did have
backing (which in itself could be taken as providential), was
quite another thing. The Lord was certainly making a clear
statement that being a wholly dependent-on-the-Lord
independent Baptist was a marvelous way to live.

**When the $70,000 loan from the Watertown bank was
canceled, the president said, "I can't understand this. I
have done business with these people for twenty years,
and I know they are shrewd bargainers, but what
mystifies me is that Roman Catholics would do that for
Baptists!"** The number of years varies from rendition to
rendition of this story. Flynn had twenty, twenty-two or
twenty-five years of dealing with the shrewd bargainers! But
why would the Catholics do that for Baptists? At this point,
Cedarholm was convinced that it was, "A SIGN TO ME THAT
GOD WANTS US TO HAVE THAT PLACE." The Lord was
giving the Cedarholms, and the entire Maranatha family, a
spiritual stake on which to pin future trust in Him.

**Our response was, "This is proof that the Lord
controls the affairs of men, whoever they are, and that
He wants us to have that campus for the training of
young people for His service."** The next Tuesday, May 28,
the FBF regional meeting was being held at Calvary Baptist
Church in Normal, Illinois. Dr. Arno Q Weniger, Jr. was the
host pastor. The first official announcement of the new
college was made at this meeting for pastors from throughout
the Midwest.[11] Two days later, on Thursday, May 30, the
Cedarholms moved to Watertown, just as Pillsbury began its
Commencement weekend. They were pulling a U-Haul trailer
with some of their more precious goods to Watertown. A car
passed them and then struck their front left fender, spinning
the car and trailer around so that they were facing back
toward Minnesota. Satan was determined to stop this new
venture, but the Cedarholms continued on. Though no

[11] "New Baptist Bible College Launched," News Release, June
1968.

contracts had been signed, no faculty hired, and no students enrolled, the Cedarholms and many others certainly sensed the leading of the Lord and felt confident in relocating to Watertown. Their rented white house on West Street became the first Admissions Office for the new school. Mrs. Cedarholm, Louise Sincock (now Louise Budahl), Gloria Dreyer (now Gloria Taylor), and Shirley Sims set up their typewriters on the dining room table and the Admissions, Recruitment, Academic, Summer Extension, and Executive Offices were up and running.

On Saturday, June 1, 1968, Ed Caughill, in his new position as Business Manager for Maranatha Baptist Bible College and working at that time from Owatonna, Minnesota, sent the Brothers a check for $5,000 earnest money; he told the brothers that the rest of the "downpayment" would be paid at the signing of the contracts.

The next Saturday, June 8, 1968, Don Bailer acknowledged the receipt of the money and wrote that the land contracts should be to them later that week.

On June 10, the first news release about the college was ready for distribution. It listed the already confirmed faculty of the new school as the Cedarholms, Dr. and Mrs. Richard Weeks, Rev. Edward Caughill, Mr. and Mrs. Ray Fulayter, Mr. Donald Scovill, Miss Louise Sincock, Mrs. Edythe Gould, and Miss Mary Donovan, "with announcements of new appointments to be made shortly." Dr. Cedarholm's letter that accompanied the release opened with Ephesians 1:12, "To the Praise of His Glory," and was prepared on college letterhead. Most of these faculty were coming from Pillsbury. Why? Though Caughill could not speak for everyone, he said, "I was for starting a new school and building it on the philosophy we believed in, though I didn't know how we could do it without any money." And what was that philosophy? "We wanted to train the Lord's workers, and to do that we had to build character as well as knowledge. We were afraid that the change of discipline would get away from strengthening character. Then, what would be the next step? We felt it rather deeply, felt some things just weren't right."

Among the numerous visitors who made their way to Watertown were a faithful pastor, former college teacher, missionary church planter, and renown violinist, Edward Burckart and his wife, Dorothy. Following an overnight visit with the Cedarholms and a casual survey of the housing situation in Watertown, they wrote back within three days saying, "Brother Cedarholm, we feel strangely moved to come to join you in this venture of faith." These were precious words. They bought a house that was not for sale (their own Maranatha miracle) and joined the Cedarholms in their new venture.

Wednesday, June 26, 1968, marked the official incorporation of the College, a process that involved several trips to the Madison capital and the Jefferson County Courthouse. This process was greatly facilitated when Cedarholm arrived in Madison, because he found that one of the people he needed to see was Bob McCarley, a man he had met 25 years earlier when they were starting a new church in Madison. McCarley, in turn, personally introduced Cedarholm to Secretary of State Robert Zimmerman, the man in charge of charters. Perhaps most amazing phenomenon to anyone living in the bureaucracy of the twenty-first century: his trip to the Industrial Commission, forerunner of the Building Commission, took only twenty minutes to gain approval to operate the institution. Since it was being used for the same educational purpose, no new requirements were imposed.

On June 28, Dr. Cedarholm himself wrote to Don Bailer, sending along two checks, one for $5,500 for the rest of the "downpayment" and another for $2,849 for items purchased from the military academy.

All of these deliberations had taken place during the month of June. The military academy had been making preparations for departure on June 30, 1968, and we were trusting the Lord for a July 1 occupancy. Day by day many gifts had accumulated until, on the very last day of June, two large gifts, one $5,000 gift from a farmer that the Cedarholms had not seen for ten or twelve years and a second gift of $5,500 **completed the amount needed to pay the realtor's fees which amounted to $4,500, and we stepped over the threshold into the "soon-to-become-a-**

college" Old Main. References to these early payments are confusing. What the Cedarholms were calling the "downpayment" was apparently the realtor's fee which the Brothers of the Holy Cross had to pay, regardless of how generous they had been in other regards to the Cedarholms. The official sale price listed with the college records is $160,500; this figure includes $150,000 for the buildings and property and $10,500 for the realtor's fees. Cedarholm mentioned years later that when he told the Catholics about the gifts, Bailer said, "Instead of paying us $15,000, take the $10,500 off and pay us the difference ($4,500). If you were figuring [your] own terms, you would never have thought of all those things." Maranatha did have to assure that adequate fire and boiler insurance were carried on the property in both Maranatha's and the Brothers' names. The Brothers had to assure their investment would be protected in case of fire. Later in the school year, in April 1969, when Dr. Cedarholm needed permission to build on some of the land, Bailer wrote to Maranatha saying that the Brothers had, up to that point, cleared only $4,500 after the realtor's fees were paid.

By the first week of July, over 150 applications had been submitted. On July 5, Mrs. Cedarholm completed the college hymn.

Caughill continued to be particularly concerned about the $1,500 (some accounts say $1,200) premium payment for the building insurance. Mrs. Cedarholm was the story lady for Vacation Bible School at First Baptist Church, Hammond, Indiana, for the week of July 22–26. In addition, Jack Hyles asked Dr. Cedarholm to join her in Hammond and present his new venture of faith to the church during the Wednesday evening prayer meeting on July 24th. Hyles took an exit offering (ushers at the doors after the service, rather than "passing the plates"), and the offering received was the $1,500 (or $1,200) needed to cover the payment.

On that first day of occupancy, July 1, **the building had the appearance of a huge skeleton. Every room had been cleared of its contents. Now the floors shone with fresh coats of varnish; the brightly painted walls reflected the glory of the Lord. Halls rejoiced with quickly moving** footsteps and shouts of joy filled the air. Shrubbery and trees seemed to bow in awe before our great God that day.

As trustees of the seemingly insurmountable task which lay before us, we could not but cry out, Lord, help us! A COLLEGE? About to open a COLLEGE? There are only sixty days before opening of classes! How, Lord? How can we possibly get everything together and ready? Where will we find instructors in such a short time? Where students? A library—for a COLLEGE? Where all the furnishings for classrooms ... and dormitories? Where textbooks, food, cooks, workers ... and no funds to support all these?

The large empty building, the growing stack of applications on the kitchen table, and the sending of two checks to the Brothers brought the enormity of what they had undertaken into clear focus. This was the moment of reality. Dr. Cedarholm was sitting on an apple crate in an office that had only a crucifix hanging on the wall! At that point, Mrs. Cedarholm walked in and said, "Now don't you go and die and leave me with this place!"

The moment also led to an intimate confrontation with God. "Who ever heard of hiring teachers in the summer? I said, Lord, this college was your idea.... You got us into this mess and now, you're going to have to take care of it. I'm not going to be stubborn, but I'm not going to make any phone calls, I'm not going to write any letters, I'm not going to see any prospective teachers. I'm just going to sit in the bleachers, pray, and watch you work."

Within the days remaining, some fifty-four teachers and staff applied for various positions with the new college. These were not novices! Many had been teaching for some ten to fifteen years; some of these had added years of pastoral experience, so they were ready. How had they even heard of the new Bible college? How could they be certain that such a new work could adequately support them and their families? There had been no advertising; in fact, the very first advertising appeared in the *Sword of the Lord* on September 18—almost **two weeks after classes had begun.** No official *printed* advertisement appeared until after the school began, but there was quite a bit of promotion of the school. Don Scovill, his wife Evelyne, and Robert VanMaasdam became the original summer team, *The Messengers*. During the entire month of July, they were in services in Illinois, Indiana, Michigan, and Wisconsin. The Cedarholms were in California at the Lucerne Conference Center the first week in July and nine other churches throughout the rest of the month. The Cedarholms, Mr. Caughill, the Burckarts, Dr. Weeks, and even Ron Hodges, the one-man maintenance department, were all in Sunday services in various churches during July, introducing the college. The first newspaper article about the school appeared on July 25, 1968, in the *Watertown Daily Times*.

After July 1, a constant stream of visitors came to the campus; over 500 people signed the guest books before school started (the first was just a spiral school notebook, until a more official one was obtained). They came from Texas, Colorado, Nebraska, North Carolina, Tennessee, Brazil, and, yes, even Minnesota to see the school. This was far more than just the expected states of Wisconsin and Illinois. They picked up applications, submitted applications, left gifts, and helped with whatever was being done at the moment.

Five families and two single women from Pillsbury needed to move their belongings to Maranatha during June and July. They combined resources, purchased an old truck, and operated a moving ministry. Since many of those had summer school commitments at Pillsbury, and because of the tense situation on the Owatonna campus, the moving was done at night. When they were finished storing all their items in the Main Building, the college bought the truck, and it became the first in a long line of Maranatha fleet vehicles.

Sacrificial and trusting souls joined hands. **With unfeigned faith and complete trust in the Lord, they set out, as it were across a vast sea into the unknown. Some lost friends of many years, others laid aside monetary gain and forfeited promise of prosperity. By the time classes were scheduled to begin, every field of instruction was covered, and some twenty-seven**

teachers comprised the faculty. By the time the next "News from Maranatha" flyer was available on August 1, 1968, the Burckarts, the Braggs, Lorna Prang, Jean Zimmerman, Judith Hornbacker, the Burkes, Dr. Joseph Huebscher, Pastor Schafer, and Pastor Sanders rounded out the first year's faculty.

The entire month of August became a literal moving miracle as students from all across the country called and wrote, indicating their intention to come to school. Some students completed their applications after arriving on campus. **Surprisingly, these represented all classifications of college life—freshmen** (81), **sophomores** (44), **juniors** (53) **and seniors** (25), of whom 13 would graduate. **Who had ever heard of upper classmen wanting to transfer from a well-established institution to a fledgling school? How could they be sure that there would be courses enough to guarantee completion of education?** There was some flexibility that year. Colleen O'Neil (now Colleen Oats), who was in the first graduating class in May of 1969, never did take Baptist History, a course required at both Pillsbury and Maranatha! **Would the education received be quality education? Would the degree received be valid? Prospective students and parents came to inquire about possibilities of being enrolled. Pastors came to investigate, some to question. Some doubted that it would actually become a reality. Miracle of miracles— 211 students trusted the Lord and stepped out on faith to become a part of that first student body. Halls began to bustle with young life. Early arrivals assisted in setting everything in order. The various rooms began to take on a new perspective with the addition of desks and chairs, business machines and musical instruments, athletic and maintenance equipment, kitchen and dining room supplies. All previous classroom equipment and supplies had been moved by the previous owners to their new location in Indiana. Now, since we had been left with nothing, they felt obligated to return much of it and so, with several truck loads, they returned the very sizes and types of study chair and desks that were needed by us. In fact, so much**

was returned, that it was necessary for us to have an auction to clear the halls. Caughill explained this unusual situation: the military academy was for 5th–8th grade boys, so the Brothers moved out all of the small desks, chairs, tables, and other furnishings necessary to continue their school in Indiana. Obviously such equipment was not the proper size for adult students. What the Brothers sent back to Maranatha were adult size furnishings that the college could really use.

Many were the hearts of those whom the Lord touched to help us in those days. There was the father of a prospective faculty member, Sherrill Fulayter, Spanish teacher until 1984, **who decided to make a visit to Watertown to investigate the situation in which his daughter and son-in-law had become involved. He was a steam engineer at the University of Minnesota-Duluth, who promptly set about to check out all the plumbing and heating system. The very next day after he had cleaned all the boilers, the state inspector made a casual visit to campus, checked them all over and said, "Fire them up, they're all ready to go."** Caughill also related an additional blessing with Maranatha's heating system. Its low-pressure boilers could be maintained and supervised with student workers. Had the equipment been a high pressure system, by law the school would have been required to hire full-time engineers to rotate eight hour shifts, twenty-four hours a day, with one man always in reserve. Those boilers did not need to be replaced until the summer of 2007.

A local manufacturer (Fiberesin of Oconomowoc, Wisconsin, whose factory manager was a Christian who had taught in a Christian school) **of fiberglass chairs called one day to ask whether we needed chairs of the sort that they made. He would give us 200, he said, since he was making a change in the style of the chair. (We had trusted the Lord for a beginning student body of 200.)**

The owner of a chain of fast-food restaurants in Minnesota (a Mr. Osmond of Country Kitchen restaurants) **called to ask whether we had dishes for our dining service. We answered, "No, but we've trusted the Lord to send us 200 students in September."**

"Well," said he, "that's interesting—I've just put in an order for new dishes and I've ordered 200 too many! I'll have them sent down to you." So, down they came—200 of everything—plates, cups, soup bowls, salad bowls, serving bowls and platters—all we would ever need! Among the items they did need to purchase were tables for the dining hall. Delivery was promised well in advance of the start of school, but the tables were nowhere to be seen, in spite of promises that they were coming. The truck finally arrived just before the first meal of the college was to be served, Tuesday, September 10, 1968, at 5:30 p.m. The delivery men unloaded the truck, men students assembled the tables, women students washed everything down and set the tables, and everything was done in time to sit down together for the first family-style dinner served at Maranatha. The college also had to purchase new bunks for the dormitories. The new men students that fall had to literally make their own beds!

One day a truck came up the back drive and began to unload some lawn mowers. We stepped out to investigate and to notify the driver that there must be some mistake for we had not ordered any lawn mowers. "Well," said he, "my boss told me that there was a new college starting over here and that we should bring these mowers to keep the grounds in order." Riding lawn mowers ... and with four-foot blades! How we needed them, especially with the sixteen acres of grass which, if left to itself, would be a hay field in no time at all. (Rains in Wisconsin are so plentiful that the grass is green and growing all summer and late into the fall.) Shortly thereafter, a sixteen year old high school boy gave several weeks to riding the newly acquired lawn mower over the vast expanse of lawn. He wanted to be a help, and his assistance in the maintenance was greatly appreciated.

A nearby furniture manufacturer offered remnants of beautiful upholstery material for the costume department. One remnant measured nine yards in length—hardly a remnant! Mrs. Gale Schaefer, pastor's wife from Calvary Baptist Church in Jefferson, recalled that her church ladies became regular volunteers, cleaning, and upholstering furniture for the first Dating Parlor.

The walls of the beautiful mahogany paneled chapel had been left greatly marred when the large statues had been removed. A study of the gilded walls across the front revealed the application of not gold paint but gold leaf. This, we knew, we could never provide nor repair and so, we decided to purchase good quality textured red and gold velvet-flocked **wall paper and apply to cover the scars. The wife of a local optometrist, an interior decorator in her own right, and her mother, offered to come to do the decorating.** "Dr. Cedarholm drove to Chicago early in the morning to pick up the red and gold flocked paper," recalled Mrs. Jane Smebak, the interior decorator. "When he returned, we started in. All we had was one old rickety ladder. Dr. Cedarholm helped by praying that the ladder wouldn't collapse. I don't even remember what we used to lay the paper on to paste it. All I remember is Dr. Cedarholm sitting off there on the side, praying that the paper would stay up and the ladder wouldn't collapse!"

Contributions of necessary items arrived from everywhere almost daily—furniture for the reception room and offices, linen for the dormitories and guest rooms, china and glassware for the dining room, pots, pans, and utensils for the kitchen. One elderly lady gave her wedding silver for the president's dining room. A pastor's daughter brought a waste basket for the president's office. Parents of an entering student loaned their lovely piano for the chapel. Later, parents of a young man brought their many years' of saving quarters, enough to complete payment on a nice organ. Even Maranatha's unusual Percussion Ensemble got its start in those first days with the donation of a Deagan marimba. The Cedarholms had purchased a Deagan vibraharp in 1949 when they first moved to Chicago and started in the CBA work.

Staples of all sorts came from gardens everywhere—vegetables by the box, bushel and truck load, meats, preserves, baked goods. We were most grateful for the fine cold storage and freezer facilities in

the kitchen. Charlotte recalled that all through that first summer, they never knew how many people would be joining them for supper, but that without fail whenever they came home from the college, there would be bags of groceries and fresh vegetables waiting for them on the porch. She said that they never found out who brought the food.

Many were the hands that contributed to carrying, placing and arranging the various items where they belonged. Mrs. Senn was cleaning what became the Presidential Dining Room and commented, "You could tell a bunch of men lived here!" as she wiped the tops of the doors and windows.

Of great concern to all of us was the matter of the library. What would we do to provide enough resources for a COLLEGE library? We prayed and waited. Perhaps, we thought, we could acquire about a thousand books, in the main, reference materials, and that would at least get us started. We prayed and waited to see what the Lord would do. Faculty members agreed to put their books on loan. We brought a new Bible from our personal library to make the first entry in the accession record. Unfortunately, the handwritten accession books have long since been replaced and no one can locate on the shelves the original Bible. **After all, this was to be a BIBLE college! A young man from LaCrosse, Wisconsin, brought over the first set of encyclopedias. The wife of a local mortician gave us a good supply of missionary books which she had already read and now believed they might be a blessing to the students. Dr. Richard Weeks provided some 3,000 volumes, many of which were choice accounts of great missionaries, preachers, and evangelists. There were also books on Baptist history and polity, which had been purchased abroad and which are no longer available. Dr. Arno Q. Weniger, Sr., then president of the San Francisco Baptist Seminary, sought out discarded volumes from public libraries in his area, had them boxed up by the seminarians and shipped to the college.** They sent 1,000 books to the new library even before the July 1 occupation date. **Pastors and missionaries, evangelists and Bible teachers, pastors' widows, Christian publishing houses,**

seminaries and colleges, boys and girls—all these provided so many books that the second-floor hall was literally filled, and before we were able to arrange for adequate shelving in the small room which was intended to be the library (the present Admissions Office), it was necessary to move over 2,000 books to a more suitable location, even before the opening of classes. Mrs. Edythe Gould, our first Dean of Women, assisted by incoming students, accessioned all the earliest arrivals. Records at the end of the first semester indicated that some 6,000 volumes had been cataloged, and Mrs. Cedarholm's goal had grown tenfold, from a meek desire to perhaps gather 1,000 volumes for the start of the school, to a confident hope to see 10,000 volumes by the end of the school year.

And so it went, on and on, as we prayed and the Lord moved upon the hearts of men. Soon all that we needed the Lord had provided. Every day we praised Him and were humbled by His gracious and timely provision.

"TO GOD BE THE GLORY, GREAT THINGS HE HATH DONE"

Much about the new Maranatha followed the Pillsbury template. Student life included barracks dorms, traveling choirs, rake days, intercollegiate sports, plays, recitals, and discipline meted out by committee. Maranatha's first Madrigal tour to California followed an old Pillsbury itinerary. Mrs. Cedarholm had even written the music for the Pillsbury College Hymn years before she set about to write the Maranatha school song.

The following pages are the original script for the Maranatha Hymn. There is no explanation of the date at the top of the first page. If you check the bottom of the last of these pages, you will see that the Maranatha Hymn was dated on July 5, 1968. The Maranatha Hymn was the first in a series of songs from the book of Ephesians. The Hymn is from Ephesians 1:12. The following song, "Far Above All," is from Ephesians 1:17-21. Mrs. Cedarholm later wrote "Rich in Mercy," which is from Ephesians 2.

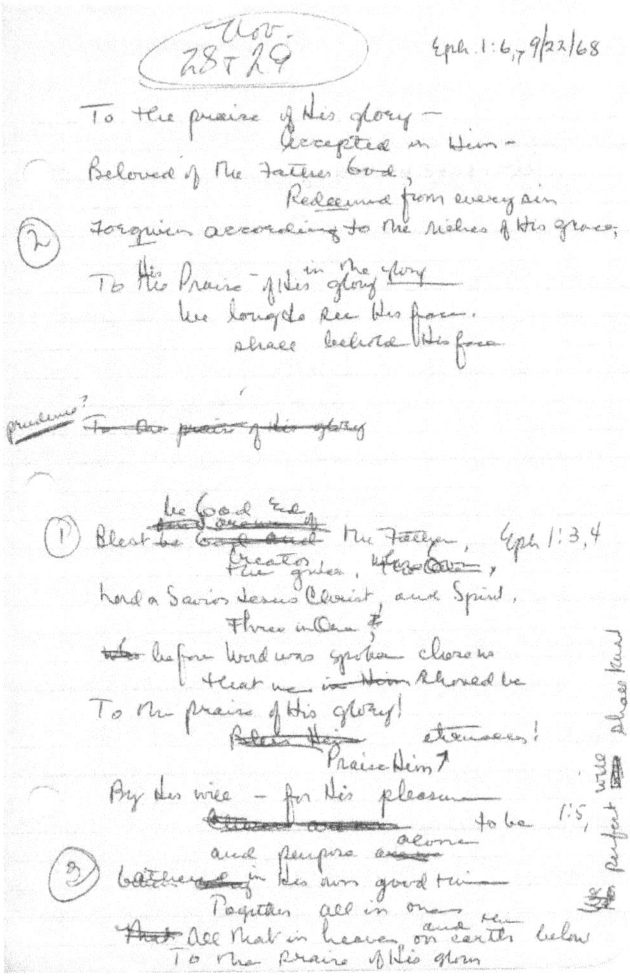

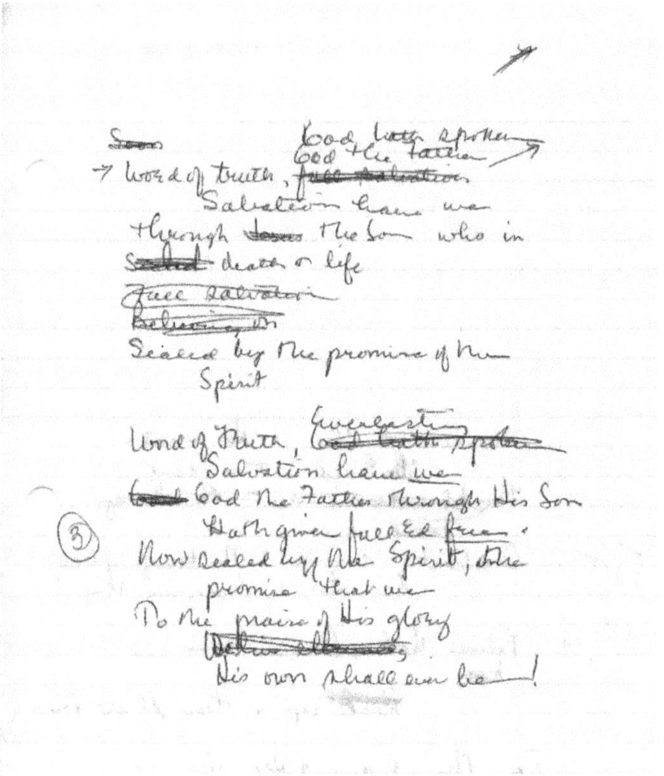

[Handwritten manuscript draft — partially legible]

Word of truth, ~~full salvation~~
God hath spoken
God the Father
Salvation have we
through ~~Jesus~~ the Son who in
~~sealed~~ death or life
~~Full salvation~~
~~Believing in~~
Sealed by the promise of the
     Spirit

Word of Truth, ~~God hath spoken~~ Everlasting
     Salvation have we
③ ~~God~~ God the Father through His Son
     Hath given full ~~Ed~~ free.
Now sealed by the Spirit, the
     promise that we
To the praise of His glory
     ~~Who will alway,~~
     His own shall ever be!

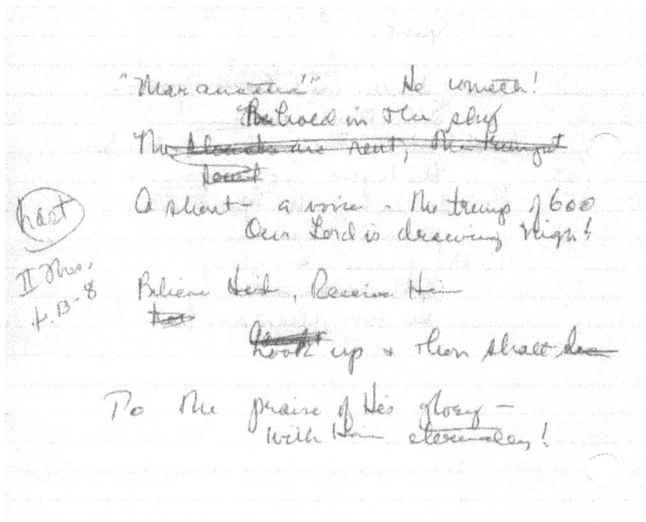

"Maranatha" ... He cometh!
     Behold in the sky
The ~~clouds are rent,~~ ~~the trumpet~~
     ~~loud~~
A shout — a voice — the trump of God
     Our Lord is drawing nigh!

(last)

II Thess,
4.B-8

Believe ~~not,~~ Receive Him
     ~~too~~
     ~~Look~~ up & then shall ~~be~~

To the praise of His glory —
     with ~~Him~~ eternally!

TO THE PRAISE OF THE GLORY
– Ephesians 1:12

Maranatha College Hymn

Words and Music by Thelma M. Cedarholm

1. Blest be God and the Fa - ther, Cre - a - tor, Whose Son,
2. To the praise of His glo - ry ac - cep - ted in Him
3. By His will for His plea - sure and pur - pose a - lone
4. Word of Truth, ev - er - last - ing sal - va - tion have we,
5. "Ma ran - a - tha" He com - eth! Be - hold, in the sky

Lord and Sa - viour, Je - sus Christ and Spir - it, Three in One, Be -
lov - ed of the Fath - er God), re - deemed from ev' - ry sin, For
gath - ered in his own good time to - geth - er, all in one
God the Fath - er through His Son pro - vid - ed full and free, And
SHOUT! a VOICE! the TRUMP OF GOD! Our Lord is draw - ing nigh! Be

fore word was spo - ken, chose us that we should be TO THE
giv - en ac - cord - ing to the rich - es of His grace TO THE
all - now in heav - en and on the earth be - low TO THE
sealed by the Spir - it, His prom - ise that we TO THE
lieve Him, re - ceive Him, look up and thou shalt be TO THE

PRAISE OF HIS GLO - RY! Praise Him e - ter - nal - ly!
PRAISE OF HIS GLO - RY, We soon be - hold His face.
PRAISE OF HIS GLO - RY shall see Him and Him know.
PRAISE OF HIS GLO - RY - His own shall ev - er be!
PRAISE OF HIS GLO - RY with Him e - ter - nal - ly!

Far Above All

Ephesians 2

Rich In Mercy

T.M. Cedarholm

1. Rich in mer - cy, God the Fa - ther
2. With great love and by His mer - cy,
3. Through the ag - es He shall ev - er
4. To good works by God cre - at - ed
5. Rec - on - ciled to God for - ev - er,
6. Rich in mer - cy, God the Fath - er

Spared not His be - lov - ed Son;
E'en when we were dead in sin,
Show the rich - es of His grace,
In Christ Je - sus now are we,
By the cross, for - giv - en, I
Rec - on - ciled my soul to Him.

From Heav'n's por - tals grace ex - ten - ded,
God with Christ hath quick - ened, raised us,
In His kind - ness through Christ Je - sus,
And or - dained that we should ev - er
Once far off, now no more strang - er
I am His and His for - ev - er.

Sought the sin - ner, vic - to - ry won.
Seat - ed us in Heav - en with Him.
Oh, what mer - cy! Oh, what Grace!
Walk and serve o - be - di - ent - ly.
By His grace am now made nigh.
Christ my Sav - ior dwell - eth with - in.

Dr. Cedarholm at a football game

It would be inaccurate, however, to assume that the Cedarholms only transferred a Pillsbury mindset to Maranatha because they had no other plan. The truth was that their already existing philosophy of Christian education, which was being fleshed out at Pillsbury, naturally followed them to Maranatha. That philosophy was the first of several legacies given to Maranatha by the Cedarholms.

Educational Philosophy. When asked, "What makes Maranatha unique?" the overwhelming response is: strong fine arts and athletics in a thorough-going Bible college, rounded out with a liberal arts platform that most Bible colleges either cannot or do not offer in a rigorous way. The Cedarholm philosophy was that of the well-rounded individual. The example of their own lives reflected their educational philosophy. They were refined in social graces and appreciated the finer things in life, so they expected the students to develop refinement and culture.

They were both physically active, vigorous, and disciplined, and they expected Christian men and women to be coordinated, healthy, active, and appreciative of the role of biblical sportsmanship in building Christian character.

They were knowledgeable and well trained in music and speech, so they recognized the level of training and skill Maranatha graduates would need to benefit any ministry in which they were involved. They wanted students who could teach or preach as a vocational ministry, but who could also skillfully prepare music and drama for their ministries.

Dr. Cedarholm attended two secular colleges, and Mrs. Cedarholm attended a religious school with a strong general education core. They both were capable of applying biblical thinking in the secular arena, and they expected nothing less from those they trained.

Confident that God could do anything, unhindered by human difficulties, the Cedarholms desired to inculcate their charges with this same unwavering trust in the Lord. They were totally consumed with the privilege of serving the Great God and wanted every student to embrace that same tireless and creative can-do spirit for the Lord's work.

Some likened the dual emphasis of music and sports to the individual interests of the Cedarholms: Mrs. Cedarholm's passion for music and Dr. Cedarholm's passion for athletics. This is not entirely accurate, however. Mrs. Cedarholm was a skilled athlete in her own right and taught physical education as well as music during her five years teaching high school. Dr. Cedarholm was an avid musician, using his trombone and his singing voice throughout his ministry. They viewed both pursuits as important in the well-rounded educational development of a Christian worker. There were opportunities in music and physical education for all from the very beginning. Participation in choir, band, soccer, intramural sports, basketball, and softball were all vigorously encouraged. Men's chorus and women's basketball both had their place. Attendance at virtually every musical and speech performance was mandatory.

This was the flavor of education Parker had set in motion at Pillsbury, and because it was so very much like the Cedarholms themselves, it was the direction they continued to develop during their Pillsbury years. It was certainly the flavor they wanted to instill on the Watertown campus. In the early years, all the pastoral students were in a preacher boys' choir, because every man going into a pastoral ministry needed at least a little music education. And every male student was in the preacher boys' classes for at least one year, because every man needed a ministry mindset. All the effort to produce full-blown dramatic productions from the very first semester (*The Merchant of Venice*), or to provide monthly Sunday afternoon Vespers, and occasional student or faculty recitals was not primarily to provide entertainment for students' free time or to garner publicity for a new school. The ambition was to infuse the richness of God into every fiber of every student He sent their way.

People-Centered. The Cedarholms were interested in people. They could never have survived the CBA years if they did not have a deep-seated love for the people to whom they ministered. At Pillsbury and Maranatha that same concern was directed toward the college students; in fact, many of those students were the children of pastors and church members they had been helping for years. For Mrs. Cedarholm there was a special bond with the students in Madrigal. Charlotte shared: "Madrigal was my mother's life, her absolute life. Every student that came through, there was family. The night she gave up Madrigal, she said, smiling and controlled to the audience, 'There are times in life when we must give up those things that mean the most to us. Tonight is that night for me.' Then she went home and sobbed on the sofa."[12]

The Cedarholms' personal concern extended to the faculty as well. A good example is when Mrs. Cedarholm was absolutely delighted to play the part of "secret messenger" with money designated for a faculty couple praying for funds for a missions trip. She wrote the source of the funds:

> By now I suppose you wonder why I have delayed so long to acknowledge receipt of that wonderful gift that you sent for Ed and Dorothy. Needless to say, I was thrilled when it came and immediately began to search out plans for the presentation so that it could be carefully covered.
> I went down to the bank to cash the check and secured ten brand new one hundred dollar bills. I put them in envelopes of various amounts—$200—$300—$500, addressed them in different ways on different kinds of paper and then over these past weeks have put

---

[12] Charlotte Cedarholm.

them in their post box without any identification.... The other day Dorothy said, "I really don't know how to say this, but I will have to tell you that I think now we have enough to cover the cost of our tickets to Hong Kong. I have always heard so many testimonies from the young people about these things, but I never supposed it would happen to us. Maybe you are responsible?! Anyway, if you are, I don't know how to take care of it. How do you do it?" I explained to her that on many occasions we receive gifts for students.... We usually suggest ... that they write a little thank you note and bring it to our office.... When we acknowledge the gift, we can send that little thank you along, and the donor will be pleased to know the gift has been received and appreciated.... I told her to pack lightly, save room for souvenirs. I know this will be a tremendous experience for them, and I am just thrilled to death that they can go.... I wish that I could crawl into the suitcase and come along. I know we could have a great time. I would let YOU take us up to the border instead of having to go with a party on a bus. I never did really get to see the border, because I was not able to walk those last blocks up the hill. But I was satisfied to be that close."[13]

The faculty members were Ed and Dorothy Burckart. The secret donor was Dorothy's sister, the Hong Kong missionary whom the Burckarts were planning to visit.

Tuition-Driven. Maranatha was an experiment of an independent Baptist school, free of outside control, and sustained only because people supported the philosophy, the man, and the product. The support came primarily in the form of students, not gifts or endowments, and so developed another legacy of the Cedarholm era: tuition-driven funding, or in layman's terms, living hand to mouth for not just the pioneer year, but for most of the school's existence.

Cedarholm was suspicious of big money ventures; he had seen their danger during his years with the CBA. He often shared his concerns,

> I believe one of the reasons the CBFMS and CBHMS are in such spiritual doldrums is the $1,200,000 [they

---

[13] Thelma Cedarholm, personal correspondence to a former Chinese missionary, April 22, 1982.

have invested] in the stock market. People and churches never gave this money for this purpose. This is open deception and misuse of funds. CBFMS says that it is good business. They say, "Why should we let this money, which is natural reserve for medical and other contingencies of the missionaries, sit in the bank at 5 and 6 percent? Why not put it in the stock market where we can get up to 25 percent?" We all agree that every missionary society has a right to have some reserves, but not a million and a quarter in the stock market!

CBFMS sent out a letter not long ago for $60,000 for the emergency in Congo. We all recognized the need, but why didn't they dip into the money in the stock market to pay for it? But no, they sent out an appeal to the churches and received more than the $60,000 and had more for the stock market. Next, CBFMS sent out an appeal for that academy over in Japan and asked for $50,000 for building. This is a worthy project. Why didn't they go into the million and a quarter in the stock market?

This money in the stock market was intended for missions! The appeal for the academy brought in more than the $50,000 so they had more to invest in the stock market! That's how uncritical organizations become when they become rich and no longer trust in the Lord! This is the very thing that happened to the Northern Baptist Convention. They finally had so much of their money invested in the stock market and business enterprises that they said to the churches, "We don't need your money nor your suggestions for reform——just quietly leave."

That's just exactly what happened in our own circle with the CBFMS and CBHMS. They are uncritical of their unscriptural practices.[14]

Cedarholm was wary of storing up this world's goods and losing that desperate need for God to supply. For most of the college's history, "contingency fund" was an empty blank on the ledger sheet. The administration plowed everything back into school, rather than try to develop contingency funds. Development at Maranatha has almost always meant procuring funds for specific projects, not building a major endowment.

---

[14] *Central Testimony*, 9.3 (November-December 1967), 3-4.

Buildings. Almost all of the fund-raising projects have involved building. The original facilities of Maranatha were ideally suited for a small college. The third floor had been set up by the Catholics as bedrooms for the priests with sinks in each room, and there were showers in the basement for the cadets. To be sure, the dining hall, chapel, gym, and auditorium were all undersized by today's standards, but they were already in place, well maintained, and ready for use. The larger versions would come as the Lord prospered. During the Sacred Heart years, the school was bursting at the seams with barely 100 students and rarely housed more than 50. The room plans that the Cedarholms sketched out were in constant flux as enrollment climbed. With Old Main filling both the classroom and housing needs for the students, the can-do spirit was put to the test from the very beginning. In every letter and every message, the Cedarholm call was, "We need to build before next fall." During the first ten years of the school, Cedarholm was regularly seeking funding, because something was always being constructed somewhere.

Board Influence. Not everything transferred from Pillsbury to Maranatha. Though it may have made little difference to the students, Maranatha was built on a very different organizational foundation than Pillsbury. Reacting to the strong board influence at Pillsbury, Cedarholm constructed a personally chosen board, comprised of pastors and lay friends from all across the nation. Though called the Board of Trustees, they did not run the college, but rather functioned more like a Board of Reference. Cedarholm did not regularly or consistently communicate with the Board throughout the year. The men were busy with their own ministries, and when they came to Watertown for the Board meetings, they came at their own expense. They met once a year, the afternoon of the day before commencement, and finished in time for dinner and the evening baccalaureate service. They voted to accept the administration's list of seniors waiting to graduate the next day and routinely voted to approve whatever decisions the administration had made during the previous school term. Official minutes for the meetings were perfunctory. Any discussion that occurred was normally about an idea for which Cedarholm needed some official approval; with minimal input the Board would routinely approve the plans. On rare occasions the minutes would identify suggestions given by the Board to the administration, such as when they wanted to see some way to pay wives for their work at the college,[15] or the time when, during a discussion of salaries, "The Board went on record that they were concerned, but willing to follow the administration's leading in this matter."[16]

Not only did the Maranatha Board function differently than the Pillsbury Board, they were a much broader body of men. Instead of limiting the Board of Trustees to men in state, Cedarholm did at Maranatha what he had been unable to do at Pillsbury; he brought in men of expertise and experience from across the country. The first Board of Trustees consisted of:

Dr. Roy Austin, California
Rev. Clinton Branine, Illinois
Rev. Donald Camp, Indiana
Rev. David Cummins, Michigan
Dr. Warren Dafoe, Indiana
Dr. M. James Hollowood, New York
Dr. Jack Hyles, Indiana
Rev. Joseph MacMullen, Michigan
Mr. John McLario, Attorney, Wisconsin
Dr. Edward Nelson, Colorado
Rev. Omer Norris, California
Rev. Wesley Potter, Illinois
Rev. Charles Sanders, Wisconsin
Rev. Gale Schafer, Wisconsin
Dr. Mitchell Seidler, Ohio
Dr. Wayne VanGelderen, Sr., Illinois
Dr. John Weidenaar, Wyoming

[15] Board of Trustees minutes, May 30, 1969.
[16] Board of Trustees minutes, June 1, 1973.

Rev. Arno Q. Weniger, Jr., Illinois

Dr. G. Archer Weniger, California

The Executive Committee, consisting of Cedarholm, Caughill, Weeks, Sanders from Calvary Baptist Church in Watertown, and Schafer from Calvary Baptist Church in Jefferson, made Board-level decisions that could not wait until the next Board meeting. These Executive Committee meetings were few and far between (an average of fewer than two officially called and documented meetings per year for fifteen years). Many unrecorded informal chats over lunch, phone calls, and visits at church must have been how a lot of school business was worked out. Then there was the "kitchen cabinet." The Cedarholms regularly ate their meals with the Caughills, the Weeks, and later the Hollowoods. More than one decision was hashed out at those meals.

With these loosely structured councils, Cedarholm had the forum he felt he needed to operate a college, a structure that allowed him to develop the programs he felt the college needed to grow and thrive. He built Maranatha on a concept of independence that gave him the freedom to discern in counsel with trusted friends what God did or did not want done. Both the strengths and weaknesses of that operational template would become part of the unfolding of Maranatha's development.

Theological Emphasis. Dr. Cedarholm had two primary emphases in his preaching and teaching: Baptist distinctiveness and the primacy of the local church. He would frequently declare at the beginning of a chapel session, "Let your Bible fall open to Matthew 16:18." As a pastor, church planter, and church encourager, he emphasized that the means to accomplish God's overall will in this age is primarily the local church.

This emphasis on the local church had been carefully expressed years before.[17] Cedarholm identified several key

---

[17] B. Myron Cedarholm, "The Conservative Baptist Association of America: Its Affiliated Churches, Its Mission," *National Voice of Conservative Baptists* (April 1953), 6-7.

characteristics of a New Testament church. First, a New Testament church is an independent church. The Apostles themselves treated each church as "independent bodies, having the rights of self-government, without subjection to any other authority." Even the apostles reported their activities to the local church and addressed their epistles to the churches. Second, the Apostles recognized the right of each church to "choose their own officers, to admit, discipline or exclude members, and to make their own policies under the leadership of the Holy Spirit and Word of God." Third, as the director of the CBA, Cedarholm noted that "Baptists have always recognized this fundamental right of the local church to determine its affiliations." He and other former NBC pastors were concerned with the "recurring tendency of ecclesiasticism to coerce and destroy the freedom of the local church." Finally, the result of his belief is that it makes "all outside bodies purely advisory in character and with no powers whatever over the local church."

Although it was probably not coined by Dr. Cedarholm, he did use the quip to great effect: "What would I be if I were not a Baptist?"[18] To which Cedarholm would respond, "Why I'd be ashamed of myself." This sentiment can be interpreted as uncharitable, sectarian, or even a bit arrogant. That was not Cedarholm's intent. For him it expressed a truth central to his life: Baptists have historically been the most accurate interpreters of New Testament ecclesiology, and thus other ecclesiologies to one extent or another are unfaithful to the Scriptures. Being Baptist was not, therefore, optional for him. He was wholeheartedly a Baptist by conviction.

When Dr. Richard Weeks came to Maranatha in its beginning and became the college's first teacher of Baptist history and polity and the first academic dean, he already had a strong Baptist pedigree. He had served as pastor in several Baptist churches in Illinois, and while pastoring in Oak Lawn, a suburb of Chicago, in 1965 he took a prominent part in the organization of the New Testament Association of

---

[18] This section was adapted from David Saxon, "Baptist by the Grace of God," unpublished.

Independent Baptist Churches. Just a year earlier, in an address at Camp Joy in southern Wisconsin, Weeks had affirmed the cruciality of a proper doctrine of the church:

> What is the most important doctrine facing us today in the struggle within Christianity? It is not the doctrine of the sinfulness of man. It is not the doctrine of the inspiration of the Bible or that of the deity of Christ. It is not doctrine of salvation by Christ or of His Second Coming. It is none of these. It is the doctrine of ecclesiology, or the doctrine of the church, that is so tremendously at issue today.[19]

To express the centrality of Baptist ecclesiology in the ethos of Maranatha, the curriculum called for every student to take two courses, Baptist History and Baptist Polity. These courses were later combined into a single course, "Baptist Heritage." The word *heritage* in this title spoke to two emphases: first, the course surveyed Baptist history, but it also summarized Baptist theology, and the historical sections very much served the purpose of illustrating and advocating for Baptist polity; second, the word emphasized the historic continuity that Baptists have—their heritage—to which the rising generations should be loyal.

In order to inculcate Baptist ecclesiology effectively, Dr. Weeks departed from the historic approach of expressing the Baptist distinctives by using *Baptist* or *Baptists* as an acrostic. Instead, after an intensive study of various lists of distinctives throughout Baptist history, Weeks designed a new acrostic that would express the distinctives in a more logical order than is possible in the more traditional

---

[19] Address given at the Labor Day Weekend Family Bible Conference, Camp Joy, Whitewater, Wisconsin, September 5, 1964. Originally published by the Conservative Baptist Fellowship, now the Fundamental Baptist Fellowship International.

approach. The acrostic—which is now ingrained in several thousand Maranatha graduates—is BRAPSIS$_2$:[20]

> B ible the sole authority of faith and practice
> R egenerated and immersed church membership
> A utonomy of the local church
> P riesthood of the believer
> S oul liberty
> I mmersion and the Lord's Supper, the only two New Testament ordinances
> S eparation of church and state
> S eparation ethically and ecclesiastically

Why was it so important to Weeks and Cedarholm to instill Baptist ecclesiology in the Maranatha students? Maranatha emerged from the battles with New Evangelicalism that shaped the Fundamentalist movement in the 1950s and 60s. One of the points of division in those battles related to divergent views of the "ecumenical evangelism" being practiced by Billy Graham and others. Fundamentalists opposed Graham's approach, which involved extensive cooperation with gospel-deniers, and the New Evangelicals endorsed it. Of course, fundamentalism was and had always been transdenominational, and the leading fundamentalist institution at the time was Bob Jones University, a nondenominational school. Weeks was convinced, however, that the most effective response to evangelical ecumenism was an emphasis on the local church, its autonomy, and its responsibility to be loyal to Christ and Christ alone.

> The first avenue of emphasis [in opposing evangelical ecumenism] ought to be a reassertion of the New Testament as the authoritative source for church doctrine and practice, without being proudly exclusivistic.... It is really only those who are Baptists by name or by teaching

---

[20] See https://www.mbu.edu/seminary/journal/maranatha-is-baptist/ for a discussion of the meaning and significance of BRAPSIS$_2$.

and practice, who can challenge Christendom to a complete New Testament pattern of correct church doctrine.[21]

So, for Weeks and Cedarholm, being Baptist was integral to how they practiced their fundamentalism.[22] The gospel is best defended when the local church has primacy. When churches give up their sovereignty and amalgamate with doctrinally unsound ministries for the purpose of evangelism, ironically the pure gospel becomes a casualty.

What would Cedarholm be if he were not Baptist, in practice if not in name? He would have seen himself as unfaithful to the New Testament.

Because of his strong emphasis on being a Baptist, he was sometimes accused of being a Landmarker.[23] He repudiated this charge in an article in the *Maranatha Messenger*.

Landmarkism

Because of Maranatha's biblical emphasis on the local church, the necessity of establishing new churches and the importance of pastor-led rather than board-controlled churches, some have labeled Maranatha as a

---

[21] Ibid.

[22] Non-Baptistic fundamentalists have also stood against ecumenical evangelism and the encroachments of liberalism, but the primacy of the local church is rarely an emphasis in these circles. And in the past decades, those non-Baptistic fundamentalists have shrunk dramatically in number and influence. Cedarholm's concerns with the CBA were reflected later when the CBA changed its name to CBAmerica, the CBFMS changed its name to CBInternational and then WorldVenture, and the CBHMS changed its name to Mission to The Americas and then to Missions Door. This move away from "Baptist" organizations was a disappointment to Cedarholm and others like him, but not unexpected. The soft core did not appreciate the emphasis the hard core laid on being Baptist.

[23] See Fred Moritz, "The Landmark Controversy: A Study in Baptist History and Polity," *Maranatha Baptist Theological Journal* 2.1 (Spring 2012), 3–28, for an evaluation of Landmarkism.

"landmark" school. This, of course, is absolutely without foundation.

A few words are in order on this subject—

We recognize that there are various theological positions among the Landmarkers, however, there are some views generally held by all. *First*: Some hold that only Baptists comprise the Bride of Christ. WE REJECT THIS. WE BELIEVE that ALL believers, regardless of their denominational affiliation or preference, will be raptured before the tribulation when the Lord appears in the air. *Second*: Some believe that Baptists will be closest to the Lord at the Marriage Supper of the Lamb. WE BELIEVE that when we stand before the Lord, all rewards will be given on the basis of obedience, NOT denomination. *Third*: Some hold that Baptist churches are not valid churches unless they are mothered by a Baptist church whose succession can be traced to the first church in Jerusalem. WE BELIEVE that the Bible teaches that a church does not necessarily have to be mothered by any church. A group of New Testament believers may meet to organize a New Testament church. A church does not need to prove historic succession. What IS important is to follow and practice the Bible. *Fourth*: Some hold that immersion is not valid unless the administrator and church are in historic succession to the church at Jerusalem. WE BELIEVE that immersion is not to be equated with historic succession but that it is to be administered by a church that believes and practices the Bible. *Fifth*: Landmarkers do not generally take a stand on personal separation. Many of their leaders and pastors use tobacco openly. Many are active members of secret societies. WE BELIEVE that such practices are forbidden by the Bible

More could be said, but *Landmarkism is in no way taught at Maranatha.*

We do not deny that there are great preachers, fine soul-winners and great church builders among the Landmarkers, many of whom we know personally. Some have made great contributions in the field of Baptist history. But, THERE ARE NO LANDMARKERS AT MARANATHA. We are simple old-fashioned fundamental, soul-winning, church-planting, missionary-minded, local church, anti-ecumenical, anti new-evangelical Baptists who take the Bible as our only authority for faith and practice; who believe that we ought to love the brethren and hate the devil, stand for all that God is for and against all that God is against, oppose all deviation from the Bible and all forms of compromise, educate our children and young people in Christian schools and fundamental colleges, be at peace among ourselves, live godly and holy lives by God's grace, do all we can to keep our country free, vote in all elections for only those candidates who uphold biblical principles of government and keep busy preaching and practicing the Word of God!

Dr. B. Myron Cedarholm[24]

Dr. Cedarholm was an evangelist. His work as General Director of the CBA included significant evangelistic work. He was an ardent fundamentalist and separatist. He was part of the FBF. He was involved in the start of the CBA as the fundamentalist reaction to the NBC. He was engaged in the beginning of the NTA as one of the fundamentalist reactions to drift in the Conservative Baptist organizations. These characteristics were reflected in the Purpose Statement for Maranatha Baptist Bible College, adopted by the Board of Trustees at its first meeting on September 14, 1968.

> The purpose of Maranatha Baptist Bible College is and always shall be to train students for the Christian, gospel ministry at home and abroad in the historic, Baptistic, fundamental position and distinctives of the Bible—giving total loyalty to the Word of God and preeminence of the Lord Jesus Christ, opposing and combating any and all forms of modernism, liberalism, inclusivism, new evangelicalism, ecumenicalism, neo-orthodoxy, compromise, atheism, agnosticism, paganism, evolution and so-called scientific adulteration of the Word of God.[25]

Cedarholm was well known for his "10-point sermons." These were often written on whatever he had on hand —envelopes, napkins, the back of letters, etc. His rapid-fire

---

[24] B. Myron Cedarholm, "Landmarkism," *Maranatha Messenger* 9 (June 1977), 6.

[25] *Maranatha Memos* 1.3 (October 1968), 1. The *Maranatha Memos* became the *Maranatha Messenger* in 1969.

preaching allowed him to say far more in a sermon than the average preacher. His favorite topics included "Why I am a Baptist," "Why Go to Bible College," "Why Send your Children to a Christian School," and more. These sermons were not exegetical gems, but they were focused and to the point.

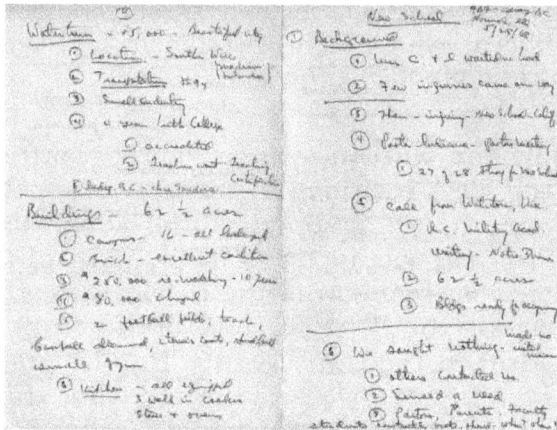

Growth. Cedarholm was eager to grow the curriculum. He was the product of a major university, and while Maranatha was called a "Bible College," it had a stronger general education curriculum and broader academic offerings than those found at a typical Bible College. The school opened with Bible, Church Ministries, Christian Education, Education, Missions, and Pastoral Studies majors. During Cedarholm's fifteen years as President, he added the Business and Nursing programs.

In 1970, Bob Jones University bestowed upon Dr. Cedarholm an honorary Doctor of Humanities degree. That same year, Maranatha began the Maranatha Baptist Graduate School of Theology, offering a Master of Arts degree. In 1972, the Graduate School added the Master of Divinity.

Dr. Cedarholm's concern for young people and the inability of Calvary Baptist Church, Watertown, to add a high school to their Christian School, led him to begin Maranatha Baptist Academy, grades 9–12, in the fall of 1973. Dr. Cedarholm's vision for Christian education was timely—the Academy enrolled 107 students that fall.

Mentoring. Dr. Cedarholm was not a "mentor" in the current use of the term, but he was very interested in bringing young men into leadership roles. In the 1969–1970 school year, one of the faculty members had to leave because of some personal problems. His classes were divided among various other faculty who could carry that extra load, but there was no one available to teach this man's first-year Greek class. Cedarholm turned to a twenty-one-year-old college senior to teach that class. In the fall of 1973, Cedarholm turned to this same young man to oversee the day-to-day operations of the newly opened Academy. This confidence in the younger generation could be repeated over and over. A complaint often raised today against older fundamentalists is that they do not trust the younger ones and therefore keep them out of leadership positions. This was not a problem with Cedarholm. He was eager to bring young men into key positions and help them develop.

In February 1971, the Maranatha family honored Dr. and Mrs. Cedarholm with an evening of "This is Your Life, Dr. Cedarholm." Pastor friends and co-workers, seminary roommates, and old friends wrote to express their appreciation for the ministry life of the Cedarholms. The centerpiece of the evening was a rare accounting of the life of Dr. Cedarholm for the students, faculty, staff, and guests attending the program. The author of "Prince of a Man" (the script that was read that night) is unknown; however, the stories and information came primarily from Mrs. Cedarholm's treasure trove of vignettes and family insights. Though intended as a lighthearted evening of entertainment, it offered a rare personal glimpse into the family and memories that helped to shape the couple who built Maranatha.

In the late summer of 1980, Mrs. Cedarholm suffered a stroke while she and Dr. Cedarholm were visiting in California. After a short hospital stay in California, a quick trip back to Watertown, weeks of rest and therapy, and, perhaps most difficult of all, cutting back on her responsibilities at Maranatha, she made a full recovery. She was well enough for a trip to the Orient that November and early December, visiting missionaries and churches in Manila, Singapore, Bangkok, Hong Kong, Seoul, and Tokyo.

Dr. Cedarholm's 87-year-old mother moved to Watertown in 1981. Her mind was being affected by age, so the Cedarholms took Grandma for a "ride" one day while a crew of workers moved her possessions from Minnesota to Watertown. By the time they finished their "ride," they took Lollie to what looked to her to be her old apartment. The Cedarholms lived in a house on campus; Grandma Cedarholm, as she was known to the students, lived upstairs in the duplex next door. She still loved to play the piano—at all hours of the day and night, sometimes to the dismay of the staff living below.

Dr. Cedarholm was invited to the Pillsbury Commencement on May 13, 1982, but his calendar does not indicate that he attended. On September 11, 1982, the soccer and football teams of Maranatha Baptist Bible College and Pillsbury Baptist Bible College met on the athletic fields at Pillsbury. Pillsbury won the soccer game, and Maranatha won the football game. Far more important than the wins was the fact that these two schools could, fourteen years after Maranatha began, participate in a joint activity.

In the 1982–1983 school year, three significant difficulties arose that greatly impacted the Cedarholms. First, the school's enrollment had been in a four-year decline that did not appear likely to change in coming years. Second, a problem had developed between Maranatha and Calvary Baptist Church in Watertown. In response, Dr. Cedarholm considered starting a campus church, an action that was not well received by a number of faculty, board members, and constituency. Finally, for several years students had been borrowing money for their school bills from local banks—with Maranatha co-signing those loans. As the default rate climbed, Maranatha struggled under the increasing financial requirements. Shortly after Dr. Cedarholm started Maranatha, he had placed the name of his successor in a sealed envelope kept in the college safe. While there had been earlier contacts with Cedarholm's selection, that individual, Dr. Arno Q. Weniger, Jr., realized in 1982 that it was time to assume the leadership of Maranatha. He came on campus with his son, Tim, a new freshman. It had been a while since his last visit on campus. A man with an eye for detail, he was struck that the school seemed to look more run down than he had remembered. The grass was not cut. Buildings seemed in disrepair. Five years had passed since Dr. Cedarholm had first approached him about the presidency, but now the time was right. Dr. Cedarholm offered his resignation effective August 26, 1983, and assumed the role of Chancellor.

Dr. Cedarholm was a gracious chancellor and ex-president. He never sought to interject himself into college affairs, unless he was invited. Weniger was a gracious and respectful new president. When any major decision was about to be made, he would consult with Cedarholm to get his blessing. Cedarholm's routine answer was, "You're the president now, Bud. You do what you think is right."

THE FINAL YEARS:
1983–2008

In 1983, the Cedarholms entered their "retirement" years. They did not slow down, but instead continued to travel and accept invitations for various speaking opportunities. They had purchased a motorhome before they retired, making their travel easier and more convenient for them. They enjoyed the additional freedom this gave them in their travels. Before they moved to Florida, they sold the motorhome; it became too expensive for the lengthy trips the Cedarholms routinely made.

In the fall of 1983, the Cedarholms made a trip that Thelma had dreamed of for most of her life. She traveled to China. They visited Beijing, Nanjing, Shanghai, Kweilin, Canton, and Hong Kong, with a side trip to Japan.[1]

Dr. Cedarholm witnessing at the University of Shanghai

---

[1] 1983 Cedarholm Christmas letter.

Mrs. Cedarholm's love for China had not diminished over time. While her love for missions expanded through the years, China still held a special place in her heart. In the Cedarholm living room hung a painting that declared, in Chinese, "To the Praise of His Glory."

In 1985, they traveled to Australia and Papua New Guinea, where they met with Scott and Melody Childs and Jerry and Marilyn Arrowood Williams. Marilyn was the first Maranatha alumnus to enter fulltime missionary service. They also traveled to Guam and then Korea, where they spent time with Maranatha's first Korean graduates Ockhyun and Yoon Jong Kim and Hwangro Lee. They concluded their trip with a few days in Japan.[2]

In 1987, the cabin on the shores of Lake Nebagaman was rebuilt and redecorated. It had deteriorated badly in its 37 years of use. That same year, the Cedarholms became snowbirds, traveling to Florida for the winter and returning to their home in Watertown for the rest of the year.

On May 7, 1988, Maranatha awarded Dr. Cedarholm the Doctor of Sacred Theology and Mrs. Cedarholm the Doctor of Sacred Music in recognition of her role in the music programs at Maranatha. Mrs. Cedarholm had served in a variety of areas at Maranatha. She was the director of admissions and librarian for the first fifteen years and also taught courses in music and Christian education. She authored the college hymn, "To the Praise of His Glory," which premiered at Maranatha's first Fall Festival Program, October 19, 1968. She assisted in the start of Maranatha Baptist Academy, wrote promotional materials for the college, served as her

---

[2] 1985 Cedarholm Christmas letter.

husband's secretary, spoke off-campus at a variety of women's conferences, and for the first nineteen years of the college, directed the Madrigal and Handbell Choir.

In 1989, Lollie Cedarholm suffered a debilitating stroke, which required her permanent placement in a nursing home in Lake Mills, a community just a few miles from Watertown. She passed away March 17, 1992.

1990 was a special milestone year for the Cedarholms: They both turned 75, celebrated their 50th wedding anniversary, and rejoiced over the 25 years that Charlotte had been with them.

In June of 1993, Maranatha purchased a condominium at the Top of the World in Clearwater, Florida, for a permanent residence for the Cedarholms. The "snowbirds" became permanent residents in Florida, coming back to Wisconsin only for the occasional visit. At that time, Charlotte came home from five years of teaching at Harvest Christian Academy in Guam, telling her parents of her desire "to be with you while you are still normal!"[3] Charlotte stayed in Florida for the 1993–94 school year and then returned to Guam for three more years. Her parents' declining health brought her back to Florida in March 1997, just three months before her father's death.

Their final years were not kind to the Cedarholms. Age, prostate cancer, and Alzheimer's took their toll on Dr. Cedarholm. He also suffered a series of strokes. Mrs. Cedarholm was diagnosed with diabetes early in 1995. Their traveling days were over, and Mrs. Cedarholm took on a new title: "Caregiver."

Caring for her husband became increasingly more difficult for Mrs. Cedarholm, but she never flinched from that responsibility. Dr. Cedarholm's mind was gravely affected, but not his spirit. Near the end of his life, while in the Mease Continuing Care facility in Dunedin, Florida, one of the nurses who cared for him told Mrs. Cedarholm that he continued to read his Bible and pray every day. He witnessed to this nurse on a regular basis (usually not remembering

---

[3] 1993 Cedarholm Christmas letter.

that she was already converted). His physical life was in quick decline, but his spirit was looking ever heavenward. The Lord took him home on June 6, 1997, just a few days before his eighty-second birthday. His body was returned to Watertown, and a fitting funeral was held on campus.

Mrs. Cedarholm and Charlotte returned to Watertown after the death of their beloved husband and father. They lived in a college-provided home across the street from the Maranatha campus. Mrs. Cedarholm had been elected to the Maranatha Board of Trustees in 1996, serving on the Education and Academic Affairs Committee. She directed her last Madrigal and Handbell Choir song at the spring 1999 concert, at the invitation of its director, Monty Budahl. She attended her last Board Meeting in December of 1999. On January 3, 2000, Mrs. Thelma M. Cedarholm joined her husband as she entered into her eternal reward. Her funeral was held on the Maranatha campus on a cold January 7th.

The Cedarholms were Baptists. Myron grew up a Baptist, while Thelma abandoned her Lutheranism to become one. They made the local church the focal point for ministry. Myron argued that Baptists best represented the order of New Testament churches. He preached this conviction in the churches in which he ministered, and he inculcated these beliefs in the students at both Pillsbury and Maranatha. He served on the board of the Fundamental Baptist Fellowship and left a record of attending the annual conference for 45 consecutive years, when some FBF leaders were attacking Maranatha for entering into the accreditation process.[4]

The Cedarholms were separatists. In obedience to the teaching of Scripture in 2 Corinthians 6:14ff and elsewhere, they left the Northern Baptist Convention and helped form the Conservative Baptist Association of America. They spent eighteen years in fulltime ministry with the CBA, but when it began to compromise, they left without concern for all that they would lose.

---

[4] "Dr. B. Myron Cedarholm, A Tribute," 1997 Fundamental Baptist Fellowship National Conference.

Both of the Cedarholms were missions-minded. Their church in Philadelphia caught the missionary vision and sent out numerous missionaries. The CBA sent the Cedarholms around the world to visit 325 missionaries in 52 countries. This trip fired their passion for missions even more, and the Cedarholms envisioned the opportunity to train Baptist missionaries to fulfill the Great Commission. With Matthew 28:19–20 as his text, Dr. Cedarholm often peached that the Great Commission consisted of "conversion, immersion, and the planting of a New Testament Church."[5] Missionaries who yielded to God's call under his ministry in churches and at Pillsbury and Maranatha are scattered all over the world. Dr. Cedarholm served on the Baptist World Mission board for 28 years.

From early in her ministry, Mrs. Cedarholm excelled as a gifted teacher and speaker. During their CBA days, she travelled extensively to women's conferences around the States. She directed children's camps and was the story lady for numerous Vacation Bible Schools. She served on the CBHMS and Maranatha Baptist Bible College boards. She was an accomplished musician with a great love for music. That love was transferred to those in her choirs and classes. She was an outstanding hostess. Her home in Philadelphia was open to church members and visitors alike. They built a home in Chicago and a cabin in northern Wisconsin that specifically fit their desire to provide a refuge for families in ministry. Their homes at Pillsbury and Maranatha were opened to the students. And anyone who had the privilege of singing in her Madrigal and Handbell Choirs fondly remembers her Swedish pancake breakfasts.

God gifted both Myron and Thelma Cedarholm with the acuity to recognize genuine spiritual potential in students where others could not. The passage of time has proven the veracity of their godly insight. Many of the men and women whom the Cedarholms guided, taught, and mentored became leaders in Fundamentalist circles. The full impact of the

---

[5] Ibid.

Cedarholms' obedience to the Lord's leading will be realized only in eternity.

The Cedarholms held to a simple but profound faith, a faith that was centered on God's Word and its promises. If God said it, the Cedarholms by faith believed it. The influence of the Cedarholms on churches, missionaries, students, pastors and families attests to their significance in the history of 20th century fundamental Baptists. As servants of the Lord they were willing to go wherever and do whatever God wanted them to do.

The Cedarholms are buried beside each other on the Maranatha campus just east of Old Main. Their lives were centered around the glorious hope of the Lord's return. They are singing praises to their Savior while their bodies await the resurrection.

Maranatha!

To the Praise of His Glory

Appendix

Beautiful Feet

The age-old custom of binding feet to make them beautiful causes this Chinese lady to appreciate the biblical version of "beautiful feet." Her tale is an adaptation of a true story that has often been told to encourage others in faithful witnessing.

The Mission School

Tired from packing, Ming-Chu sat down on the porch of the mission school. She smiled as she listened to the shouts of the children on the playground, remembering her own first years at the mission school. Her thoughts were interrupted by the sound of running feet.

"Ming-Chu! Watch out!"

Ming-Chu looked up as a ball bounced close to her feet. Reaching down, she picked up the ball and tossed it to the bright-eyed little girl who came racing after it. "Run," Ming-Chu called.

The little girl called back over her shoulder as she ran back to the playground. "Come and watch us, Ming-Chu!"

Ming-Chu followed the running child down the path, moving slowly and carefully in her tiny shoes. At the edge of the playground she stopped to watch the game.

She giggled softly as the two leaders of the teams urged the children on to victory. One leader was the missionary, head of the mission school, and the other was a young Chinese man. Both men were special to Ming-Chu. The American missionary had been almost like a father to her during her years at the mission school, and the young Chinese was the man Ming-Chu was to marry. As the game ended, the two men walked toward her, still arguing cheerfully.

"Just wait until tomorrow!" challenged the missionary as they stopped beside Ming-Chu.

"You hear him, Ming-Chu?" said the young Chinese. "Another day! Always another day!"

Ming-Chu smiled. "And I will not be here to see either of you win."

The missionary turned to her. "Have you finished packing?"

"Yes," she replied. "It's hard to believe that today is my last day at the mission school."

The missionary took her hand. "Now, Ming-Chu, is not a time for sadness. You are returning home to prepare for your wedding."

The young man nodded. "I too will miss the mission school. But I am looking forward to a new life with you, Ming-Chu. The missionary has brought the gospel to us. Now we will give the gospel to others."

As Ming-Chu smiled up at him, the porters came down the trail, carrying a sedan chair. "It is time for me to go," she said. "I will return as swiftly as possible with my family."

When the porters stopped in front of them, the young man carefully helped Ming-Chu into the sedan chair. Then he warned the porters to take special care of Ming-Chu. "I want no harm to come to my bride-to-be."

Ming-Chu laughed. "We have made the trip often. I will arrive back in one piece!"

"And in time for the wedding," Ming-Chu called back as the caravan began moving up the mountain trail.

Days later the caravan reached Ming-Chu's village. Children and neighbors crowded around the sedan chair as it moved slowly through the streets to Ming-Chu's house. Ming-Chu called greetings to her friends. Then the gates of her house were opened, and a servant appeared to take her to her eagerly waiting parents.

Early the next morning Ming-Chu's mother sent for the tailor. Soon material was spread across the room in a silken rainbow of bright colors.

The tailor carefully measured Ming-Chu for her wedding dress.

"Now the shoes," he said, spreading parchment on the floor. "What beautiful feet," he murmured as he traced Ming-Chu's feet on the parchment. "You must be very proud of such tiny feet."

Min-Chu's mother beamed. "I bound her feet when she was just a baby. They are the smallest feet in the village, even smaller than my own."

Ming-Chu thought of the little girl back at the mission school who had run so lightly after the ball. What freedom the children had whose feet were not bound!

Preparations continued for the wedding trip. Soon the caravan was packed and ready to go. As Ming-Chu and her family traveled across the mountains, she watched eagerly for the first glimpse of the mission school. At last they reached the last mountain pass. There far below them lay the mission school.

"There it is!" called Ming-Chu to her parents. "We are almost there!"

A Special Gift

Ming-Chu and her family were welcomed, and the wedding festivities began. After a week of joyful celebration, Ming-Chu's family returned to their village. Ming-Chu and her new husband prepared for their first trip together into the mountains of China.

"Thank you for everything you have done for us," the two young people told the missionary. "We will miss you and will think of you often."

"May God be with you," said the missionary.

"Good-bye," called the children as Ming-Chu and her husband started down the trail, Ming-Chu in her sedan chair carried by the porters and her husband walking alongside her.

That trip was the first of many. From village to village the young people went, carrying the gospel to the Chinese. In each village Ming-Chu's husband preached, and Ming-Chu taught the women from the Bible.

The women were delighted with Ming-Chu's tiny feet, and came often to hear her teach. They began to look forward to the visits of the "lady with beautiful feet," and many of them came to know Christ as their Saviour.

Ming-Chu enjoyed the long walks over the mountains to the different villages. As her husband walked along beside the sedan chair, Ming-Chu would read the Bible aloud.

One day she was reading a passage from Romans 10: "And how shall they preach, except they be sent? As it is written, How beautiful are the feet of them that preach the gospel of peace, and bring glad tidings of good things." Ming-Chu closed her Bible and looked along the path. It was a beautiful day, clear and crisp in early fall. "I wish I could walk with you," she said to her husband.

"There are pebbles along the path," he answered. "What if you slip and fall?"

"I would be careful to lean on you," Ming-Chu replied wistfully.

Her husband hesitated, then stopped the caravan and let her walk slowly along the path. He held her arm firmly as she walked.

"I wish my feet had never been bound," Ming-Chu said sadly. "Then I could walk easily beside you, and we would not have to travel slowly because of my sedan chair."

"But Ming-Chu," replied her husband, "you have beautiful feet!"

"No," Ming-Chu said, "you have beautiful feet."

"Me!"

"Yes, you," Ming-Chu said tenderly. "The verse I just read says that the feet of those who carry the gospel to others are beautiful. That makes your feet beautiful, and mine are beautiful only because I help you, not because they are so tiny."

"I understand," said her husband. "But the Lord has used your tiny feet to bring many women to hear you teach. They come to marvel at your feet and stay to hear the gospel. The Lord uses what each of us has to further the gospel."

Ming-Chu thought for a moment as her husband helped her back into the sedan chair. "Do you know who else has beautiful feet?"

"The missionary," replied her husband, smiling at her. "He brought the gospel to us. Soon we will go back to visit him."

"I would like that very much," Ming-Chu replied.

But it was many years before they saw the missionary again. One day they received word that he was returning to the United States.

"We must go now," said Ming-Chu, "or we will never see him again."

"Yes, we will leave tomorrow," said her husband.

As Ming-Chu packed for the trip she found the little silk wedding shoes that had been carefully tucked away in a tiny box. "Husband," she said, showing him the shoes, "these shoes remind me of the verse in Romans about beautiful feet. I would like to give the shoes to the missionary."

Her husband nodded. "The little shoes will make a fine gift of remembrance."

When Ming-Chu and her husband returned to the mission, they were joyfully met by their old friends. When at last they were able to sit down with the missionary alone, Ming-Chu gave him the little shoes. She explained what beautiful feet now meant to her and asked the missionary, "Will you find some little girl in America that loves the Lord and give her these shoes? Perhaps my story will encourage her to carry the gospel to others as you have done."

When the aged missionary returned to America, he gave the tiny shoes to an eight-year-old girl. She cherished the tiny shoes and never forgot the story of Ming-Chu's "beautiful feet." The girl grew up to serve the Lord faithfully in many ways. She still has the tiny shoes and often shows them to others. After she tells Ming-Chu's story, she encourages her listeners to be faithful in spreading the gospel so that they too may have beautiful feet. [The eight-year-old girl was Thelma Melford.]

"Beautiful Feet." In *Reading for Christian Schools 3-2*. Greenville, SC: Bob Jones University Press, 1983. 50-60. Used by permission.

INDEX

www.ingramcontent.com/pod-product-compliance
Lightning Source LLC
Chambersburg PA
CBHW021138090426
42740CB00008B/839